AIRING DIRTY LAUNDRY

Ishmael Reed

Ishmael Reed is one of the most innovative, irreverent, and outspoken iconoclasts of our time. Throughout his thirty-year career he has refused to be categorized. Reed may be a nationally acclaimed novelist, but he is also an all-American writer and critic moving to a World beat.

Airing Dirty Laundry, Reed's fourth collection of nonfiction—following *God Made Alaska for the Indians*, *Shrovetide in Old New Orleans*, and *Writin' Is Fightin'*—is his biggest and richest yet. Almost half of the material appears for the first time here. Once again, Reed confirms his status as an indefatigable "Establishment" agitator, an undying advocate of multiculturalism, and a supportive and nurturing presence in a variety of artistic endeavors from writing to rap. The lead essay, "Airing Dirty Laundry," is a scathing indictment of how the media establishment not only sells out black America, but, in the process, coddles its predominantly white constituents by blaming the bulk of America's social problems on blacks—hypocritically airing the black community's dirty laundry and not their own. Whether it is the

Continued on back flap

Airing Dirty Laundry

By Ishmael Reed

ESSAYS
Writin' Is Fightin'
God Made Alaska for the Indians
Shrovetide in Old New Orleans

NOVELS
Japanese by Spring
The Terrible Threes
Reckless Eyeballing
The Terrible Twos
Flight to Canada
The Last Days of Louisiana Red
Mumbo Jumbo
Yellow Back Radio Broke-Down
The Free-lance Pallbearers

POETRY
New and Collected Poems
A Secretary to the Spirits
Chattanooga
Conjure
Catechism of D Neoamerican
    Hoodoo Church

PLAYS
Mother Hubbard, formerly Hell Hath No Fury
The Ace Boons
Savage Wilds
Hubba City

ANTHOLOGIES
The Before Columbus Foundation Fiction Antholog
The Before Columbus Foundation Poetry Antholog
Calafia
19 Necromancers from Now

TELEVISION PRODUCTIONS
The Only Language She Knows
Personal Problems
A Word in Edgewise

LIBRETTOS
The Wild Gardens of the Loup Garou
Gethsemane

Ishmael Reed

Airing Dirty Laundry

Addison-Wesley Publishing Company
Reading, Massachusetts   Menlo Park, California   New York
Don Mills, Ontario   Wokingham, England   Amsterdam   Bonn
Sydney   Singapore   Tokyo   Madrid   San Juan
Paris   Seoul   Milan   Mexico City   Taipei

Many of the designations used by manufacturers and sellers to distinguish their products are claimed as trademarks. Where those designations appear in this book and Addison-Wesley was aware of a trademark claim, the designations have been printed in initial capital letters (i.e., Kleenex).

The following essays first appeared in the publications listed below: "Clarence Thomas Lynched Again," *Washington Post,* October 18, 1992; "Rodney King and I," *San Francisco Examiner,* May 3, 1992; "Drug 'Experts' Don't Live with Gunfire," *USA Today,* February 16, 1990; "Elaine Brown," *Philadelphia Inquirer,* February 14, 1993; "Paul Robeson," *Los Angeles Times,* February 19, 1989; "Bill Gunn," Whitney Museum of American Art, New American Film and Video Program, June 19–July 8, 1990; "Frederick Douglass," *Los Angeles Times,* February 3, 1991; "Reginald Lewis," *Utne Reader,* May/June 1993; "Ambrose Bierce," *War News,* March 16, 1991, reprinted in *Classics of Civil War Fiction,* University of Mississippi Press, 1991; "Langston Hughes," *Newsday,* September 25, 1988; "John Edgar Wideman," *Philadelphia Inquirer,* September 23, 1993; "Zora Neale Hurston," introduction to *Tell My Horse,* Harper and Row, 1990; "Chester Himes," *Los Angeles Times,* June 30, 1991; "Jess Mowry," *Nation,* September 21, 1992; "Eldridge Cleaver," introduction to new edition of *Soul on Ice,* Laurel Books, 1992; "Miraculous Fiction," *American Book Review,* August-September 1992; "Money Can't Buy You Love," *San Francisco Examiner,* October 27, 1991; "Reading, Writing, and Racism," *Image,* August 19, 1990; "The Be-Bop Revival," Newport Jazz Festival Program, 1979; "Savages and Liberators," *Before Columbus Review,* Fall/Winter, 1992; "To Be an American Is to Be Fair," *Newsday,* October 25, 1993; "Black Irishman," *Callahan's Irish Quarterly,* 1982; "American Poetry: Is There a Center?" *Black American Literature Forum,* January 1978, reprinted in Pushcart Prize, 1978, and *God Made Alaska for the Indians,* 1982.

Library of Congress Cataloging-in-Publication Data
Reed, Ishmael, 1938–
    Airing dirty laundry / by Ishmael Reed.
      p. cm.
    Includes index.
    ISBN 0-201-62462-1
    1. Afro-Americans—Social conditions—1975- 2. Afro-Americans.
    I. Title.
    E185.86.R38 1993   93-13874
    305.896'073—dc20   CIP

Jacket design by Jean Seal
Text design by Janis Owens
Set in 10-point Palatino by Haddon Craftsmen, Inc., Allentown, PA
1 2 3 4 5 6 7 8 9-MW-96959493
First printing, October 1993

This book is dedicated to the memory of Bennie S. Reed, Sr., auto worker and Sunday school teacher; Paul Lofty, musician and instruments repairman; Marquel LeNoir, class president and pre-med student; Ted Jackson, outsider and intellectual; Carman Nelson, youth advisor; Leothe Owens, entrepreneur book activist

Why do you see the speck that is in your brother's eye, but not notice the log that is in your own eye? You hypocrite, first take the log out of your own eye, and then you will see clearly to take the speck out of your brother's eye.
The Gospel of Matthew

Happy are you, Hester, that wear the scarlet letter openly upon your bosom! Mine burns in secret!
The Scarlet Letter, Nathaniel Hawthorne

CONTENTS

Preface / xi

PART 1: Airing Dirty Laundry

Airing Dirty Laundry / 3
Is There a Black-Jewish Feud? / 33
Beyond Los Angeles / 43
Clarence Thomas Lynched Again / 53
Gays and Feminists Play with Racist Fire / 59
Rodney King and I / 65
Mike Tyson and the White Hope Cult / 68
Drug "Experts" Don't Live with Gunfire / 75
An Outsider in Koreatown / 77

PART 2: Profiles / Reviews

Elaine Brown—Activist / 87
Eldridge Cleaver—Writer / 95
Gwendolyn Brooks—Poet / 104
Paul Robeson—Actor / 107

Contents

Bill Gunn—Director / 112
Frederick Douglass—Politician / 120
Ambrose Bierce—Writer / 126
Reginald Lewis—Businessman / 133
Langston Hughes—Writer / 136
John Edgar Wideman—Writer / 140
Zora Neale Hurston—Writer / 146
Chester Himes—Writer / 152
Jess Mowry—Writer / 157
Reginald Martin, Toni Cade Bambara—Writers / 165
Miraculous Fiction—Writers / 172
The Fourth Ali—Boxer / 176

PART 3: Odds & Ends

Money Can't Buy You Love / 209
Reading, Writing, and Racism / 216
The Be-Bop Revival / 220
Savages and Liberators / 224
Silencing the Hordes / 229
Ms. Gore's Crusade / 232
To Be an American Is to Be Fair / 235
Black Irishman / 238
American Poetry: Is There a Center? / 242
Distant Cousins / 266
Index / 275

PREFACE

More than 50 percent of the pieces in this book, including a major essay, "Airing Dirty Laundry," make their first appearance herein. The earliest essay, "The Fourth Ali," was published in 1978 in the *Village Voice*, and the most recent essay, "Airing Dirty Laundry," was completed on June 2, 1993.

Some of the essays were inspired by a call from Eric Kopage, now an editor at the *New York Times Magazine*. Indeed, it was this call—made to a hotel in Bern, Switzerland, while I was visiting Swiss universities—that precipitated a turning point in my outlook on how America's staggering social problems are perceived. Eric wanted me to respond to a piece called "Letter to a Black Friend" that had been printed in *Esquire* in 1988. It was a highly emotional work in which the author, Pete Hamill, angrily denounced the behavior of a class of people known as "the underclass." He listed a number of personal behavior traits identified with "the underclass"—this based upon his hanging out at some New York welfare hotels for a hot minute. For him as for others of the growing black-pathology business, the underclass was black.

I was offended by the piece. Some of the behavior Hamill considered peculiar to the black underclass—such as alcoholism (which has historically been associated with Hamill's group,

Irish Americans), obesity, and promiscuity—I knew to be rampant in American society in general. Further study on my part revealed that even serious social scientists were not unanimous as to what the term *underclass* meant. Did it refer to those who live below the poverty line? to those engaged in socially deviant behavior, many of whom are wealthy? Or was an underclass person one who is both poor *and* engaged in socially deviant behavior? In his book *Money and Class in America*, Lewis H. Lampham discusses "heirs of large family fortunes, ranging from old-money scions to second-generation Texans," who "abuse their children," driving them to "alcoholism, suicides, drug addiction, and insanity." Why aren't these dysfunctional families considered members of the underclass? Since the typical underclass person is white, why is the underclass label always applied to blacks?

I began clipping articles from newspapers and reading dry academic material about the underclass. Many of these writings countered some of the opinions in Hamill's piece, and quite a few referred to such opinions as "media myths."

I also noticed that even newspapers that published hundreds of op-ed essays about the black underclass would, from time to time, report on a study that attacked such op-ed opinions as "myths." One of those myths, promoted by neoconservatives connected with the Eastern media, is that while black society is rife with problems, the Asian American community, through hard work and devotion to Anglo values, has proved that assimilation correlates with American success. In the April 1993 issue of the *Atlantic*, James Allen McPherson adheres to the neoconservative line that "drugs, drive-by shootings, teen-age pregnancies, unemployment, and self-hatred" are black problems exclusively. A few pages later, in an article entitled "The New Minorities," smiling Vietnamese are shown assimilating into the sunshine of the American dream.

This is typical of the kind of coverage Asian Americans receive in the media. They are portrayed as well behaved and as not making trouble, while blacks are regarded as perennial fuck-ups, even though among some Asian American groups there exists sizable underclass activity, including Vietnamese extortion gangs, soaring school dropout rates, spousal abuse, homelessness, and even indentured servitude and slavery. Yet in the media, Asian Americans are rarely associated with underclass activities.

When former California attorney general Van De Camp's office released a report about the shocking extent of Asian American gang activity in California, the report was suppressed, due to an outcry from members of the Asian American community, who wanted to keep such activities hidden. In 1992, David Nakasjima, project director of the East Bay Asian Youth and Family Project, was quoted in the *San Jose Mercury* describing Asian American "crack" use as being "sheltered by [a] conspiracy of silence."

My research and rethinking of social pathology, prompted by Kopage's phone call, informs many of the essays in this book. My comments about the Los Angeles riots in "Beyond Los Angeles" include observations that were not made by the number of op-ed pieces that blamed the whole thing on blacks (Joe Klein's *Newsweek* carried the incendiary cover BLACK VS. WHITES). Very few media outlets commented about white participation in the riots. The media successfully squeezed this complex social catastrophe into their flat and lazy White Hats/Black Hats perspective.

By the time a PBS "Frontline" documentary on the riots aired on Tuesday, April 27, 1993, white participation in the riots, including the looting and burning of Korean stores by white mobs, had been deleted from history (even though 12 percent of those arrested for looting were white). Though the majority of those arrested for looting were Latino, a Latino spokesperson was featured lecturing blacks about their behavior. The sternest lectures, as usual, were delivered by white males, who were shown debating issues of the riots with two black women and one Korean woman; no black, Latino, or Asian males were invited. When Korean American lawyer Angela Oh said that the media depicted blacks as a dangerous people, journalist Richard Reeves responded emotionally and defended the media. He launched into a tirade about how his eighty-five-year-old mother feared black males without having been prompted by the media to do so. This scene was cut so that Reeves had the last word, which is the way the media usually deal with criticism of their profession—cut off the debate, stonewall, deny.

The producer and the director of the L.A. riots entertainment were white women, the kind who've bought *The Color Purple* version of American reality—in other words, that most of America's social problems are the result of black male behavior. Predictably, *Times* critic Walter Goodman loved the show.

In "Mike Tyson and the White Hope Cult," I write that Mike Tyson's lynching is the result of a steady buildup of animosity toward black men. Black men are singled out by the modern feminist movement as the main perpetrators of American misogyny. This belief was attributed to a small faction of disgruntled, paranoid black men, of whom I, according to *Ms.* magazine, am the "ringleader." By the end of the 1980s, however, some black feminists and white male intellectuals and scholars began to agree.

The liberal wing of the feminist movement may have improved the lives of its middle- and upper-class constituency—indeed, 1992 was the Year of the White Middle Class Woman—but since the leadership of this faction of the feminist movement has singled out black men as the meta-enemy of women, these women represent one of the most serious threats to black male well-being since the Klan. White men receive more favorable treatment from this group than the brothers—who have few jobs, perks, or rewards to dispense—do. When I was hit by my debating partner, Barbara Smith, in *Ms.* magazine, I responded that even though I was a black male living in a ghetto, I felt that I should be regarded with the same courtesy as the men who own *Ms.*, the feminist magazine, Lang Communications. My reply was never printed, or acknowledged.

It simply amazes me how few feminists criticize men from their own ethnic group, making black men take the rap for all men. For instance, Gloria Steinem said in a *New York Times* op-ed piece that she was always embarrassed when a male of her background received bad publicity. She was a harsh critic of Joyce Johnson's book *What Lisa Steinberg Knew*. Had it been fiction, Steinem said, the book would have been more acceptable, because then it would not have been about the truth. Yet when she gave *The Color Purple* its send-off in the June 1982 issue of *Ms.*, Steinem said that this fictional work told the "truth" about black men.

Disappointingly, National Public Radio also harbors prejudices against black men. Terry Gross, host of the program "Fresh Air," not only maneuvered black gang members and a naive young black filmmaker into underwriting her prejudice that black men have a problem with misogyny but even finagled Gerald Early, a middle-class black college professor, into commenting about fatherless homes and violence in the black community, as though this were the only community where such pathologies exist. On the other hand, she was so awestruck by her guest Philip Roth that she failed to question him about his comment, made in *Esquire*, "Fuck the feminists." I write about one of black men's persistent critics at NPR, Margot Adler, in "Gays and Feminists Play with Racist Fire."

Because he defended Clarence Thomas, Arlen Specter was subjected to a hostile interview by Ms. Gross. Ms. Gross and other feminists at NPR make it a point to bond with black women, even to the extent of overpraising Maya Angelou's inept inaugural poem, "Pulse of the Morning," but have made no attempt to recruit more black women for jobs at NPR. A FAIR (For Accuracy In Radio) report revealed that NPR remains segregated.

I was annoyed by the *New York Times* op-ed page becoming a

sort of rallying point for Anita Hill. The *Times* actually printed Stephen Carter's op-ed piece twice. Carter believed Anita Hill because she was his friend. This was typical of the specious thinking of Anita Hill's supporters. Even Barbara Ehrenreich, whom I otherwise admire, appeared on Terry Gross's show saying that she believed Anita Hill because she was a woman. I wrote an op-ed piece for the *Times* challenging this orthodoxy. The newspaper wouldn't publish it. By coincidence, the *Washington Post*'s Jeff Morley called and asked whether I would like to comment on the Anita Hill–Clarence Thomas conflict. The piece, "Clarence Thomas Lynched Again," was published in the *Washington Post*.

As a black male writer, I am in a position to profile individuals—black intellectuals, writers, and scientists—who are often ignored by the media. Part 2 of *Airing Dirty Laundry* profiles a number of articulate black men and women, most of them writers, men and women with whom the media are uncomfortable because they aren't athletes, criminals, entertainers, or neoconservatives. When was the last time you've seen any writers from this group on Larry King's show? Black authors and intellectuals, especially male ones, are seldom seen on television network programs, unless it's to comment on black pathology.

Propaganda in which one denigrates the achievements of those considered an enemy, or problem people, while at the same time denying questionable moral behavior on the part of those with whom one has racial ties, is nothing new in history. In "Silencing the Hordes," I discuss how the contributions of the Mongol invaders were treated with what Charles Halperin calls a conspiracy of silence. In "Savages and Liberators," I demonstrate that even Columbus didn't downplay the achievements of the Native Americans he encountered in this hemisphere as much as his contemporary defenders, such as Michiko Kakutani, do. "Silencing the Hordes" was to be one of the commentaries aired on the NPR show "All Things Considered," which had invited me to do guest commentaries. It was never aired. If blacks had as much power in the media and were to behave in a similar manner, they'd be accused of black nationalism.

I wrote an article for *Life* magazine in which I maintained that I'd rather be a black male than a white male because nobody expected me to be superman, and if I experienced setbacks in life, I could always attribute them to racism and most of the time I'd be right. One of the white pathologies that the media ignore is the growing rate of suicide among middle-aged white men. This national health problem deserves more attention from the media. I can understand why white men would be stressed out: People expect them to be superman. But I don't have to be superman; nobody expects a black man to be Atlas, carrying the weight of the world on his shoulders. White men today find themselves threatened by the growing demands of blacks, Latinos, Asian Americans, and feminists, and although many are sympathetic to these demands, for some the response takes the form of denial and defensiveness. Minorities who've complained about being lumped together with some of the more obnoxious members of their group think nothing of generalizing about white male behavior, blaming all white males for the crimes against humanity that have taken place since the beginning of time. All white males are born with a lengthy rap sheet compiled by history. People can't tell them apart. I do it myself. White male intellectuals are hurt and confused. They smear multiculturalism as a threat to Western values when multiculturalism may, in the end, do more to preserve Western values than all of the defenders of Greece and Rome. In a recent class of mine (which was 90 percent white), the only person who was able to identify John the Baptist was a Chinese American student. She's typical. Most of us black, brown, yellow, and red people know Western books, music, and other aspects of Western culture, while even sober, well-meaning critics like Robert Hughes plunge over the cliff when discussing African history and culture. (Next time Mr. Hughes and Michiko Kakutani visit Paris, they ought to examine the Louvre's statue of Osiris, the

Jesus Christ [though some would argue that it's the other way around] of Egyptian religion, whose rites are still observed in Luxor. He's black!)

Instead of reaching out to multiculturalists, common-sense feminists, and others, neoconservatives strike out in hostile books and op-ed articles that trivialize their opponents' arguments. Instead of accepting the exciting intellectual challenge that feminists, multiculturalists, and Afrocentrics have posed, many white male media people, academics, and intellectuals wing it on arrogance, dismissing their opponents with feisty crossfire types of one-liners and hostile, goofy, ignorant op-ed pieces.

It must take considerable courage for a white man to genuinely break ranks with the united front against what is regarded as the heathen horde. One who does so must be paid tribute: Allen Ginsberg has not only championed black and Asian culture but even sought to popularize African American culture by teaching a course in African American literature at Brooklyn College.

"American Poetry: Is There a Center?" was a response to an article appearing in a mass magazine and describing the Naropa Institute—an accredited institution administered by Ginsberg and his associates—as "the center for American poetry." At the time, many of us who were involved in the multicultural movement felt that a scene so white could not possibly be the center for American poetry. I was assigned to write a story about Naropa for *Oui* magazine. I tried to collect all points of view about the Naropa scene and to flesh out some of the rumors about a party that turned violent. The article bothered Allen Ginsberg and Anne Waldman, even though it included some praise for both of them and for their work. Since then, Ginsberg and Naropa have become much more inclusive. In February 1993, Ginsberg sent me a note that included information about his Rainbow Readings Series. And the Naropa Institute Summer Program in Writing and Poetics now stands out as one of the more integrated programs in the United States.

There are thousands of white men and women like Allen Ginsberg and Anne Waldman, but their voices are neglected in the "gong show" pyrotechnics and shrill whistles of the American racial debate. Still, they are role models for white Americans.

Even though the article Eric Kopage commissioned me to write was never published, the experience of researching it was extremely valuable to me. So I am indebted to Kopage for leading me into a direction that changed my thinking about social pathology. That the article was never published (and that I was never paid) doesn't bother me a bit.

Ishmael Reed
June 6, 1993

PART 1

Airing Dirty Laundry

Airing Dirty Laundry

A professional media organization recently gave an award to a magazine that endorsed the Simi Valley jury's acquittal of Rodney King's tormentors, because, according to the organization, that took courage. Shelby Steele was congratulated in the *New York Times* for discussing matters that are "unspoken"—his unoriginal notion of blacks feeling guilty for receiving advancement as a result of affirmative action was borrowed from a mean-spirited editorial by Midge Decter, over five years before. Nevertheless, Steele's ideas appear and are promoted regularly by *Harper's, New York Times Magazine,* the underwriters of PBS, and other powerful sections of neoconservative opinion.

The profitable literary scam nowadays is to pose as someone who airs unpleasant and frank facts about the black community, only to be condemned by the black community for doing so. This is the sure way to grants, awards, prizes, fellowships, and academic power.

A grants-giving agency sent me the confidential letter nominating a black conservative writer for a very generous grant. The nominator said nothing about the literary merit of the author's work but praised his ability to needle blacks. Currently, blacks are depicted as members of an uptight community, where thought control is rampant. They're "paranoid" and can't take criticism.

3

As someone who for years has aired the dirty laundry of the black, white, yellow, and the brown community, as well as that of men and women and a whole host of -isms, I can testify that among all of my targets, blacks are the least thin-skinned. Though I have had trouble with a minority of black people who want to exercise thought control over blacks, they amount to a sect. No black person has tried to drive me out of business as the feminists have. No black group has called for a boycott of my books as feminists at the University of Louisiana at Baton Rouge did (the boycott collapsed because none of them had read my books).

The true thought police are corporate sponsors and a minority of men who control American public opinion. They are the ones who decide which op-eds are printed or the kind of slant that's to be placed on news involving blacks. Though they pretend that criticism of blacks is prohibited by political correctness, their publications and news and commentaries carry a steady stream of criticism of black behavior.

Even when certain outlets, such as National Public Radio, pretend to solicit a variety of viewpoints in the name of free speech, those black, brown, and yellow writers who do not adhere to politically correct views of race are excluded from the public discussion. For example, a few years ago, the senior editor of a well-known men's magazine approached me about doing an opinion column. I sent a tongue-in-cheek piece that argued that if street drug dealers were to be executed for their crimes, then upper-class money launderers should receive the same punishment. Not only did the editor turn down the piece; he sent a note to my agent, suggesting that black behavior was responsible for the drug crisis and that I was merely trying to make whites feel guilty. A few months after the letter was sent, President Bush and then drug czar William Bennett, who certainly can't be accused of desiring to make whites feel guilty, made the same proposal. (In 1992, U.S. Attorney for New York Robert Morgan-thau said, when bringing indictments against BCCI, that the

35,000 arrests of New York street dealers that year were not as important as breaking up money laundering banks like BCCI. Though television networks run footage of black small-time drug dealers all day, seldom do they carry stories about money laundering, presumably because the banks are some of the principal stockholders of the networks.) Not content with merely reprimanding me with a note, the editor hired a black writer to challenge, out of context, a line that I'd written in a *Life* magazine piece that being a black man in the United States was like being a spectator at your own lynching. The black writer said that black men were lynching themselves, and that their problems were crime, drugs, and sex. (This was printed in an issue that carried a full-page photo of a nude woman in chains; about six months later, a woman sued the publisher, successfully, for holding her as a sex slave.)

This black writer, and the editor who hired him, are laboring under a misconception if they believe that drug addiction is a black problem exclusively. While the media bombards the public with images of black women as irresponsible cocaine mothers, statistics indicate that the white suburban rate for cocaine pregnancies is about the same as that in the inner city. According to a *New York Times* survey, the typical crack addict is a forty-year-old white male professional, married, and suburban. Cocaine addiction is a sizable problem on Wall Street, but stories about this white collar crime are usually carried on the business shows and not reported as news.

I wasn't surprised at the revelation that social problems are occurring in the white suburbs. I've been reading the fiction of white students for twenty years, and they paint a picture of the American suburban life where drug addiction, alcoholism, and fatherless homes are widespread. In most of these stories the father is missing or is, as one student wrote in a poem, "a tourist" in his own home. The son of an investment banker told me that he and his friends rarely see their parents, and that they spend their lavish allowances on drugs and alcohol. Even though studies show that white teenagers are more prone to drug abuse than black teenagers, the image of drugs as a black problem prevails, not only in the media, and political circles where the war on drugs means a war against black neighborhoods, but in the country's leading intellectual publications. One would think that intellectuals would inject a tone of reason into this public discussion, but, in the United States, the intelligentsia often sell their intellects to the highest corporate bidder.

In the old days, muckrakers like Lincoln Steffens used their talents to fight big steel, big oil, and big meat; today's intellectual goes after welfare mothers, the homeless, and the hungry. They might write an op-ed article justifying the murder by a vigilante of an unarmed homeless man. They might write a lengthy article opposing the distribution of food stamps or argue that poverty is often a lifestyle choice. They might hire out their talents to places like the Heritage Foundation or the American Enterprise Institute, outfits with apparently unlimited access to the television networks.

This group of think-tankers, op-eders, television commentators form the chief impediment to black progress. In the words of Carl Rowan, they have brilliantly used the media to "out-propagandize" the group whom they perceive as the enemy. Lacking the access to the media, those whom they target have little recourse to combat this propaganda. They are like the Bosnians trapped in a conflict with the Serbs, who have the arms and the ability to engage in a steady debilitating war.

When a *New York Times* reporter recently congratulated a prominent black woman for having the courage to air the dirty laundry of the black community, as though such laundry was unaired, I was wondering whether that reporter reads her own paper. The *New York Times* regularly prints front-page stories accompanied by pictures, associating blacks with spousal abuse, drugs, child abandonment, and illegitimacy. This coverage reached its *National Enquirer* low with the front-page photo of a black baby who'd been murdered by his parents after having been abused with a toilet plunger. This was rivaled by another front-page story in April 1993 about a black man murdering a white woman during a domestic dispute. Pictures of the couple were printed on the front page; the story jumped to the inside where it took up an entire page of the newspaper. Though editors at the *Times, New York* magazine, and producers of the network news shows feel their goods to be superior to tabloid shows like "Hard Copy," "Inside Edition," "A Current Affair," "Unsolved Mysteries," and "America's Most Wanted," I believe that these programs have more dignity since they're not prone to blaming everything on blacks.

When the *Times* is not maligning black character in print— Sam Roberts's column is a virtual sniper's nest against blacks— they do the job with pictures and Willie Horton–style layouts. For example, in Anne Matthews's *New York Times Magazine* article "Crime Turns the Campus into an Armed Camp," the victims of crime were represented by photos of white women and the group causing the problems, alcoholism, robbery, were represented by photos of black males and one Asian male. With this layout the *Times* was suggesting that if black and Asian males weren't on American campuses, campus crime would vanish. This conclusion runs counter to a study aired on CNN, which reported that the typical perpetrator of campus crime is a nineteen-year-old white male. College presidents were accused of remaining silent about the crime situation as a way of staving off bad publicity. This response is typical of the way the media and other institutions deal with white pathology. Silence.

In the print and electronic media, pictures of blacks are associated with social pathology, while whites are represented as society's stewards. They are shown counseling and assisting blacks who mess up in other ways, or speaking on their behalf. The coverage of whites by the media is similar to the plot of the movie *Grand Canyon*. Whites were born to prevent blacks and Latinos from getting into trouble, and Asian Americans are depicted as the group that blacks and Latinos ought to be like.

Jim Sleeper is one of many journalists who have realized the potential profits from becoming a professional critic of black character. In *Tikkun* magazine Sleeper argued that blacks ought to try to imitate the scholastic achievement of Vietnamese Americans. But according to Bill Ong Hing, a professor of Immigration Law at Stanford University, among Asian Americans the Vietnamese have the fastest growing dropout rate in California. I don't know whether Jim Sleeper is ignorant of the facts, lazy, or whether he merely realizes that he has a good salable product going for him.

Asian American intellectuals like Peter Kwong *(The New Chinatown)* and Ronald Takaki *(Strangers from A Different Shore)* and journalist William Wong complain about what they regard as the "model minority" stereotype, but their opinions are ignored by the very media that praise their groups for their devotion to the work ethic. Gwen Kinkead *(Chinatown, A Portrait of a Closed Society)* writes about a crime-infested community quite different from the one portrayed in publications such as the *New Republic* and the *National Review.* Chinese American gangs control 60 percent of New York's heroin trade—a fact that doesn't attract the attention of conservative writers who always lecture blacks about drug-related crime. When it comes to criminal gangs, however, the media and the segregated American opinion industry seem incapable of seeing any color other than black.

(Ironically, in the 1890s, when the Japanese were feared and hated, San Francisco papers designated blacks as the model minority. "The negro always takes an interest in every crop that he cultivates and he is more easily managed than the Japanese," editorialized the *San Francisco Chronicle* in 1897.)

Just as whites speak for blacks, they also speak for Asian Americans, thereby protecting white Americans from the harsh criticism of American society made by militant Asian American intellectuals. No one seems to care about what veteran dissident Frank Chin or a new generation of Chinese Americans like Hoyt Sze feel about issues such as assimilation. When Andrew Hacker wrote a typical why-can't-you-blacks-be-like-Asians article,

Frank Chin wrote a reply to the *New York Review of Books*, which went unpublished. I published it in my magazine, *Konch*. Chin answered Hacker's argument that the "real and deep racial dilemma remains," because "whites feel blacks and others should adapt to white ways," an indirect blessing of Asian Americans who have, in the eyes of Hacker, Sleeper, and others, done exactly that. Chin wrote: "Just because we read, write and speak your language as well as you do, Mr. Hacker, does not mean we believe your rhetoric, agree with your racist cowardice. . . . The Asian or black or any non-white 'model minority' Shangri-la people is a fiction, a product of white racist self-serving wishful thinking, not reality."

Chin's *The Year of the Dragon*, a play that was broadcast on the PBS network in the '70s, had the same effect on audiences as Richard Wright's *Native Son*. It showed white audiences Chinese tour guides smiling at them during their tours of Chinatown and pouring out their resentment in private. The four horsemen of Asian American literature, Jeffery Paul Chan, Frank Chin, Lawson Fusao Inada, and Shawn Wong wrote in the *Big Aiiieeeee*, a magazine they edit, "We began another year angry! Another decade, and another Chinese American ventriloquizing the same old white Christian fantasy of little Chinese victims of 'the original sin of being born to a brutish, sadomasochistic culture of cruelty and victimization' fleeing to America in search of freedom from everything Chinese and seeking white acceptance, and of being victimized by stupid white racists and then being reborn in acculturation and honorary whiteness. Every Chinese American book ever published in the United States of America by a major publisher has been a Christian autobiography or autobiographical novel." This sort of social protest makes contemporary conservative writings by the media-ordained black critics and writers seem tame.

Asian American militant writing is not the only minority writing, however, that criticizes white American society in an incisive manner. In fact, compared to other minority writers, blacks, no matter how militant, are in the political center. No black writer has challenged the values of white society as trenchantly as Leslie Silko, a Native American writer. Her book, *The Almanac of the Dead*, one of the most powerful novels ever written by an American, prophesies an apocalyptic doom for American Civilization, because of its atrocious treatment of Native Americans. In the novel, white serial murderers are guided by the voices of dead Native Americans, craving revenge. The same voices urge suburban whites to suicide and "accidental" death. By comparison James Baldwin's and Eldridge Cleaver's indictments of white society amount to little more than gentle nudging.

While Asian Americans are promoted as a model minority by an establishment media, their tangle of pathologies being virtually ignored, Latinos are all but invisible to the media. To show that another community is beset by problems, which in some ways are more devastating than those suffered by millions of blacks, is to challenge the notion that all other colored minorities can make it except for blacks. Latinos suffer from poverty, high school dropout rates, and other problems that the media portray as peculiarly black problems. Writer Brent Staples was correct to point out that though "Gang Violence is often thought of as a black problem . . . Latinos lead the country in gang killings, with Asians tending toward extortion and theft."

An example of how Latino culture is viewed as one of invisibility can be seen in an exchange between Martin Peretz, editor in chief of the *New Republic*, and writer Nicolas Kanelos. In the June 5, 1989 issue of the *New Republic*, Martin Peretz wrote: "Let's imagine a literature professor designing a course in keeping with the new ideological marching orders. She chooses some black authors and is eager to bone up on some Hispanic ones from the United States, *especially if someone will tell her who they are* [my italics]. She also doesn't know the work of many Asian American writers. But, then, who does?" (German critics like Gunther Lenz and English critics like Bob Lee, who are acquainted with American multicultural literature, must chuckle at this kind of remark.) Nicolas Kanelos answered Mr. Peretz in the 1989 issue of *Before Columbus Review:* "It is obvious that Mr. Peretz did not take the time to research and evaluate the history and accomplishments of the non-white American ethnic people—traditionally the 'other' in official American Civilization. Had he done so, he would have found out, for instance, that Hispanic letters north of the Rio Grande date back to 1598, with an epic poem on the colonizing of New Mexico, and, since then, thousands of volumes have been written, mostly in Spanish, but also in English (since the nineteenth century)."

Just as the yellow underclasses are ignored by the media, so are a prodigious number of white poor. Proportionate coverage of white poverty in America would make the story of blacks in America a triumph instead of the failure that the media focus upon. But white poverty isn't the only pathology in the tangle of pathologies one finds in white America. Instead of discussing these the media rarely mentions them.

Much of my data is garnered from the very newspapers and television news shows where think-tank operatives discuss crime, drugs, illegitimacy, and welfare as predominantly black problems. Even when a reporter on a news show presents the facts regarding a particular social malady—for example, that two-thirds of American welfare recipients are white and two-thirds reside in the rural areas of the United States—the pictures accompanying the narrative usually depict blacks.

The *New York Times,* for instance, which used pictures of two black men to accompany a story about child abandonment, presented a different picture when citing a serious study about the issue. The study, conducted by Frank Furstenberg and Kathleen Mullan Harris of the University of Pennsylvania, involved a representative sample of the population according to race, geography, income, and education. It concluded that "Although it has long been common knowledge that many poor children, especially those whose parents never wed, had little contact with their fathers, . . . the phenomenon of the disappearing father is alarmingly widespread."

Two-thirds of American children will spend a period of their lives in a single-parent household. Secretary of Health Louis Sullivan, a black member of the Bush cabinet, put the number at 60 percent. Clearly this is not a problem peculiar to the black community. With the rise of single-parent households and the United States's soaring divorce rate, child abandonment is an issue that cuts across racial and class lines. According to the American Association of Retired Persons, one-third of the women who get divorced are left in poverty. (In fact, the next time a conservative brings up black child abandonment to me I'm going to ask him when he last saw his children.) The media seldom mention the millions of white women—many of them middle class—on the dole as a result of being abandoned by their husbands. While poor black men are scolded in op-eds and by think-tank infotainers for abandoning their families (often the reason is because a woman can not receive financial aid if there is a man in the household), the fact that middle-class and upper-class white men leave their wives and children in poverty receives little editorial comment. In relation to the entire U.S. population the proportion of white single mothers (37.9 percent in 1990) who live in poverty exceeds that for the entire black population (29.3 percent).

In addition, those who assert that the two-parent household is the solution to black poverty can't explain the fact that 50 percent of the children who live in poverty, live in two-parent homes located in rural and suburban America. A study conducted by Mary Jo Bane and David Ellwood of Harvard's Kennedy School of Government, and printed in *Science,* finds that "Half of America's poor children live in two-parent homes, often in suburban and rural areas," and concludes that "the key to understanding poverty lies beyond an exclusive focus on the ghetto poor." Though the media portrays the urban environment as violent and the white suburbs as quiescent, battery in the home is the leading cause of injury of American women, and child abuse, committed by both men and women, also occurs in the home. This happens in equal proportions in the suburbs, rural areas, and the urban areas. Feminists may have a point when they say that the two-parent household may be the most dangerous place for a woman to be. That also goes for children.

Contrary to feminist propaganda, men aren't the only perpetrators of domestic violence. A report issued by Sheriff Sheman Block, dealing with child abuse in Los Angeles County, revealed that in 1991, for the first time, "mothers represented the greatest perpetrators of child abuse with 41 percent of the cases linked to mothers." Though the proportion of black children killed by parents and caretakers dropped, "the proportion of white victims jumped from 20 percent to 31 percent."

Responding to one of Alice Walker's frequently venomous attacks on black men, this time printed on the op-ed pages of the *New York Times*, May 5, 1993, Elaine Brown said that violence is frequently learned from the mother ("Mammy's not-so-nurturing switch"). Feminists like Cornel West and Henry Louis Gates, who believe that critics of Alice Walker are "misguided," seem to be restricted by feminist ideology, for they rarely, if ever, comment on violence meted out by matriarchy. They would be hard pressed to explain why two-thirds of the rapists in the California prisons were abused by their mothers, according to *Gender Monthly*. West and Gates air their views about black misogyny in the *New York Times* where no ethnic group of men has been maligned for misogyny as much as black men. I know for a fact that letters to the *Times* about, for example, Italian American misogyny go unpublished. This is typical.

Violence isn't the only suburban problem. Dr. Arnold Washton, director of a New York treatment center, said that there are more crack addicts among white middle-class people than any other segment of the population "despite all of the poor black crack addicts you see on TV and Page One."

A study conducted by National Rural Development Institute

13

contradicts the claims of Mr. Walter Goodman and others that the black urban underclass is our "least tractable social problem." It concluded that the social and economic strains facing rural children are every bit as bad, perhaps worse, than those facing city youth. Predictably, Goodman, a neoconservative, raises the issue of young unwed black women, regularly, in his *Times* column. While the rate of unwed black mothers is on the decline, the fastest rising rate of "illegitimacy" is among white women (who also have the highest percentage of cocaine pregnancies). According to the Children's Defense Fund, "two-thirds of the teens who give birth each year are white, and two-thirds do not live in big cities." So why are Mr. Goodman and other neoconservatives so concerned about unwed black women yet shun the problem of unwed and poverty-stricken white mothers? Is it because he believes that these black women are soaking up the welfare budget? This myth and others like it were ably refuted by black women scholars and professionals in an issue of the *Nation* that was aptly entitled "Scapegoating the Black Family."

Moreover, Terry K. Adams and Greg J. Duncan, in their study "The Persistence of Urban Poverty and Its Demographic and Behavioral Correlates," say that "Media images of urban poverty often present households headed by young, never married black women. . . . [D]ata show that this image does not fit most or even a substantial minority of the persistently poor living in urban areas." To argue that the fractured family exists only in the inner city is to engage in the worst kind of racially based hypocrisy. Indeed, one of the first novels written by a black author, William Wells Brown, dealt with Thomas Jefferson's fractured family. Even Tamar Levin, Goodman's *Times* colleague, writing about fathers who desert their children, says that the phenomenon of the disappearing father is not confined to poor people, but is "alarmingly widespread."

Many of the new poor are white mothers who are either divorced or separated from their husbands. (Only 44 percent of the fathers who are obligated to pay child support actually do so, according to *USA Today*.) National Displaced Homemakers, an organization devoted to improving the circumstances of these impoverished women, reports that "[o]ne in five are living with unrelated people in doubled up households. Three quarters of the displaced household members, which rose from 13 million in 1987 to 15 million in 1989, are white." According to the American Association of Retired Persons, one third of divorced women live in poverty. Sometimes it seems that the only difference between a poor man not marrying a woman and leaving her broke and a middle-class and upper-class man marrying a woman and then leaving her broke is that the poor get chastised more by neoconservative columnists who ignore the delinquency of white men, some of whom belong to their class. For them to see the fractured family, in a country where almost half of the marriages end in divorce, as a peculiarly black phenomenon sounds racist.

Often, it seems that the media are willing to promote a racial war in America in order to boost their ratings. A sensational piece of bilge carried on CNN, April 24, 1993 was entitled "Mounting Urban Violence." The program showed blacks with guns as perpetrators of crimes and whites at shooting ranges preparing to defend themselves. Even though white-on-white crime involving guns is pervasive, rarely are whites as a group portrayed as violent people—this in spite of the fact that a study printed in the *New York Times* concluded that whites, among racial groups, are the ones most likely to engage in violence against all other groups, Asian Americans, African Americans, Latinos, gays, lesbians, Jews, pro-choice advocates, etc. Still, violence and drugs are perceived as black problems.

Typical was a story about violence printed in the *Parade* section of the *Sunday Examiner & Chronicle* entitled "Tame the Beast Inside." Accompanying this story about dealing with managing one's own "fear and rage," written by former world champion boxer Jose Torres, was a photo of black youth rioting in Los Angeles after the first Rodney King verdict. (Here again, the white and Latino participation in the riots has been removed.) In a sidebar eight teenagers were asked, "Why Is There So Much Violence?" All eight teenagers were black. Black kids are constantly associated with violence in the media.

After years of front-page pictures about black violence in inner-city schools, the *New York Times,* on April 21, 1993, quoted a Justice Department report of 1989, which found "surprisingly little difference between cities, suburbs, and non-metropolitan areas in a number of measures of school violence." Yet even when the media does report stories of white violence the participants are often provided with excuses. For instance, a rise in battery against women that occurred in Alaska was blamed on male depression about unemployment that resulted from the Exxon oil disaster. The murder of a Little League baseball player by a youngster on a rival team was blamed on violence in adult sports. But the network news shows illustrated this story with pictures of black athletes fighting instead of showing white athletes engaged in brawls.

By offering justifications or explanations for this violence instead of condemning it, the news media and the neoconservative policy wonks often seem to be condoning it in a manner similar to how some members of the German government blame violence against foreigners on the foreigners. When a black man was murdered by a white mob in the Howard Beach section of New York City, a *New York Times* writer said that it was because whites were afraid of the underclass. When a trigger-happy white Louisiana suburbanite killed a visiting Japanese student, Yoshihiro Hattori, who had mistakenly knocked on the wrong door, NBC News said that the Japanese ought to learn slang so that they will understand what is meant by *freeze.*

Attacks upon Asian Americans by white individuals and mobs is on the rise. Vincent Chin, a Chinese American, was beaten to death because two white men mistook him for a Japanese. They were acquitted. On August 25, 1992, Milton Fujii,

Japanese American director of community affairs for the University of California at Berkeley, was attacked by a left-wing white mob that mistook him for the Chinese American Chancellor, Chang-lin Tien, with whom they had a dispute. A member of the mob yelled at him, "Lock up the Japanese. Intern the Japanese." Echoing the 1990 study that concluded that members of the white group are those most likely to assault members of all other groups, a study released in May of 1993 by Northeastern University's Center for Applied Social Research concluded that 60 percent of those who commit urban hate crimes are young white males.

Hundreds of thousands of women are raped each year by white males, but unlike some black urban males who assault women, these suburban males are neither referred to as "a bizarre new form of human" life by white writers like Pete Hamill, nor accused of lacking values by people like Joe Klein.

White suburban women who are tackled and pummeled by their drunken husbands on Superbowl Sunday must be shocked to hear that all of the violence in the United States takes place in the inner city. They are encouraged and glamorized by firearms organizations and the media when they arm against the black male underclass, but statistically they are most likely to have these weapons used against them by their boyfriends and husbands. The media also ignore the fact that with such weapons in the home gunshot wounds are the third leading cause of death of American children, black and white, and that 75 percent of suicides among men over age sixty-five between 1979 and 1988, according to the American Society on Aging, were from such firearms.

Though violence is stereotyped as a black issue, whites commit, according to the *Wall Street Journal*, 54 percent of all violent crimes, and the sharp increase in violent crime over the past decade has been the same among blacks and whites alike. Reporting the same facts on August 29, 1992, the FBI said that the rise in crime not only occurred among poor youths in urban areas, but "in all races, social classes, and lifestyles." Yet when CNN network carried the story, they used pictures of blacks only and virtually ignored the white perpetrators of violent crime, another example of how the media and the think-tank wonks protect whites. And when the Centers for Disease Control issues a report that "white teenagers have the fastest growing death rate [from gunshot wounds], up 24 percent a year from 1988–1990," this gets completely ignored by writers from the *Atlantic Monthly, Harper's, New York* magazine, the *New Republic,* the *McLaughlin Report,* and other infotainment outlets.

Claims made by journalist Jim Sleeper in an issue of *Tikkun* that crime is "heavily black" and urban, an attitude endorsed by Michael Kaus *(The End of Equality),* is contrary to conclusions of a Senate committee chaired by Joseph Biden, Jr., which described the increase of violent crime in the rural areas of the United States as "astonishing." "Most rural states—those with 50 persons or fewer per square mile—had greater increases in violent crime over the past year than did New York City," the Biden committee reported. Another Senate committee, chaired by Senator Herb Kohl, concluded that racial disparities in the criminal justice system account for the large number of incarcerated black youth, who are four times more likely to be incarcerated than whites who commit the same crime. Mr. Kaus, of all people, should know that the inner cities are not the only places where social pathology occurs. He grew up in Beverly Hills.

Though black ethnic character has been discussed in a negative fashion frequently in the print and electronic media, journalists, like the *Times* reporter who congratulated a black woman for courageously airing the dirty laundry of the black community, have a habit of hailing every new black-pathology author for "breaking the silence" or saying the "unspoken" about the root of problems in the black community. Rarely do the commentators who are on the payroll of these magazines comment about the social distress among the ethnic groups to which they belong. One wonders when black-pathology thinkers like Lee Eisenberg, Norman Podhoretz, Ben Wattenberg, Roger Rosenblatt, and the Jewish American commentators who lined up behind Anita Hill are going to "break the silence" about the pathological violence among Jewish Americans, which, according to Barbara Harris, executive director of the Transition Center, a kosher shelter for battered women and children in Queens, New York, exists in over 10 percent of Jewish American homes.

"Nobody likes to talk about it because Jews as a group take a lot of pride in looking good," explains Julie Spitzer, associate rabbi at Baltimore Hebrew Congregational and author of *Spousal Abuse in Rabbinic and Contemporary Judaism* (1985). "We live with so many myths. Jewish families are not supposed to be dysfunctional, and Jewish husbands are supposed to be, by definition, nurturing," Sherry Berliner Dimarsky, executive director of SHALVA (Safe Homes Advice and Legal Aid for Victims of Abuse) was quoted as saying in the winter issue of *Lilith* magazine. Don't feminists at *Ms.* magazine, NPR, and the *Village Voice* who have made black misogyny into a fetish care about what happens to Jewish American women? Why doesn't Ted Koppel do an edition of "Nightline" about the subject? He could invite Mickey Kaus on to give his opinions. What about the *New Republic, Harper's,* the *New York Times Magazine?* Walter Goodman? Why haven't they addressed the problem of the Jewish American dysfunctional family?

Members of the Jewish American group are not the only ones who have a stake in looking good. Mary Sansome, of the Congress of Italian American Organizations, says that she has a difficult time obtaining funds for Italian Americans because the government and city agencies feel there's no need. When is the last time that black underclass theorist Ken Auletta commented on the Italian American underclass?

As long as some ethnic groups continue to hide their underclass for fear of looking bad, a true picture of the American underclass will never emerge, and blacks will continue to be scapegoated by opportunists out to make a quick buck, or to enhance some career move, or to hype ratings and newsstand sales.

Irish American writer Pete Hamill's scolding of black Americans in *Esquire* included only sixteen lines about the white underclass. Unlike many black-pathology writers, he at least admits that it exists but says that it's been contained. Contained? A study released in October 1992 by the Center on Budget and Policy Priorities disagrees with Hamill's throwaway line. While the increase among black and Latino poor rose 22 percent each between 1989 and 1991, whites accounted for 51 percent of the increase. "Half of the nation's 35.7 million poor people are non-Hispanic whites and recent poverty trends among this group have not been encouraging. Nevertheless, poverty among non-Hispanic whites has received scant attention in recent years. Many Americans think of the poor as being predominantly members of minority groups, and poverty debates in this country frequently become ensnared in controversies about race and ethnicity," the report concluded.

Organized crime, which includes Irish American, Italian American and Jewish American members, is expanding its influence in American society by taking over businesses, unions, and other legitimate segments, as well as continuing to participate in the kind of professional violence that amateurish black muggers and crackers don't have the sophistication or the equipment to create. Commented Rudolph W. Giuliani, United States attorney in Manhattan, "if we take back the labor unions, the legitimate businesses, eventually they become just another street gang. Spiritually, psychologically, they've always been just a street gang."

Not only does organized crime, a coalition of mostly white ethnics, earn tax-free revenue in the hundreds of billions of dollars; it also influences foreign policy. Yet, concluded Hamill in his *Esquire* article "Breaking The Silence" (March 1988), the black underclass is a greater threat to our national security than the Russians. What a preposterous conclusion. It's ironic that the same claim was made by Irish-pathology writers only two generations ago.

The claim that white ethnics made it to the suburbs from Ellis Island solely through legitimate hard work and traditional values is just a Reaganite, Fourth of July lie. In his book *The Rise and Fall of the Jewish Gangster in America*, Albert Fried wrote, "It is no secret that Jewish criminals did what others did before them and have continued to do, that they all have used crime as another way of moving upward and onward in the American manner. First the Irish . . . ; then the Jews and the Italians; and now, presumably, the Blacks and Hispanics and the Chinese too have successively climbed the same queer ladder."

One could argue, however, that blacks were never able to accumulate as much profit from the underground economy as the white underclass because of racism, even when it came to exploiting their own neighborhoods. The movie *Cotton Club*, written by Irish American William Kennedy, is about the Irish and Jewish underclass fighting for domination over the multibillion dollar Harlem policy racket. Ted Robert Gurr, professor of political science at the University of Colorado, has written, "From the 1840s to the end of large-scale European immigration after 1918, each new wave of immigrants—Irish, Germans, Italians—added disproportionately to crime and mayhem in our cities." The fact that Hamill lectured the black underclass for its pathologies and devoted only sixteen lines to a far more lethal white underclass, and none to other nonwhite underclasses, could be considered racist. Yet Eisenberg, in his sensational flame-throwing and irresponsible introduction to Hamill's article, said that anybody who opposed Hamill's arguments is a racist ideologue.

Hamill's criticisms of the black underclass have been made about some Irish Americans, the group to which Hamill and William Buckley and Moynihan belong. Hamill, who apparently agrees with William Buckley that blacks are heavily into drugs and illegitimate children, ignored the fact that this is the same stereotypical charge made against the Irish, only in this case the drug is alcohol, which is responsible for many more pathologies—such as wife abuse and vehicular homicide—than drugs. As for illegitimacy, Bob Callahan, author of *The Big Book of The American Irish*, points to the stereotype that the typical Irish American was a person with thirty-five children that he couldn't support, all of whom were headed for the poor house. As for crime, Callahan remembers growing up in a New England in the 1930s and 1940s where the newspapers separated information about "American Crime" from "Hibernian Crime."

While some blacks may enter a career of street crime (just as some Irish American gangs like the Westies), Irish Americans are now more associated with white collar or government crime, particularly pertinent when you consider that the last presidential administration included Irish Americans in key posts and was one of the most scandal-laden in history. According to Callahan, all the pathologies on Moynihan and Hamill's list exist in the Irish American community.

In a recent PBS documentary series, "Crime, Inc.," "hundreds" of people, far more than those who are being murdered in Washington, D.C. and Los Angeles, were murdered in the streets of New York as "underclass" Irish American, Jewish American, and Italian American gangs fought over the spoils of the bootlegging racket. But white gang activity isn't merely a thing of the past. It exists today. Martin Sanchez Jankowski *(Islands in the Street: Gangs and American Urban Society)* discusses the existence of white gangs. Such gangs, however, rarely, if ever, show up in the discussions of social pathology by professional intellectuals. For example, the most violent gang of the last twenty years, according to the New York City police, was not a black or Hispanic gang but the Westies, an Irish American gang, whose activities are explored by T.J. English *(The Westies)*. According to English, the Westies were "the most brutal men this violent nation has ever seen." I've never heard such Irish American critics of blacks as Charles Murray, William F. Buckley, or Pete Hamill discuss the Westies or even acknowledge the fact that close to 100,000 illegal Irish immigrants reside in Northern California, some of whom are blackmailed by their employers into working for sub–minimum wages.

If Pete Hamill, author of *Letter to a Black Friend*, thinks it's a good idea for black middle-class people to return to the ghettos to aid their "underclass" brothers and sisters, then why isn't it a good idea for Mr. Hamill to relocate to South Boston or the Bronx to aid the Irish American "underclass"? Hamill went so far as to suggest that some kind of genetic mutation, a "bizarre new form of life" explained crime in the inner city. Yet when William A. Tatum was slated to become the editor of the race-baiting and inflammatory *New York Post*, Hamill compared Tatum's coverage of Jews with that of the Nazi magazine, *Die Sturmer's*. I thought that was ironic, since casting unpopular minorities as "animals" (Hamill's word for inner-city youth) and as members of a separate species was *Die Sturmer's* trademark.

Doesn't Hamill care about the suffering of millions of Irish Americans? Don't Ben Wattenberg, Nathan Glazer, and others care about the Jewish American underclass? During David Dinkin's first political campaign for mayor, he said that 44,000 Jewish Americans live in poverty in New York City alone. Don't the people at the *New Republic* or the *New York Review of Books* consider the plight of impoverished Jewish American senior citizens in Florida to be worthy of some of the space it devotes to denouncing black culture and values? The attitudes of some white ethnic critics of black behavior could be considered hypocritical. I asked a young white critic and friend, who was accosting me at a Cambridge party about my misogyny, what he was doing to alleviate the suffering of thousands of women who belong to his particular ethnic group—Polish American women. He said that he didn't identify with them. Why don't the critics of black culture and behavior identify with the less fortunate members of their groups? Why doesn't William Buckley, Jr., do a special broadcast of "Firing Line" from Appalachia to high-light the suffering and impoverishment of thousands of Irish Americans who live there?

As I began to accumulate more material, I discovered that even I had succumbed to myths about the black community.

I grew up in petit bourgeois surroundings where people were not just devoted to the work ethic but were members of a virtual work cult. My late stepfather is regarded as a saint because he worked hard all of his life, rarely missing a day. He became a devoted patriot and church worker because American society had rewarded him, he believed, for his hard work. (But even with his capabilities, he wasn't offered the job of plant foreman at Chevrolet until a few years before his retirement. He blamed the fact that he had been passed over for the job on racism. When they approached him about the job, he told them, bitterly, to give it to his sons.) A childhood friend of mine who was recently killed in an automobile accident is regarded as a martyr because his death occurred when he fell asleep at the wheel, while driving to a second job. Among the people whom I grew up around, people who are seldom featured by the media, working with your hands was considered more difficult and honorable than working with your head. The moral exemplars in our community were those who put in a lot of overtime. Welfare cheaters and idlers were spoken of in less than endearing terms. I was influenced by these values, but upon closely examining the attitudes of my relatives and their friends and even myself toward those less fortunate, I realized that some of these attitudes were in fact based upon myths.

Shortly after my stepfather died an excruciating death—a man who was married to the same woman for thirty-seven years and who left a will assuring that she would live the rest of her days in comfort, a man who taught Sunday school for thirty years—I heard a black-pathology hustler whose career has been advanced by his loud and ugly denouncement of black leaders and black people talk about a "poverty of values" within the inner city. I thought of the millions of black people who, like my father, and my childhood friend, pay their dues, only to be smeared by show-boating media hotdogs out to make a quick buck as opinion makers. I think that if I had found myself face to face with this man, at that moment, I would have punched him out, even though I'm not a violent man. But this man, and others like him, have generous access to a media that shuts most blacks, Latinos, and other minorities out.

The lack of minority representation in the media for me was exemplified during an exchange between George Will and Sam Donaldson on an edition of "This Week with David Brinkley." Donaldson asked Will how the black community felt about a certain subject. If George Will is a spokesperson for blacks in the media, then black people are really in trouble. This is a man who described the racist reaction to the Goetz shooting of four unarmed black men as "healthy," and the shooting down of an unarmed Iranian airbus, deliberately, by American forces, as "ethical."

After I began to collect and examine material I began to notice that the media, even a place like National Public Radio, had accepted the corporate think tankers' "underclass" theory of America's social problems, that is, that a majority of America's social problems were related to the personal behavior of black people. NPR's Daniel Zwerdling's coverage of Africa, shuttling back and forth between Kenya and Liberia, consisted of dishing up the most sensational and ghoulish stories for the entertainment of his upscale audience. His negative report on Zambia, aired on May 9, 1993, was typical. Journalists should cover corruption in Kenya, but that's all we get from them. Lurid stories with hints of cannibalism. African journalists complain that the American media only cover the basket cases of the continent and never mention the role that the United States and the Soviet Union played in creating those basket cases. The civil wars, the arms race, and other problems that ravage the continent. Listening to NPR's Africa coverage, you wouldn't know that there are fifty countries in postcolonial Africa.

I began to tape news shows and commentaries. One particularly shocking to me was a commentary by Roger Rosenblatt, of the "MacNeil/Lehrer News Hour," during which the black youth involved in the Central Park rape of a young stockbroker was used to smear *all* black youth, whose activities were equated with Satanism.

After examining all of this evidence, which clearly showed that the media was scapegoating blacks, and occasionally Latinos, for America's problems, I talked about my frustration during a panel held by Bumbershoot, an annual Seattle Arts Festival. I casually mentioned that maybe there should be a boycott of television network news, as a way of highlighting the abuses of blacks and Latinos by network news. I was not prepared for the enthusiastic response. The summer before the Seattle festival, I had gathered some young black professionals to show them the Roger Rosenblatt tape, which, for me, was the last straw.

They were interested in organizing a boycott against network television news, but their interest didn't survive one meeting. After I returned from Seattle, I asked novelist Floyd Salas, president of PEN Oakland, whether he would appoint me to head a committee that would organize a one-month boycott against television network news. Salas not only agreed, but it was largely due to his efforts, along with Claire Otalda, and Gregory Nicosia, that, despite opposition from some members of PEN West, a resolution was finally passed at the PEN International conference, at Rio, in 1992.

I contacted writers, scholars, and artists and, with very little cash, PEN Oakland and the Before Columbus Foundation sponsored town meetings, panel sessions, and poetry and fiction readings, to deal with the lack of balance in images of blacks and Latinos. These meetings took place in ten cities. By coincidence, I was asked to write a piece for the op-ed page of the *New York Times*. I told the editor about the boycott and asked whether this would be a suitable subject for an op-ed. "Why Boycott TV Network News," in which I announced the PEN Oakland Boycott and the reasons for it, was published in the *New York Times*. The response to the article far exceeded my expectations.

The PEN Oakland post office box was flooded with mail. The boycott tapped into black, Latino, and even white anxiety about media coverage of blacks and Latinos. The *New York Times* critic Walter Goodman, who believes that dysfunctional families are the reason that blacks don't prosper (but can't seem to explain the material success of thousands of dysfunctional white families), accused us of "frightening network executives" in an April 14, 1991, column entitled "Drawbacks to a Boycott of TV Network News." I answered Mr. Goodman with "Blaming Everything on Blacks," an abbreviated version of which was published in the *Oakland Tribune*. Goodman accused me of desiring Affirmative Action quotas when I pointed out how pictures—such as those broadcast on the "MacNeil/Lehrer News Hour" to accompany the Rosenblatt commentary—frame black people for social pathologies that are widespread in American society. But the tapes, and other data that I have accumulated, provide irrefutable evidence that such is the case.

Some of this may be due to the fact that some TV news film crew personnel, from my experience at least, are more to the Right than the reporters. For instance, after I was taped for an NBC News network show in 1989, the cameraman began to taunt me about crack, illegitimacy among young black women, and so on. When I informed him that the typical person involved in such behavior was white, a spirited discussion ensued that spilled out onto my front porch. The last thing I said to him was that his network, NBC, with CNN, is a major contributor to myths that all antisocial behavior is black. (Ironically, six months after PEN Oakland's first annual boycott of network news shows, a NBC network representative contacted me about sharing some of my documentation with them. Their representative seemed surprised that rural youth suffer more, using all of the indexes, than urban youth. NBC never reimbursed me for the cost of faxing my research to them.)

Mr. Goodman is one of a number of reporters and columnists at the *New York Times* who are disciples of Moynihanism. Just like religious fundamentalists, who, incidentally, are also ridiculed and grossly caricatured in the *Times,* they refuse to entertain any facts that would dispute the dogma. If, as Sam Roberts claims, Daniel Moynihan showed "courage" when he predicted the rising proportion of single-parent households in the black community, did Moynihan's *inability* to predict the rapid rise in white illegitimate births show a lack of courage? Though underclass activities exist in yellow, white, and brown communities, the *Times* hasn't assigned a Sam Roberts to monitor those as much as blacks are monitored.

In his reply, Goodman also mentioned that the number of blacks engaged in these activities is disproportionate to their numbers in the population. I'm not so sure. Take crime for example. Some studies assert that whites commit crimes in the same proportion as blacks, but because of racist practices in the criminal justice system, blacks get arrested more. Sheriff Michael Hennessey blamed the fact that African Americans make up nearly half of the San Francisco County jail population on "institutional racism. . . . The lopsided numbers . . . are an indictment of our society's priorities and its inability to create equal justice under the law," he said.

For our first boycott we were able to assemble a coalition unheard of in these days of division and polarization. Buddhists in Boulder, Colorado; blacks and whites; Latinos in Houston, Texas, and New York; gays and lesbians; integrationists in Berkeley, California, and nationalists in Atlanta, Georgia. Writers in Boston, Brooklyn, New Orleans, Washington, D.C., and Detroit. During some of the events, writers addressed the stereotypes of African Americans, Latinos, and Asian Americans that pour into the nation's living rooms each night; others concentrated on specific shows. Boycott Coordinator Professor Eugene Redmond's East St. Louis group responded to what African Americans of that city considered to be an unfair and biased portrait of East St. Louis that appeared on CBS's "Sixty Minutes."

Of the Oakland kickoff event *Oakland Tribune* columnist Alix Christie noted that "two hours of poems, songs and appeals by Blacks, Whites, Latinos, and Asians" dealt with the "exclusion of a diversity of viewpoints from television news." She hailed it as "the truest town meeting I've seen."

The applause in Seattle that greeted my suggestion that a boycott take place was not the only surprise in store for me during my organizing activities: In a one-hour exchange with phone-in participants on Jay Marvin's WTKN radio show in Tampa, Florida, even the right-wing callers agreed that the picture of African Americans on television is not balanced.

Representatives of the networks who were asked by reporters to respond to PEN Oakland's complaints agreed that there is a problem, but their explanations for the problems were not, in my opinion, convincing. Answering the issues raised by PEN Oakland's boycott on National Public Radio, ABC's ombudsman said that ABC television news merely "reflected reality" because "crime, poverty, and violence are urban problems." When challenged by Washington drug policy experts, who'd been invited to appear on the show by Bill Drummond, of the University of California at Berkeley's School of Journalism, he had to back down. CNN's Ed Turner and Steve Haworth said that black faces go with drug stories on their network "because they rely upon local police forces when busts are going to be made, and don't get calls saying there's going to be a bust of a high school in a white neighborhood." Home Box Office did a feature called "Crack USA" and apparently had no difficulty in locating a number of white crack faces.

In September 1991, CNN aired a series called "Black Men in Crisis." Its simplistic conclusion was that black men in Atlanta commit crime out of "boredom" and "impulse." A psychiatrist was brought on to give the conclusion a predictable neoconservative sound bite. He said that all of their problems came not from unemployment, poverty, and racism but from "inside" of them. I've never seen any of the networks do a long-distance psychoanalysis of white and Asian ethnic criminals who commit far more profitable crimes. Nor have I seen any of the white males, whose inside trading crimes threaten the foundation of the capitalistic society, brought onto the couch. The following year, Larry Woods, the commentator on "Black Men in Crisis," travelled to the Midwest to do a show that represented blonde, hard-working farmers as the salt of the earth.

Don Browne, executive director of NBC News, finally said, in response to the boycott, that the best way to avoid negative stereotypes is to hire more black journalists, editors, and producers. A move I would applaud. If, since that date, NBC has hired more minorities, it certainly doesn't seem to have affected their nightly news programming.

The most thorough response to our boycott was made by the San Francisco ABC affiliate. During a lengthy feature about the boycott, KGO-TV agreed that television news reports unfairly focus on blacks in drug stories and furnished statistics and graphs to show the lack of minority hiring by the news media. Now "ABC World News Tonight" might even show a white cocaine infant from time to time. But in a series called "The American Agenda," their use of disproportionately black images to go with "social pathologies" is no different from that of the other television networks. Toward the end of 1992, "The America Agenda" report on heroin addiction showed blacks, exclusively. This integrated staff should be informed that members of yellow and white ethnic groups are the ones who drive the heroin market, not blacks.

If I have a beef about newspaper coverage I can always write a letter. And the newspapers, to their credit, often publish stories that indicate that some of their emotional and sensational op-ed writers and columnists occasionally do push myths about minorities ("The Mythology of Black Violence in America," "Myths of the Black Underclass," "Negative Stereotypes About Welfare Recipients," and "Crack Is Not a Black Monopoly," are among the clippings that I possess.) And local television stations usually include community programs that are moderated by blacks, Latinos, and Asian Americans. Radio stations include call-in programs that are as close to participatory democracy as you're likely to get from the electronic news. The network news organizations, however, provide *no* opportunity for critics to challenge their news stories. With the elimination of the Fairness Doctrine, the networks are not even obligated to provide equal time to opposing viewpoints.

This arrogance is a danger for the future of democracy. The exclusion of a variety of viewpoints from the black, Latino, and Asian communities and the inability of members of those communities to respond to unbalanced images amounts to censorship. Moreover, health professionals are beginning to cite these images as contributing causes of the lack of self-esteem among minority youth. In the July 17, 1989, *New York Times,* Dr. John T. Chissell said that this condition is partially brought on by the images of themselves that they see in the media.

I announced the second boycott in *New York Newsday* on August 31, 1992. In addition to the cities that were included in the first boycott, Philadelphia and New York were added for the second.

The networks responded to our first boycott by agreeing that some of our charges about the coverage of blacks and Latinos were true. We'd caught them by surprise. By October 1992, however, they were ready for us. They stonewalled. Replying to reporter Lynda Seaver, who confronted the networks with our charges, spokespersons for CBS, NBC, and CNN all stood behind their reporting. Roy Brunett, manager of communications for CBS News in New York, said: "We cover minority issues fairly and we take great pains to make sure we don't single out any one group." Ha! NBC was defended by Heather Allen, the West Coast bureau chief in Los Angeles. She said that NBC had created the Women in Minorities Task Force to monitor nightly newscasts and magazine shows aired by the network. The task force, which is made up of African and Asian Americans, Hispanics, gays, and lesbians, concluded, she said, that "there is a fair mix." But on May 30, 1993, the NBC network did yet another story about teenage pregnancy in which all of the pictures were of black women, promoting the canard that it is a black problem. The response to our second boycott indicates that the networks have decided to satisfy the growing and angry complaints about their coverage of blacks, Latinos, and others, by policing themselves. Even Walter Goodman said of the boycott that "there are not many other ways that viewers can express dissatisfaction with what shows up on the tube."

We live in a country where General Electric, which sponsors one of the chief outlets for anti-black propaganda, "NBC News," has been in trouble with the law more times than your average mugger. Gerry Spence, citing a Bureau of National Affairs estimate, writes in his book *With Justice for None: Destroying an American Myth* that "the cost of corporate crime in America is over ten times greater than the combined larcenies, robberies, burglaries, and auto-thefts committed by individuals. One in five of America's large corporations has been convicted of at least one major crime or has paid civil penalties for serious misbehavior." The reason that we hear less about the underclass behavior of corporate suite gangs who do more damage to the society than street gangs is because they provide the revenue that keeps big-business television on the air. I suggested in the *Nation* that the way the Crips and the Bloods (Los Angeles gangs) could improve their image is by sponsoring television network news so that their underclass activities will never be mentioned.

Up to now, only the dirty laundry of the black community has been hung in public. The Crips and the Bloods side of the story. In order to free American society of its social secret—secrets which condemn millions to suffer in silence—it's time for us to let it all hang out. We also need to challenge the obsolete and unscientific blame-the-victim explanation of America's racial crisis. We need to encourage a new consensus that is not based upon fear, myth and hunger for ratings and profits, or upon some upscale opinion merchant's ambition, or the need to build the self-esteem of whites by promoting the disesteem of blacks and others, but a consensus that is built upon reason and probity.

Is There a Black-Jewish Feud?

Over the years, the highly regarded and eminent scholar Henry Louis Gates, Jr., has not only made flattering and thoughtful comments about my work but also provided me with valuable assistance by pointing out errors I have made during the course of writing more than a dozen books. I am pleased to be in a position to return the favor.

Henry Louis Gates's conclusion that general anti-Semitism is "generally" on the wane while black anti-Semitism is on the rise—carried in an op-ed piece entitled "Black Demagogues and Pseudo Scholars"—proceeded from a false premise. Shortly after the article appeared, I checked with Jack Cohen, assistant director of the San Francisco Anti-Defamation League, who told me that anti-Semitism rose by 11 percent between 1990 and 1991. He said that the statistics for 1992 weren't in. When the Anti-Defamation League did release them, later in 1992, the statistics revealed that, contrary to what Gates said, anti-Semitism among blacks had declined since 1964. Why my friend Gates—one of the nation's most publicized scholars—would make such an assertion without checking the facts, and why the *New York Times* would fail to check his implication that the last vestiges of anti-Semitism exist only among African Americans, is puzzling, since in February and March of 1992, news reports about the rise of anti-Semitism among whites, based upon information gathered by the Anti-Defamation League, were published in the news sections of the *Times*. Even more puzzling is why the *Times* didn't correct Gates's statements. Every time I've submitted an article to the *Times*, it has been fact-checked to death.

Given the segregated character of the American opinion industry, it becomes very difficult for blacks to respond to such an allegation, which Mr. Gates bases upon an unidentified poll about whose methodology no information was provided and whose conclusions I believe to be false. To add to the damage resulting from what amounts to a slander against the African American character, Mr. Gates's article was used as a basis for talk shows by the nation's television and radio networks, including CNN and NPR. Neither NPR's John Hockenberry, who, like some of his colleagues, uses the "underclass" theory to explain black American society, nor CNN's Sonya Friedman—two of the talk-show hosts—detected Mr. Gates's error. (In the May 28 *New York Times*, Dennis King and Chip Berlet questioned whether blacks were being blamed for anti-Semitism while that of others was being ignored. "In 1984 the ADL [Anti-Defamation League] was justified in scolding Jesse Jackson. . . . But it remained silent in 1985 on the appointment of Patrick Buchanan, already a defender of Nazi war criminals, as White House communications director." The writers also accused the ADL of shrugging off "frequent meetings between some of Ronald Reagan's national security staffers and followers of the neo-Nazi Lyndon LaRouche organization.")

Gates's generalization—using the few to indict the many—is a tactic that's been used against Jews since the time of Josephus and Philo. This claim not only insults the majority of decent, tolerant black citizens but lulls those Jewish Americans who are unacquainted with the facts into a false sense of security. For Jewish Americans, Gates seems to be arguing, the United States is the Promised Land where the only problem, so the lines go, is some Afrocentric scholars, nationalists, and students who are misled into believing that the "protocols of the Sages of Zion" are genuine. *Village Voice* writer Nat Hentoff has developed an obsessive-compulsive disorder over these students, while powerful and influential people like former secretary of state James Baker, whose comment "Fuck the Jews," and Justice Sandra Day O'Connor, whose letter of encouragement to a right-wing group agreed that the United States is a Christian nation, have been long since forgotten.

Indeed, the *New York Times*, which has hounded Jesse Jackson for his "Hymietown" remark, in late 1992 included a glowing profile of Mr. Baker in which he was depicted as "an aristocrat." Mr. Baker, as someone who may one day become president of the United States, and Ms. O'Connor, as someone sitting on the highest court of the land, have more power than all of the black anti-Semites in history combined. So do the two Jewish Americans who designed Willie Horton–like tactics for the Clinton and Bush campaigns. Stan Greenberg, a pollster, engineered the incident that embarrassed Jesse Jackson, when Mr. Clinton appeared before Mr. Jackson's Rainbow Coalition dinner and criticized Sister Souljah. This Willie Hortonizing of Jackson was meant to demonstrate to Reagan Democrats that Clinton would stand up to Jackson, who in the commercial media has become a symbol of black aspirations. For the Republicans, William Kristol used the L.A. riots to carry Dan Quayle's campaign about family values, or, as Joe Klein termed it, "the poverty of values" within the inner city.

Kristol tried to Hortonize the New York welfare issue in February of 1992, but the vice-president and his coach, Kristol, were not prepared for the energetic reaction from New York State officials.

Granted, there is tension between blacks and Lubtitzchers, but with its large West Indian population, Crown Heights is not your typical black community. (Notice how the largely West Indian population of Crown Heights are referred to as West Indians—honorary whites—on every other occasion, when West Indians are used to embarrass blacks about their lack of devotion to the work ethic, but when they clash with elements of the Jewish community, they're referred to as blacks.) The underlying irony of the highly publicized and exaggerated black-Jewish feud is that Jewish Americans and black Americans face far more problems from members of "white" ethnic groups than from each other. Neither group has as much power to destroy each other as their enemies have to destroy them both. This was borne out during the summer of 1993 when federal agents exposed a neo-Nazi plot to blow up a black church and to assassinate Jewish and black leaders. Challenging Cornel West and Henry Louis Gates, Jr.'s theory that anti-Semitism is a black problem, none of the conspirators was black. No op-ed appeared in the *Times* discussing the participation in this plot by members of the group most prone to attacking both blacks and Jews: white youth. While black and latino youth are constantly cast as social misfits by the *Times*, the young skinhead leader, son of a professor of computers, was treated very gently by the *Times*.

Blacks have faced mob violence from Irish Americans, Scottish Americans, and Scots-Irish Americans for more than a hundred years. These clashes weren't just located in a neighborhood, like Crown Heights, but occurred all over the North and South. The New Orleans Carnival Riot of 1900 and the New York Draft Riot of 1863, during which blacks were lynched and murdered in the streets of New York and an orphanage for black children was gutted, are just two examples of Celtic violence against African Americans. During the draft riot, Irish American mobs held the city for three days and 105 people were killed. The Chicago race riots, chronicled by the great Irish American writer James T. Farrell, were scenes of bloody carnage involving Irish Americans and blacks. These were only a few of the large-scale civil disturbances during which Celtic Americans clashed with blacks. Though American history boasts the presence of many progressive Irish, some of the most scurrilous of racist political campaigns have been designed by Irish Americans. It was a *New York World* Irish American journalist, David Goodman

Croly, who invented the Willie Horton campaign technique. In 1863, he authored a fake pamphlet that sought to prove that the Republicans and Abraham Lincoln were soft on miscegenation.

According to Patsy Sims, author of *The Klan,* all of the founders of the Ku Klux Klan, an anti-Semitic, anti-black organization that originated in Scotland, were Scots-Irish, including the infamous General Nathan Bedford Forrest, who massacred black men, women, and children at Fort Pillow. The cross that appears in the Stars and Bars, the Confederate flag, is the cross of St. Andrew, the patron saint of Scotland. The image of the Klan's fiery cross was derived from Sir Walter Scott's *Lady of the Lake.* It was an Irish American, Pat Buchanan, and a Scottish American, David Duke, who ran presidential campaigns whose messages contained anti-Semitic overtones. Given this information, it's not surprising that Scottish American David Duke, during a trip to Scotland, said that his values originated there.

Just as it took courage for Gates to denounce an Afrocentric scholar who has threatened him, it took courage for William F. Buckley to accuse Mr. Buchanan, his fellow Irish American, of anti-Semitism. It also took courage for Ellen Goodman to scold her fellow Jewish American Ben Wattenberg for what she interpreted as racist remarks in his book *Birth Dearths,* in which Mr. Wattenberg said that rising birthrates among blacks and other minorities threatened the survival of Western values. But neither Buckley nor Goodman suggested that, on the basis of Mr. Buchanan's and Mr. Wattenberg's remarks, anti-Semitism and racism were rampant among the ethnic communities to which they belong. Dr. Fishbein, a Jewish American, is one of the leaders in research that would seek both to prove that inner-city black males are genetically prone to violence and to offer some drugs to curb that violence. While Leonard Jefferies and those who make statements that are construed as having an anti-Semitic basis are villified by the media, the careers of people like Ben Wattenberg and Dr. Fishbein seem to be advanced when they talk like the Nazi sociologists and scientists of Europe. Mr.

Buchanan, formerly a member of both the Nixon and Reagan administrations, is another influential politician, and possible future president, who has more power than all of the black anti-Semites mentioned in the Gates article combined—the same people who are used by Cornel West to smear all Afrocentrics, people whose followings have been exaggerated by the American opinion industry for the purpose of making the entire African American community seem foolish and ignorant. (As a Christian, I am sure that Mr. West realizes that the basic book of what American intellectuals refer to as "Western Civilization" has been used to justify racism against both blacks and whites, slavery, homophobia, anti-Semitism, an ecology that has loused up the world, misogyny, and persecution of followers of the Mother Goddess religions, and that the central figure of Western civilization, Jesus Christ, is the author of comments that could be considered intolerant and anti-Semitic, yet he calls the Afrocentrics misguided?)

Mr. Buchanan's most recent chores were performed for an administration that included a Casey, a MacFarlane, a Noonan, and a Regan and that was headed by an Irish American president who honored the S.S. at a Bitburg cemetery—an incident that has been all but forgotten by the media, which will never forgive Jesse Jackson for his "Hymietown" remark, no matter what gesture he may make on behalf of black-Jewish relations. No op-ed piece has ever appeared associating the entire community of Irish Americans or Scottish Americans with the rhetoric and actions of Buchanan, Duke, Reagan, and Richard Nixon, an Irish American president who was given to anti-Semitic remarks and deeds (for example, ordering a probe of the Labor Department in order to determine its percentage of Jews; the man who conducted the probe was brought quietly into the Bush administration without a single op-ed article complaining about his reentry).

No poll has been taken to determine whether there is a concentration of people with Irish American and Scottish American ancestry in the Klan and the American Nazi party, as well as other ultra-Right groups. Why don't Gates, Hentoff, West, and others who see the friction between blacks and Jews as coming exclusively from the black side explore the possibility of such a poll being conducted? Doesn't anybody find intriguing the fact that the Klansman who became engaged in an altercation with Geraldo Rivera was of northern European extraction? Mr. Rivera says that Mr. McLaughlin called him "a spic and a dirty Jew."

No Irish American leader has been asked to denounce Mr. Buchanan for his wild, Munich-beer-hall-type Kulchur Kampf speech that was delivered at the Republican convention (similarly, the WASP establishment hasn't been required to denounce one-time congressional and senatorial candidate Gore Vidal's recent characterization of Judaism as an "ugly" religion). Why? Because African American leaders and intellectuals are the only ones who are called upon by the media to oppose loony statements by a handful of African Americans, whose leadership role has been designed by the media in the first place, a full-time job that would require a staff as big as Macy's.

Most of the African American intellectuals who are trotted out by the media to comment about racial issues are unknown in the black community and don't even reside there. As someone who lives in what journalists refer to, lazily, as an "underclass" neighborhood—which means that my neighborhood includes blacks who are high class, middle class, and lower class, some with a lot of class and others with no class—I can testify that I have never heard any of my neighbors make an anti-Semitic remark; nor have my black neighbors burned a cross in the yard of those homes or apartments in which the few whites on this block reside. When we have our neighborhood crime watch meetings, people from all backgrounds show up.

To impute anti-Semitism on the basis of pockets of black anti-Semitism that may be found among the black intellectual elite residing in the Northeast, and in academic zones located in

Southern California, is like blaming the Irish Americans for the actions of those who booed the gay Irish Americans who marched in last year's St. Patrick's Day parade and of those who rioted in the streets of Boston over the issue of busing.

Black intellectuals are sophisticated enough to know that among the Irish Americans and Scottish Americans there have been and are abolitionists, labor leaders, members of the clergy who marched with Martin Luther King, Jr., and others struggling to make the United States a more humanistic society. It was a young Irish American president who challenged the South's segregated status quo.

I have a cure for those Jewish Americans and African Americans who believe Jews and blacks are the source of their woes: Leave New York and take up residence in a place like Pullman, Washington, a town located in eastern Washington State near the border of Idaho. There are hundreds of towns like Pullman all over the country, places that give you an idea of what the United States would look like if there were no Jews and blacks. My 1984 visit to Pullman occurred on the weekend of the shootout between the FBI and the American Nazi group the Order, an incident that created a martyr for the American Nazi cause. A Chinese American professor informed me that many of the townspeople sympathized with the Nazis. "Turner's Diaries," the bible of the neo-Nazi movements, was written by Andrew MacDonald.

Nat Hentoff wants to know why more blacks don't condemn anti-Semitism. Maybe it's just that the media's discussion of the issue is so one-sided. Rarely has a black been charged with overt anti-Semitic acts, such as defacing a synagogue with swastikas or burning down Jewish places of worship. Nor do I know of any African Americans, including those cited by Gates, who are accumulating an arms cache in preparation for an apocalyptic battle with what members of the Order—a group with a high concentration of Irish Americans and Scottish Americans—refer to as ZOG (the Zionist Occupied Government).

Moreover, I get the impression that Nat Hentoff also believes that blacks are prone to conspiracy theories. If so, then the singling out of African Americans for perpetrating the terrible social pathology of anti-Semitism may be another reason for their paranoia to remain alert. Maybe African American paranoia, like Jewish American paranoia, has been earned. (In 1992 the *New York Times* used up a number of column inches speculating about whether the image of the Penguin in Batman was anti-Semitic.) The media contribute to the tensions between blacks and Jews. New York publications like *New York* magazine and the *New York Times* inflame the situation with sensational articles and op-ed writings.

I tried to address the absurdity of the Jewish-black feud in a novel entitled *Reckless Eyeballing*. In the novel appear black characters who mouth certain arguments—some of them anti-Semitic and others pro-Semitic—that I'd heard from black New York intellectuals. A *Times* reviewer, a Japanese American with considerable influence, could read only the anti-Semitic speeches and attributed those lines to me. On the Saturday morning the review appeared, a dear friend of the family, a Jewish American, called, nearly in tears, and said that the *New York Times* was calling me an anti-Semite. I requested that Christopher Lehmann-Haupt provide me with space to respond to the charges, which I thought to be unfair and extreme. Ms. Kakutani said that the book was a major disservice to my career. Lehmann-Haupt never answered my letter, an experience that taught me that once you get tagged with the label anti-Semitic, it's difficult to remove it. (Feminist Ms. Kakutani, however, has praised Saul Bellow and John Updike, whose images of women have been considered misogynist. But I was aware that misogyny with big bucks behind it is tolerated, whereas the amateur variety practiced by black males is greeted with hysteria and vilification.)

In 1987, while I was teaching at Harvard, a Jewish American graduate student made clear to me his opinion that one scene in my novel *Reckless Eyeballing* was ridiculous and would never happen. In that scene, a Jewish American director, who has been sheltered by New York's liberal ambience, is invited to lecture at a southern college. At least, that's what he thinks. It turns out that he has been lured into a trap by Christian fundamentalist fanatics and is sacrificed during a bizarre Christian rite. A few years later, I ran into this scholar, who later died of AIDS, in New Orleans. We had dinner, and during the course of the meal he said that after living in Louisiana for a few years, he understood the point that was being made in that scene. He, like many other Jewish Americans, had spent his life in the relatively cozy confines of the Northeast. When he showed the intellectual courage of residing in a different place, he discovered that outside of tolerant zones in Berkeley, Los Angeles, and New York, there are regions of the country where people still embrace medieval attitudes toward Jews, and to blame anti-Semitism solely on blacks is to engage in similar medieval thinking.

Beyond Los Angeles

I thought it ironic that members of the media and opinion-making intelligentsia would assume a superior attitude over the white Simi Valley jurors, whose decision in the Rodney King case shocked some of them. Their attitudes toward African American culture and the issues affecting black life are just as ignorant. What's the difference between the media and the president bonding with the white victims of the Los Angeles tragedy, yet making little of the fact that most of those killed were black and Latino males, and the Simi Valley jurors expressing loyalty to those with whom they shared a similar background—the police? Doesn't this send out a message that the media and the politicians place little value on black life? Also, didn't the media's constant playing of the beating of a white truck driver convey the impression that most of the victims were white?

What's the difference between those jurors basing their judgment upon the two seconds of the videotape that seemed to show Rodney King lunging toward the police, yet ignoring the section of the tape that showed a vicious beating of Mr. King while he was lying on the ground, and the media's mostly white male opinion makers ignoring the fact that members of all races participated in the Los Angeles disorders so that the media could promote the line that the "riots" were the result of black women having a lot of babies so as to get on welfare (the position of the state's governor), and/or, as Bush press secretary Marlin Fitzwater said, that the riots were a result of 1960s social policies and welfare dependency?

We got a lot of such lazy, simplistic, cliché-ridden, Monynihan-type "analysis"—all of the social problems of the inner city originate in single-parent households—of why the blacks "rioted" but nothing about why the whites (including yuppies in Santa Monica) rioted, reinforcing the impression that whites in the media desire to protect their fellow whites from the stigma of antisocial activities. Mayor Bradley said that "most of the people who were engaged in the violence [in the center of the city] were young whites," yet none of the talk-show callers or professional opinion makers referred to them as "savages" and "animals."

During the riots, television focused upon black looters, even in situations where the majority of rioters were white. Mayor Frank Jordan said that few blacks participated in the San Francisco disorders, and Sheriff Richard Hongisto said that he wished the Caucasians involved in these disorders showed as much restraint as the African Americans. Even with these testimonies, the majority of network news TV pictures showed the few black looters, which is not surprising, since the typical image of blacks on television is that of a violent or physical people, involved in criminal activity or in athletics.

The four policemen's defense attorneys played to these fears by describing the police as those who hold the line between these white citizens and "the jungle," the old slave-trade image of where blacks reside. Television commentators also made much of what they refer to as the Korean-black conflict. If the looting of the Korean south central district by black youth indicates an anti-Korean bias among blacks, then why doesn't the looting and burning of Korean stores by whites in Koreatown—which was witnessed by Pacifica Radio's Kwazi Nkrumah—indicate a bias of whites toward Koreans? A gang counselor, who was on the streets and not broadcasting from some opulent New York studio, told Ted Koppel that he saw not only whites "looting" Korean American stores but also whites wearing yarmulkes.

Also, why are the media all of a sudden interested in violence against Asian Americans? Asian Americans are attacked by whites year-round, and Ronald Steel, a university professor who explains the actions of what he calls "the black and Latino underclasses" to whites, hasn't told us whether these whites are members of fractured families. His op-ed article, printed in the *New York Times*, where Moynihanism is the house gospel, was typical of the neoconservative line regarding the riots, a line that was also promoted by NPR, an outfit that's more segregated than your typical Georgia country club. Mr. Steel attributes the disturbances in the Los Angeles inner city to "a breakdown of the black family, pervasiveness of drugs, [and] cycle of welfare dependency." How would Mr. Steel explain the discontent of Latinos, as revealed in the Los Angeles disturbances? Forty percent of the "looters" were Latino, yet the majority of Latino children in poverty live in two-parent households. Doesn't it occur to the disciples of Moynihanism that, in a country with as astronomical a divorce rate as the United States, the so-called fractured family is widespread? The fact that two-thirds of American children will live, at one time in their lives, in a single-parent household shows that the fractured family, like drugs, welfare, and illegitimacy, is not merely a black condition but an American condition.

As for Mr. Steel's reference to "a pervasiveness of drugs," 80 percent of the consumers of drugs—not only illegal drugs, but prescription drugs that can get you just as addicted—are white. Two former first ladies and a current Supreme Court justice have experienced episodes of addiction.

Do Mr. Steel and other neoconservatives believe that Rodney King was brutally beaten because he was a member of a fractured family?

Not all of the media distortions about black life arise from sinister motives, but many stem from some of the same misinformation about black life that Mr. Steel publishes. Mr. Steel believes that "blacks who enter the mainstream are widely accepted." He should read some of the research that black author George Davis has conducted about blacks in the boardroom. Even black corporate executives complain about how racism impedes their careers. My brother, Dr. Michael Lenoir, a distinguished Oakland physician, feels that his career is hampered by racism, as do a number of black professors with whom I have contact.

"This Week with David Brinkley" went a long way in shattering myths, such as those promoted by Steel and Marlin Fitzwater, that cloud the welfare issue (the majority of welfare recipients are whites and reside in the rural areas, a guest said), only to be undermined by George Will, the resident conservative, who is devoted to these myths, and by the featured guest, Charles Murray, whose opinion is that there are jobs available but blacks just don't want to work, an old wives' tale dressed up in fancy sociological jargon.

Instead of fostering awareness between different groups, the media and the political intellectual and cultural elite often seem to be engaged in rumormongering, spreading what amounts to gossip and faulty intelligence about members of our multiethnic civilization and dividing Americans into hostile camps. I wonder how much the riots that followed the verdict had to do with CNN and Los Angeles Police Chief Daryl Gates speculating as to whether such riots would take place. The networks frequently engage in such irresponsible speculation when political events that might anger blacks are in the offing. They predicted that race riots might follow the election of Mayor Richard Daley's son in Chicago. None occurred. Now they're all drooling over the prospect of "a long hot summer" whose violent images would make their ratings soar.

How does one end the cognitive gap between the different

races in the United States, a gap that's become so acute that we're calling each other crazy? Typical was Frank Rich, the nation's leading drama critic, describing the black response to the AIDS crisis as a "mass hysterical denial." Had this critic been following black newspapers, he would have read about black church and social organizations addressing the AIDS crisis for at least five years. Similarly, blacks accuse whites of rejecting evidence about the problems they face, even when such evidence, as in the case of the Rodney King tape, appears right before their eyes.

The average person would say that one ends such division through education, yet the U.S. Department of Education during the Bush administration drove a wedge of ignorance between our various communities by promoting the line that to study the cultures of African Americans, Native Americans, and Latinos is to engage in frivolity, "ethnic feel-goodism," and "political correctness," the kind of catchy phrase used to dismiss complex educational alternatives that was created by the same people who used the term *communism* to dismiss the opinions of even mainstream politicians. I wasn't surprised that a man who wrote articles favorable to David Duke had a job in the Bush Department of Education, because some of the attitudes promoted by this department sounded like David Duke's standard speech about defending something called "Western civilization," which anybody who has traveled to Europe will have a difficult time locating. (Since 1977, I have visited some of the oldest universities in Europe, and not once did I hear anybody use this phrase!) Members of our intellectual elite show their lack of sophistication when they dismiss African American culture as a marginal culture. This is the line followed by the Aryan Resistance, which caused a disturbance at Berkeley High School in Berkeley, California, by passing out pamphlets arguing that African Americans had contributed nothing to culture. The Aryan Resistance and some of the powerful people who influence our culture and intellectual life are wrong.

African American culture is an international culture. A recent issue of the *Japan Times Weekly* printed an article about how rap music had more consumer appeal in Japan than American automobiles did.

I attended a Paris conference in February, 1992 that saluted the achievements of American authors James Baldwin, Richard Wright, and Chester Himes. Present were scholars from all over the world. If East Indians, Chinese, Russians, Japanese, and Africans haven't been culturally contaminated by reading black literature, then white Americans have little to fear from reading this literature, not just that written by those who, like me, have received generous publicity, but a variety of black literature, including that ignored by the critics who want to spare their white readers the experience of hearing from a voice that might make them uncomfortable. Whites should examine not only the theater that entertains them with show tunes and vigorous dancing, or a theater that panders to neoconservative policy positions, or films whose depiction of African Americans is no different from that of television news (which is pretty bad), but the theater of Baraka, Ed Bullins, and Aishah Rahman—inner-city writers who delve into the guts of the African American urban experience—as well as the films of Charles Burnett. Most blacks of my generation are acquainted with Hemingway, Faulkner, and Twain, but when whites wish to learn about blacks, they turn to the fire-mesmerized television news or judge all blacks by the 2 percent of the people in the streets of Los Angeles who engaged in stupid and vile acts like murder and looting. Stuart Varney, a commentator for CNN's "Money-line," asked black businessman Robert Johnson whether "the black community was cutting its own throat by burning down its own businesses," as though these thugs who participated in violence represented the entire black community. Do the 0.1 percent of Italian Americans engaged in organized crime represent the Italian American community; inside traders or "Murder Incorporated," the Jewish American community; or the Asian Americans who control the

New York heroin trade, the Asian American community? Do we represent the Irish Americans as "Dirty Harry" Callahan and the Westies, or by Gerry Mulligan, Frank O'Hara, and our great Irish American writer James T. Farrell?

How did blacks feel about the violence? According to a *Los Angeles Times* poll, 58 percent of blacks felt that the violence was unjustified.

It will be impossible to change the perceptions of some whites who view blacks through the same racial lenses through which some of the characters in Shakespeare's *Othello* viewed the Moor, but I believe that, when presented with information, millions of fair-minded whites will gain a better understanding of African American life in the United States. That the majority of whites—even in places like Ventura—disagreed with the Simi Valley decision because they saw the video of that police beating of King, an incident that has become for police brutality what Selma was for civil rights, is encouraging. Anjelica Huston spoke for many white Americans when she said that, after the verdict, she was ashamed to be an American. She had the guts to criticize the media coverage of the case and the riots while appearing on CNN, which, based upon my monitoring, because it reaches ninety countries is the mother of media stereotypes against black people. Typical was a "medical" series about violence that was rushed on the air the Monday after the riots. The majority of violent individuals depicted were black, and rather than addressing the problems of violence in American society— Rap Brown said that "violence is as American as apple pie"— this "medical" series merely provided CNN with an excuse to run footage of blacks shooting and cutting each other and ghoulish, *National Enquirer*-type photos of the remains of carnage on the hospital floors. It was racist and disgusting.

I know Ms. Huston spoke for my white students, who were anguished and bewildered over the decision, as were the thousands of white students who rioted in places like Iowa City.

I was also glad to see a famous black woman writer—who has

maligned black men as a group as alcoholics, drug addicts, and prone to make too much about the oppression they have suffered—write an article sympathetic to Rodney King and Mike Tyson in the pages of the *New York Times.* (I resented media feminists, the same ones who judged Clarence Thomas without Thomas receiving due process, using the King incident to argue that sexism and racism are the same. I can imagine a black woman receiving the same kind of treatment as King—an elderly Los Angeles woman, Eula Love, was shot and killed by the Los Angeles police—but can you imagine a white woman being beaten in such a manner?)

While the white Right and neoconservative response to the violence in Los Angeles was predictably petulant, ignorant, and nasty, the white Left's response merely heightened its reputation for wackiness and reinforced the long-held belief that its solution to the problems of blacks in the United States is for blacks to commit suicide. Anybody who calls those people who burned down the Aquarius Book Store, one of the oldest black bookstores in the United States, "revolutionaries" is sick. My sister, Linda, and her husband live around the corner of one of the first buildings set afire by these "revolutionaries." We thought they were going to be killed.

A new dialogue among blacks and whites will begin when those whom millions of white Americans depend upon for their information and education follow the lead of Winthrop D. Jordan, who, unlike the white jurors, understands the significance of referring to black people as gorillas. In his book *White over Blacks,* he traces the racist history of this appellation. Martin Bernal, Robert Ferris Thompson, Russell Banks, Allen Ginsberg, Bob Fox, Jack Foley, Lewis MacAdams, Bob Callahan, David Meltzer, and Werner Sollors are among the other brave white intellectuals who have risked condemnation for merely advancing the notion that blacks have a history and a culture.

The media have a special obligation to include more blacks, yellows, and browns, not merely as voice-overs, but in decision-making positions, so that more points of view are available to viewers and readers. The American media, even according to their professional journals, remain one of the segregated institutions in American life. The domination, during the aftermath of the riots, of panels and discussion programs by mostly men of similar backgrounds peddling their pet, often quack, and ideologically driven theories only confused the situation.

I would like to have heard from Asian American journalists like William Wong and Frank Abe or novelists like Frank Chin or social theorists like Ron Takaka about the tensions between Asian Americans and blacks. On May 7, representatives of forty-one Korean organizations met at the Korean Center in San Francisco. They protested the media's depiction of black people as "looters" and Koreans as "callous, successful, gun-toting vigilantes," or as those who have passed blacks in economic gains. The speakers at this gathering seemed conscious of the social and economic obstacles facing black people in Los Angeles, possibly because in Japan, where Koreans are the scapegoat class, Koreans are those who are associated with antisocial activities. A representative from the Korean American Bar Association described some of the joint Korean American–African American projects occurring in Los Angeles that deal with low-income housing, jobs, money, and scholarships for black students. This meeting also condemned the light sentence that a Korean store owner received for murdering a black teenager. That the television media didn't even bother to cover this meeting is further evidence that television regards only footage in which individuals or groups are at each other's throats as good television.

I would also like to have heard from black spokespersons other than those whom the media feel safe with and whose reputations were created by the media.

Reforms in the media and educational establishments and the rise of a new multicultural intelligentsia will help to change the perceptions Americans of different racial and ethnic backgrounds hold of one another. Members of the Fortune 500—

51

among whom are those who are financing the very right-wing think tanks whose intellectual functionaries are dividing Americans with myths and superstitions—must be convinced that Ross Perot is correct when he says racism is bad for business; that idea may be a more effective argument than those which appeal to conscience and morality. None of the analysts I heard even brought up the fact that the banks contribute to the underdevelopment of black industries through such racist practices as redlining, while, as in the case of the S & L scandals, bankers are very willing to finance the projects of their friends, a sort of affirmative action for the well-off, no matter how little collateral upon which these loans are based.

Finally, as a longtime critic of American institutions, I know, based upon my experiences in other countries, that the United States, despite its problems, is still one of the most creative, experimental, and dynamic societies in the world. Even James Baldwin's stinging criticism of the United States was always tinged with sadness, because Baldwin, like many of us, knew that this society could do better and measure up to its great promise. Even the hostile jabs at American society one hears in rap music are based more on disappointment and frustration than a desire to see the United States, in the words of Pat Robertson, "crash and burn." Rodney King, who showed more class in defeat than those who beat him did in victory, said it all: "Can we get along?" I believe that we can.

Clarence Thomas Lynched Again

Not satisfied with the humiliation of a black Supreme Court nominee—his private parts paraded before the world—white media feminists have decided to make the lynching of Clarence Thomas an annual event. Novelist and essayist Cecil Brown has compared it to Guy Fawkes Day: the celebration of the execution of a scoundrel.

The first anniversary of Anita Hill's charges of sexual harassment was marked by opinion polls noting her increased credibility. A *U.S. News & World Report* poll showed Hill and Thomas tied in the credibility race. The Gallup Poll gave Hill a four-point lead; the *Wall Street Journal* gave her a 10-point lead.

Unlike the polls of a year ago, no racial breakdown was provided. I suspect if one had been, the results would have shown that the majority of blacks still believe that Hill lied. A recent "Frontline" documentary on the Hill-Thomas extravaganza documented the perceptual gap between the average black citizen and the media-certified "talented-tenth" black elite, who claim to speak for blacks but who don't live among them. Though the show was generally favorable to Hill, the interviews with grassroots blacks, men and women alike, revealed strong support for Thomas.

If there has been a shift in public opinion since a year ago, one can attribute it to a year of pro–Anita Hill effusions from white media feminists, including the producers of popular sitcoms. In the media, Hill is now portrayed as something of a saint. During a recent interview with Katie Couric on the "Today" show, none of the contradictions in her testimony or her actions was discussed. It was reminiscent of nothing so much as Barbara Walters's love-in disguised as an interview last spring with Desiree Washington, the woman whom Mike Tyson was convicted of raping.

The lending of white feminists of their considerable prestige and power to Anita Hill's cause also revealed the pervasive double standard regarding black and white males who have been accused of sexual harassment. (Their case received a severe setback with the appearance of David Brock's *The Real Anita Hill: The Untold Story.* Though the book was shrilled at by feminists, Brock's major charges against Ms. Hill have not been damaged.)

Last June, on the day that representatives of two feminist organizations were chastising Thomas for his son's decision to attend an all-male military school, came new revelations about one of the most horrendous incidents of misogyny in recent years: the now-infamous Tailhook convention in Las Vegas where dozens of women were pawed, insulted, molested and assaulted.

As a black male, I'm still wondering why this incident involving white men hasn't become the symbolic cause célèbre that Anita Hill has. The abuses at Tailhook, first reported a few weeks before the allegations against Thomas, were far worse than anything the Supreme Court nominee did or did not say. Yet Tailhook is not the subject of commemoration, perhaps because most of the women involved are from military backgrounds, far different from those of many middle-class feminists. Similarly, the case of a black woman allegedly raped by four white male students at St. John's University in New York did not become a feminist cause célèbre.

It's not unreasonable to see a media double standard at work. According to a story in *Vanity Fair*, Hill was badgered into revealing details of her affidavit by Nina Totenberg, correspondent for the audaciously named National Public Radio (audacious because NPR's audience is about as integrated as your typical Georgia country club). Totenberg later told her fellow reporters on the TV show "Inside Washington" that she had received information on some high-profile Republican males who weren't living the family values that they preached. Maybe there are good reasons why Totenberg hasn't gone on the air with these allegations as quickly as she did with Hill's, but I've never heard them.

White middle-class feminists, suggests bell hooks, a leading black feminist intellectual, are harder on black men than on the white men who are able to provide them with career opportunities. Maybe that's why white feminists excused Anita Hill's zeal to get ahead, dismissing the fact that Hill continued working for the man whom she accused of harassing her, and waxing indignant anytime anyone mentions that Hill was on very friendly terms with Thomas seven years after his alleged harassment. They could identify.

Ironically, one political power broker in San Francisco, supportive of the Anita Hill crusade, found himself in the same position as Clarence Thomas. Walter Shorenstein, a prominent real estate developer, held a fund-raising event for women Democratic candidates last May, during which Thomas was pilloried. A few weeks later Shorenstein's former assistant sued him, alleging that he had physically harassed her for seven years. Shorenstein denied the charges and recently settled the case out of court with no admission of wrongdoing. The two differences between Shorenstein, patron of the feminists, and Thomas, villain of the year, is that Shorenstein is white and he at least received due process.

In the background of the Hill-Thomas affair (and my own powerful reaction to it) is the ongoing hostility between feminists and the defenders of black men. I was described in the pages of *Ms.* magazine as a "ringleader" of black men allegedly opposed to black women writing about misogyny. I was also accused of calling such writers "traitors to the race," which, of course, I have never said. In fact, in my capacity as a magazine editor, I have published leading black critics of misogyny among blacks, and I'm supportive of feminist demands such as the right to choose, the Equal Rights Amendment and day care. I think that black men are no better or worse than other men when it comes to their attitudes about women. My problem with the gender-first faction on the feminist movement, compounded by the demonization of Clarence Thomas, is that it singles out black misogyny as if it were the only misogyny that exists.

My suspicion that the mythology of the Hill-Thomas affair perpetuates a racial double standard is based on the revealing words of feminist leaders themselves. Gloria Steinem, one of Hill's most enthusiastic boosters, said that *The Color Purple*, the novel by Alice Walker, "told the truth about black men," presumably meaning that they are rapists and that they sleep with their children.

Similarly, Susan Brownmiller, in her book on rape, *Against Our Will*, writes that "the mythified specter of the black man as rapist, *to which the black man in the name of his manhood now contributes* [emphasis added]" poses a threat to all women, black or white. Brownmiller doesn't say "some black men"; she says "the black man," meaning me, Clarence Thomas and a whole lot of other people. Such sentiments have shaped public commentary around sexually and racially charged issues. Brownmiller, for example, supported the verdict that acquitted William Kennedy Smith of rape charges. But the morning after Mike Tyson was convicted on rape charges last March, she was interviewed on Pacifica Radio and sounded positively gleeful.

(It was later revealed that Desiree Washington had signed a deal with her attorney agreeing to give him one third of the proceeds of a civil case against Tyson. This lent credence to the boxer's defense that his accuser was planning to file a civil suit against him and reap a financial windfall from her accusations. The Rhode Island court said that withholding this information from the jury in Tyson's criminal trial may have influenced the outcome of the case. But since then not a word has been heard from Tyson's media judges, including Susan Brownmiller.)

Thus blacks are rightly suspicious of the Anita Hill phenomenon in the 1992 elections. Black leaders in Pennsylvania have not failed to notice that Lynn Yeakel, the defeated Democratic senatorial candidate who said she decided to run after watching the all-male Judiciary Committee interrogate Hill, was mum on the issue of civil rights. Yeakel was so obviously trying to appeal to white suburban votes that many black leaders, in reaction, supported Arlen Specter. It is worth remembering that there weren't any black senators on the committee either, and that there were more white women on the Judiciary Committee's staff than blacks.

Another candidate from the Anita Hill party is Dianne Feinstein, the former mayor of San Francisco who ran and won election to the U.S. Senate in California. During Feinstein's tenure as mayor, a record number of complaints were filed against the police department by black citizens; Feinstein consistently took the side of the police in those disputes. When a reporter asked how she would have handled Clarence Thomas on the witness stand, Feinstein said she would have haunted the porno shops seeking information about the judge's video rental habits. Shades of the old KGB.

The feminist organizations that boast that Hill's case has brought millions of dollars into their coffers are discreet about the fact that they have few black women in their membership or in their leadership. This comes as no surprise. Black feminists have been accusing the feminist movement of racism for more than a century. Media feminists are reluctant to air this issue, despite the evidence that it is tearing the feminist movement apart. There are countless stories about women of color walking out of feminist organizations and conferences because they weren't placed in leadership roles or on panels or treated with respect. So heated was a clash between white and black feminists in Akron, Ohio, a few years ago, that the governor's wife had to be summoned to mediate.

A year after the Hill-Thomas debacle, media feminists can't be relied upon to launch an open and candid discussion about racism in the movement. I also doubt whether the producers of "Murphy Brown," "The Trials of Rosie O'Neill" or "Designing Women"—all of which did pro–Anita Hill shows—will treat the subject. In "Black Women Abolitionists," an excellent study of racism in the 19th-century feminist movement, Shirley J. Lee accuses the early feminists of exploiting the rhetoric of black women while excluding them from the movement. The present-day feminist movement is using Anita Hill in the same manner.

1992

Gays and Feminists Play with Racist Fire

Congressman Barney Frank, of all people, wrote on the *New York Times* editorial page—a black-bashing hangout where blacks receive disproportionate blame for everything from welfare dependency to anti-Semitism—that "liberals are notsaposta take note publicly of the fact that black males commit street crimes in significantly higher proportion than any other major demographic group." Apparently Mr. Frank and the mean-spirited letter writers who supported his views get their news about crime from television. Probably NBC and CNN.

Serious studies cast doubt on Frank's "fact." University of Colorado sociologist Delbert Elliot, in a study cited in the August 29, 1988, issue of *Time,* and Rutgers University scholar Evan Stark blame inequities in the criminal justice system for the disproportionate number of incarcerated blacks. Mr. Stark writes that even the data on arrests and imprisonment may be the product of racial discrimination.

Senator Herb Kohl's recent hearings on minorities in the juvenile justice system reached the same conclusion. Regardless of an irresponsible *New York Times* editorial that also linked race to crime (March 29, 1992), he said that "black teens are four times more likely to face incarceration than their white counterparts who commit the same offense." Senator Kohl also cited the conclusion of the National Council of Juvenile and Family Court Judges that "the disparate handling of minority juveniles plays a major role in their over-representation from arrest to detention to incarceration." Moreover, a recent California study revealed that whites receive better plea-bargaining deals than blacks. Those who are seriously interested in fairness, as opposed to hotdogging ideology, should ask themselves why most of the black youth in jail are there for drug crimes, when whites constitute 80 percent of the consumers of illegal drugs and when the main channels of drug distribution are controlled by some whites and members of Asian American minority groups. Asked by Ted Koppel on "Nightline" whether the reason arrests of black drug dealers are high while those of white drug dealers are low is that "not many white people are selling drugs," Jerome Miller, of the National Center on Institutions and Alternatives, replied, "No. I think a lot of it, incidentally, has to do with the media. I think it's a cheap and easy way to go in terms of getting pictures, that much of the dealing is done on the streets. No way would we countenance the kind of things one sees on some of the more exploitive [*sic*] crime shows, of busting people's doors down and grabbing people and handcuffing them, and throwing them to the ground in front of their crying children and wailing wives. There's no way this would be allowed were we talking about middle-class suburban whites." The *Wall Street Journal* also accuses the media of driving the fear of black crime. "Television may also serve to exaggerate the fears of suburbanites by its frequent portrayal of crime," wrote Michel McQueen in an August 12, 1992, front-page story entitled "Political Paradox: People with the Least to Fear from Crime Drive the Crime Issue; Appeals to Suburban Whites Highlight Split between Perception and Reality."

Failure to take into account the role racism plays in the criminal justice system casts doubts not only on Mr. Frank's conclusions, but on those of the quack "studies" linking race to crime, one of which the *New York Times* gave credibility to by printing on page 1 of its February 1, 1992, edition. Media anti-Semites of the 1900s also used questionable "studies" and "statistics" to link Jewish Americans and Irish Americans to crime. Something was wrong with their genes, these early bigots claimed.

Shortly after his op-ed article appeared, Mr. Frank, a gay rights activist, appeared on NPR's "Talk of the Nation," where he was permitted to expand upon this "fact"—a "fact" based upon spectral evidence that was the kind of proof used during the Salem Witch Trials. During an interview with Margot Adler, a feminist and a professional witch (according to a *New York Times* profile) who seemed just as ignorant of the true picture of American crime as he, both Mr. Frank and Ms. Adler seemed to be suggesting that the Democrats could woo back alienated white voters by playing the Willie Horton card. A few days before Mr. Frank appeared on this show, Ms. Adler was so furious about Sally Quinn's editorial "Who Killed Feminism?" that she told men not to call in during the phone-in section of a show that featured one-sided attacks on Ms. Quinn.

Barney Frank and Margot Adler join others of their professions who've raised white fears of black violent crime (an irrational fear, since such interracial incidents are rare) along about election time. Among the others are Jeff Greenfield, Joe Klein, and Pat Buchanan. Joe Klein became senior editor at *Newsweek* and CBS as a result of his Hortonizing of Spike Lee and David Dinkens. When he tried his black-crime-against-whites trick during an appearance on the "MacNeil/Lehrer News Hour," his debating opponent, a black scholar from Boston's Monroe Trotter Institute, handed his head to him.

I wrote letters to the *New York Times* both during the campaign—to protest a demagogic piece by Greenfield about the threat of black violence to whites—and last month—to challenge his assertion, made in the *New York Times Book Review*, that the Willie Horton campaign was justified. None was published. The week after an ABC-TV appearance during which Greenfield, black-pathology careerist Jim Sleeper, and neoconservative

Shelby Steele sought to discount black fears that the AIDS epidemic was a result of a conspiracy, the *New York Times* (November 28, 1991) carried a story on a study made by Dr. Charles Gilks of Oxford University and the Kenya Medical Research Institute pointing to "a series of little-known malaria experiments in which people were inoculated with fresh blood from monkeys and chimpanzees" as being the origin of AIDS.

It's obvious that Klein, Greenfield, Sleeper, Mickey Kaus and others who advance themselves by hustling white fear of black crime enjoy the benefits of immunity, since the publications and networks they work for silence their critics ("We don't have room to publish all of the letters that come in"). But let someone who didn't go to Harvard slip up and these hypocritical cultural elitists swarm all over them. On "Nightline" recently, Jeff Greenfield chastised Marge Schott for her insensitive remarks about black baseball players, yet Greenfield, with his enormous audience and his bent toward raising racist fiction, is a far greater threat to blacks than Schott. Besides, if the personnel at television networks were as integrated as the baseball field, the networks' coverage of African American and African issues wouldn't be such a racist disgrace. (Another black-pathology entertainer is Diane Sawyer, the woman who followed Richard Nixon into exile. Every week, it seems, her show "20/20" blames blacks for things like welfare. During one show, the narrator even admitted that most of those who go from state to state committing welfare fraud are white, but the pictures showed only blacks.)

Margot Adler's colleague at NPR is Cokie Roberts, an old hand at playing the Willie Horton card. During October of 1988, while appearing on "This Week with David Brinkley," she accused the Democrats of not facing up to black crime. When questioning Democratic candidates during the recent primary debates, her example of softness on crime wasn't one of those light sentences or no sentences received by those who insulted the Constitution in the Iran-Contra scandal, or the light fine—a tap on the wrist—received by BCCI, whose operators participated in the largest drug-laundering business in history (a case that was covered up by the Justice Department during the same period it was setting up Marion Barry with women and a crack pipe). Instead, Ms. Roberts's example cited a case involving the parole of a Hispanic man, Martinez, who has been accused of raping an eleven-year-old child (Willie Martinez). As horrible as this may sound, it comes nowhere near the scale of crime committed by those who've placed the economic and political system in jeopardy through money laundering, inside trading, and what amounted to a coup against the U.S. government. But when Ms. Roberts views crime, it's black and Latino crime that draws her interest. Since NPR is segregated, few black men have an opportunity to respond to the stereotypes against black men promoted by NPR feminists. (Isn't it time for NPR and its local affiliates to either desegregate or go private?)

Given Ms. Roberts's views and her influence at NPR, no wonder the typical image of black men on NPR is that of a person or persons engaged in violence either in the United States or in Africa. (Often, in what I would call a black-pathology package, NPR plays African and Afro-American crime stories side by side; Scott Simon's weekend show was often to the right of the Klan show "Race and Reason," when it came to black issues. As a reward for his services to yuppie racists, Mr. Simon is now moderator for the Saturday edition of NBC's "Today Show," just as Cokie Roberts was promoted by ABC after her inflammatory "black crime" remark.)

As a gay activist, Barney Frank should be ashamed of himself for playing the Willie Horton card. Suppose that, based on studies indicating high drug usage and alcoholism among gays and lesbians and the refusal of young gays to change dangerous sexual practices, a black op-ed writer had suggested that the best way to woo back bigots and racists (euphemistically called the "middle-class vote") is to play the Jeffrey Dahmer card, or the Uncle Ed card, or the San Francisco Democrats card. Or suppose that a black writer had written—as a prominent black gay writer said about black men recently—that he was more afraid of gays than AIDS, in a column that was circulated by the "progressive" Pacific News Service and the hip *Utne Reader*.

Gays like Barney Frank and feminists like Margot Adler should be careful about playing to the irrational fears of white bigots who hate them as much as they hate blacks—possibly more. Judging from the speeches inveighing against gays and "femo-Nazis" that were delivered at the Republican convention, it would seem that the gays and feminists would desire to invite allies wherever they can find them. From the tone of Pat Robertson's comments about feminists engaged in witchcraft and infanticide, there may even be a new inquisition in the offing.

Before it's all over, I, who have been smeared by powerful feminists, including the editors of *Ms.* magazine, and Clarence Thomas, who was treated by feminists in the manner that the Klan has traditionally treated black men—denying them due process—may find ourselves members of an underground railroad, offering fugitive feminists and gays refuge in our homes.

As someone who was sued by a fundamentalist group, the Conservative Caucus, for what its members referred to as criminal behavior, Barney Frank would seemingly be the last to promote stereotypes about black people.

1992

RodNEy KiNq ANd I

Like most black men, my relationship with the police has been mixed—sometimes friendly, sometimes hostile but mostly bizarre.

The first California city I lived in was Los Angeles. Carla Blank and I lived in an apartment near Echo Park Lake. Carla worked at a church school camp in the mountains while I stayed home, working on my second novel under contract from Doubleday.

One day I was walking to the downtown Los Angeles library when I was stopped by a car full of Los Angeles detectives. They snatched my briefcase. The incident took place in a black neighborhood and so some blacks gathered. When the police removed the contents of my briefcase to find only a notebook, the blacks laughed. I said something like, "Gee, you can't even go to the library anymore." The police claimed they thought my briefcase was a woman's purse, jumped into their cars and drove away.

I get the chills when I think of this incident. I could have been beaten to death for expressing the wrong attitude. For getting smart.

These minor encounters between white police officers and black men occur daily, and often escalate into major confrontations. They are responsible for the fact that black men are four times more likely than whites to be arrested for the same crime, a fact that's overlooked when media and political ideologues are discussing crime.

Sometimes these minor confrontations erupt into full scale civil disturbances, during which mostly black people die and millions of dollars are lost all because some policeman gets his thrills from beating up on some black guy. All of the 1960s riots were begun by a police incident, and it would seem that conservatives, if they were truly that and not just bigots using conservatism as a substitute for a white sheet, would be the first to complain about this loss of revenue, instead of backing the police no matter what they do.

Last year, I was better prepared. Shortly after my arrival at Burbank Airport, I was stopped by three men who described themselves as members of the Burbank Airport Narcotics Security.

They separated me from my escorts, a professor and student who'd been sent to accompany me to an engagement at the California Institute of the Arts, and demanded to know why I exited from the airport terminal through a door different from the one used by the other Oakland passengers. (Huh?) It never occurred to me that exiting from an airport terminal through a door would cause one to be regarded with suspicion.

My first response must have been inspired by a show on National Public Radio where whites discuss issues pertaining to blacks without the slightest idea of what they're talking about. Terry Gross interviewed a man who said that the police only hassled members of the "underclass."

I told the white officers that I was a lecturer at the University of California. That statement made them testier. Only when they were satisfied that the bag I was carrying contained books and that I had a plane ticket did they leave. It was an ugly moment. In fact, the black professor said he thought the thing was going to go down. That I was going to suffer bodily harm.

My most recent unpleasant encounter with the police occurred the day after I appeared on ABC's "Nightline," during a discussion of the Rodney King case and police brutality. All I said was that it would be great if the police lived in the communities they served.

The next day, as I parked in front of the Bank of America on Lakeshore, across from Lake Merritt, I noticed a policeman glaring at me as he stood in front of a fast food establishment. My African sense told me the policeman had seen me on "Nightline," didn't approve of my opinion and was going to hassle me. I removed my earphones from the glove compartment and as soon as I got out of the car, put them on.

He started toward me. Hey, you, he said. He told me it was against the law to drive while wearing earphones. I wasn't driving with earphones on, but instead of arguing with the officer I thanked him for advising me of the law. He disappeared into a bar. I think he was just looking for the slightest excuse to perpetrate a confrontation.

The city of Oakland has a project that might ease some of the tensions between black citizens and the police, some members of which have been accused of brutality against black citizens. As part of the Home Alert program, police come out to our neighborhoods and discuss our problems with us. These conversations take place in a friendly and relaxed atmosphere. Sometimes it takes forever for them to act on our problems, but at least we're talking.

1992

Mike Tyson and the White Hope Cult

Since the days of Jack Johnson, as soon as a black man wins the heavyweight championship, a movement begins among some whites to dethrone him. In this American fairy tale, the black Prince of Darkness is vanquished by a white Knight in the guise of the White Hope. Since Rocky Marciano's time, the White Hopes have fallen upon hard times. Jerry Quarry, Jerry Cooney, and the most recent White Hope, Tommy Morrison, have been no match for their black opponents. Lacking a candidate who would challenge Ali or Holmes, the cult of White Hopes came up with a computer to show that had Marciano fought Ali, Marciano would have won.

Later they used the traditional racist machine to resurrect Marciano, and so we got Rocky Balboa defeating a black fighter played by Mr. T and Apollo Creed. The filmmakers even trotted out a Willie Horton motif by portraying the Mr. T character as a threat to white womanhood.

Among those who've been custodians of the White Hope mythology have been white sportswriters. This hankering for someone who would, to paraphrase Jack London, one of the early White Hope advocates, "wipe that smile" off the face of the black heavyweight champion has become part of a tradition. (After the guilty verdict came down in the courtroom presided over by a blatantly feminist judge, many sportswriters were furious because Tyson went to jail with a smile.) Not surprisingly, sportswriters have been authors of some of the most vicious remarks about black athletes, not excluding Joe Louis, even though Louis was a patriot who donated some of his purses to the armed forces. But of all the black athletes who have been the targets of vilification, none has been the recipient of abuse so much as Mike Tyson. He has been called a "psycho puppy" (mad dog) by a *New York Times* sportswriter, Robert Lipsyte, and even "subhuman." And so when Mike Tyson became vulnerable after his rape indictment, the media were in a position to usher in a series of surrogate White Hopes.

Tyson's accuser, Desiree Washington, became a White Hope. "The Woman Who Stopped Tyson" was the title given the cover of *People*. "In her, Tyson had found a most worthy opponent," said gender-first feminist Joan Morgan in a one-sided, headlined piece carried in the *Village Voice*, a newspaper that prints articles about black sexism regularly but keeps the sexism of the ethnic groups to which its male publisher and board of directors belong a secret. James Baldwin, William Demby, Ed Bullins, Bill Gunn on his deathbed, and John O'Killens shortly after his death were among a number of black men brought down by the feminist separatists who influence the newspaper and their bitter black feminist surrogates. As someone who has gotten his chastisement from these aging feminist daughters of Dracula, who always seem to have a supply of fresh bloods, I sympathize with the predicament they find themselves in. They practice their feminism in the newspaper whose male owners fired Ellen Willis and Thulani Davis and whose masthead lists no Asian American, black, or Latino women in important positions; moreover, the newspaper carries advertisements that some feminists would consider to be degrading of women.

Tyson's prosecutor, Greg Garrison, became a White Hope. According to *Sports Illustrated,* he told the Beauty Queen that he and she were going to "kick Tyson's ass." The media became a

White Hope. I knew that Tyson would be found guilty when CNN, which covers blacks and Latinos the way the Nazi press of pre-Holocaust Germany covered the Jews, announced that the Beauty Queen's testimony was one of the "most convincing in the history of Indiana trials." (An early map of Indiana includes a black dot for the location of each Klan Klavern. The map looks as though it has the measles.)

I also figured that Tyson would be sacrificed for feminists who were cheated out of roasting William Kennedy Smith and Clarence Thomas and for the alleged vices of other athletes. When Garrison said that the Tyson verdict was a message to these athletes who get away with things and write books about it, he was signifying Wilt Chamberlain. Not only did Garrison appear on Barbara Walters's program—which abandoned all objectivity and became a forum for anti-Tyson propaganda—to coach and support the Beauty Queen, but he also arranged for her to get her picture in *People* magazine. Judging from Mr. Garrison's words and actions in this case—that he has a thing about black men—his relationship with Ms. Washington goes beyond the normal relationship between a prosecutor and a plaintiff.

He's not the only public white male who has become passionately involved in the affairs of a woman in the center of a controversy with a black man. Timothy Phelps, the *Newsday* reporter who leaked the Hill statement to the FBI and then later cashed in on a book he wrote about the Hill-Thomas hearings, behaved, during an appearance on C-Span, as though he were her defense attorney.

The fact that Susan Brownmiller denounced Tyson but supported the innocent verdict in the William Kennedy Smith trial reinforces the suspicion that she, like the feminists at *Ms.*, the *Village Voice*, and the *New York Times*—all of whose boards of directors are male and white—is hard on men beneath her and black men but kisses up to powerful white men.

White males who bond with black-male-bashing feminists sometimes get caught in their own hypocrisy. The night before

Anita Hill's testimony, Larry King ran a virtual salute to Anita Hill in his show carried on Mutual, only to have a caller remind him that a woman had accused him of sexual harassment in a report in *Spy* magazine. When asked about this incident by Jeff Morley, an editor at the *Washington Post*—who was fact-checking an article I wrote about liberal feminists' continuing obsession with Clarence Thomas—Larry King said that the *Spy* magazine report had been false and that the woman had lied. Yet it would never occur to King and other white male supporters that Anita Hill might have lied.

I appeared on a radio talk show in Washington, D.C., and discovered, during the call-in segment of the program, that all of the callers—black, white, male, female—were of the opinion that Tyson didn't receive a fair trial. This opinion didn't show up in the national media, which were engaged in a lynching fest of Tyson in the same manner used in the Clarence Thomas case, during which NBC and PBS used the feminist Catherine MacKinnon to hit Thomas with malicious enthusiasm. On another program, when a black woman called in to express the opinion that Tyson was a victim of racism, Larry King and his feminist guest shrugged off the caller's opinion. They wondered how racism could be the case when his accuser was black. King has forgotten that Jewish Council members drew up the list of names of those who would go to the concentration camps and that in racist societies, the victims often copycat the racist attitudes of their oppressors.

Larry King wasn't the only media white male who was delighted by the verdict against Tyson. David Brinkley thought it was funny that Tyson might lose his money, and the odd mind who shares the David Brinkley spot, George Will, gloated that it was among the best news he'd heard all week.

A *Newsweek* reporter appearing on NPR even reconstructed an evening he spent in the company of Mike Tyson and Don King and suggested, without evidence, that Tyson had raped a woman guest. The NPR discussion about Tyson was typical of the on-the-air reaction to the Tyson indictment and verdict: white guys sitting around laughing and talking. This was also the format of a documentary that was produced by two white feminists at the beginning of 1993, called "The Fallen Champ." Tyson's career was commented upon by mostly white male judges. One boasted about having placed a gun against his head, after Tyson had allegedly come on to an underage girl. After the white guys got through with Tyson, Ms. Washington was portrayed as a perfect candidate for a convent. The show ended with your standard anti-black-male diatribe, offered by a black feminist staff member of *Sports Illustrated.* This show provided another example of how, from the point of view of a black male, the middle-class segment of the feminist movement is the greatest gift to the patriarchy.

On the day of the verdict, some perverted mind at CNN thought it was funny to show a photo of Tyson being frisked by a white guard (the evil Prince disarmed, undressed, and emasculated) next to a story about Fay Wray and King Kong. It would take the stinging pen of a James Baldwin to dissect the erotic overtones of that pairing, a scene that has played repeatedly by CNN. Maybe the reason David Duke was given such a free ride during his appearance on "Larry King Live!"—where he was allowed to issue a tirade of lies about blacks while King sat there like a dummy—is that Mr. Duke articulates the views of some members of CNN's staff.

Though black men who view the Tyson case from my perspective are dismissed as paranoid by some white men and feminists, and by a few black surrogates, they may find solace in the fact that Third World men, who have undergone similar experiences in this country, often sympathize with their view.

Two Chinese American male friends of mine observed that the cameras would never have followed somebody like Michael Milken into prison, but the media couldn't resist knocking out Tyson. Now that the Rhode Island Supreme Court has suggested that Ms. Washington might have committed perjury, the media have abandoned the story.

Carl Rowan said that anybody who supports Tyson is a "black lunatic." I don't support Tyson, but I think that it's difficult for a black man to receive a fair trial in a state that has been a traditional stronghold of the Klan (some of whose members were feminists) and from a jury that included some whites who were so paranoid about blacks that they blamed the fire that broke out in the hotel where they were deliberating on Don King, a fact that should have been enough for a mistrial. I'd also like to see Ms. Washington cross-examined by a defense lawyer who would reconcile some of the inconsistencies in her testimony—inconsistencies that were largely ignored by the Ku Klux media, which view one of their goals as lynching black men who don't know their place.

Despite boycotts, the efforts of black media reformers, and fewer complaints by blacks and Latinos, the media remain one of the most segregated institutions in American life, and their daily scapegoating of minorities imperils the safety of millions of blacks and Latinos. Former governor Jerry Brown is right when he compares the media to a secular College of Cardinals. Once they establish an orthodoxy, those who dissent from it are smeared and persecuted. It wasn't enough for the *New York Times*, which during World War II referred to the Japanese as "Nips," to hammer the National Baptist Convention for its support of Mike Tyson, but as usual, the *Times* brought in a black op-ed writer to rubber-stamp its persecution of the Baptist convention. The head minister's acquittal on perjury charges was barely noticed by the *Times*. If, as feminist Karen Baker-Fletcher wrote in a *Times* op-ed piece, the support of Tyson reflects an insensitivity toward black women, then why can't the unanimous support of the Beauty Queen by the media and powerful feminists be viewed as their insensitivity toward black men?

If Mike Tyson raped Ms. Washington, he needs help, but so do the sick surrogate White Hopes who try to achieve through the criminal justice system—or in the case of Jack Johnson, through congressional legislation, or in the case of Muhammad Ali, through the draft board—what they couldn't achieve in a fair fight. Regardless of the outcome, and the media's attempt to get in on the prosecution of Tyson, millions of Americans—black, white, brown, yellow, and red—will continue to wonder, What was this Beauty Queen doing up in Mike Tyson's hotel room at 2:00 A.M.?

Drug "Experts" Don't Live with Gunfire

You've heard gunshots before. They've become so common in this Oakland ghetto that you and your neighbors have begun to ignore them.

At first, you dismiss the explosions—crack . . . crack . . . crack—as firecrackers, even though you know it's not the Fourth of July or New Year's Eve, when Oakland sounds like the Tet Offensive.

Denial.

That's usually the first response. A few seconds later, you call out to your daughter, whose bedroom faces the street, to hit the deck. But she, like the rest of the kids on this block, is a veteran. When you reach her bedroom, she's already under her desk.

And then you hear the inevitable fire trucks and police sirens, hurtling toward your neighborhood. Three doors down from you, a young black man has been wounded. You see the police rush toward his house with a stretcher. You know him as a quiet kid. A couple of years ago, he asked whether you could find him a job. You didn't have any leads.

The newspapers report that most of the homicides so far this year are drug-related. More people gather in the street. You and your kid, Tennessee, go to see how the widow, who lives next door to the victim's house, is faring. As you enter her house, you notice the blood-soaked clothing lying on the porch of the house next door. He had called her for help. She called the police. She's one of the faithful.

"I'm a Christian and he is a child of God, and I did what I could."

Her house is so clean that you could eat off of the floor. Jack Kennedy's and Jesus Christ's pictures adorn the wall. She's obviously shaken up. Your next-door neighbor had to lean against the door of her car, to support herself, while watching the scene. She was experiencing shortness of breath. These events are hard on the retired people who live on this block. After all they've been through, they deserve some peace.

You and Tennessee head back toward the house, leaving the scene to the gawkers. She's subdued. Her second book, *Electric Chocolate*, includes lines about machine guns. Your wife is attending a parents' meeting at New Age Academy, a private school in Berkeley. If she'd left five minutes later, and driven north instead of south, she might have been caught in the cross-fire.

The young man was still breathing, you're told, when the ambulance left. The newspapers didn't even bother to cover the attempt on his life.

You know that if drugs were legalized, your neighbors wouldn't have to endure these lethal trade wars. But you don't expect it to happen. The debate about the issue is dominated by middle-class men. You watch them on television and read their opinions in newspapers. They're opposed to it.

They should live in the "inner city" they get paid so well to discuss and to be experts on. (Their employers should insist upon it.) After six months of drive-by shootings and imprisonment in a neighborhood overtaken by crackers, they'd change their minds. Believe me, they would change their minds.

1990

An Outsider in Koreatown

Over the years, I have found myself to be the only outsider present during a meeting of this or that ethnic group. A sort of ethnic gate-crasher. I just won't mind my own business. In Alaska, I sat in on an esoteric discussion of tribal law and sovereignty at the Shee Atika Lodge. In San Francisco, I attended a meeting at the Irish Cultural Center. Later I was introduced as an Irish American poet, by the late John Maher of the Delancy Foundation, at a dinner of the Celtic Foundation, of which I am a member, having, like millions of African Americans, Irish American ancestry. The discussion of race in this country—which never seems to rise above the tabloid level, even among academics—generally omits the fact that the African is only one of the heritages of those whom we refer to as African Americans.

I never know how I'm going to be treated at these gatherings. I remember a Chinese American telling poet David Henderson and me to mind our own business when, during a meeting held in San Francisco's Chinatown, we were offering suggestions on how Chinese Americans could combat media images such as those which stereotype Chinese Americans as Charlie Chans. At that moment, I understood how the white liberals must have felt when they were ousted from SNCC. On another occasion, when I appeared on the panel for a meeting of *Tikkun*, the progressive

Jewish magazine, I jested about there being only two black persons on the panel. I said that if the predominantly Jewish audience didn't like my remarks, we'd have to fight our way out of the place, since the only person who would come to our aid would be the black security guard. That broke the ice. My remarks that more candor was needed in a discussion about black and Jewish relations were greeted enthusiastically, as were my comments that, contrary to the view of the talented tenth black media royalty, anti-Semitism wasn't merely a black problem, and that if we were to oppose instances of black anti-Semitism, then Jewish racism should be opposed just as vigorously. A reporter for a local paper ignored both my remarks and the reception to them, and focused instead upon fibs about black crime and the underclass, raised by a heckler during the Q & A segment of the program. (She felt I hadn't shown the heckler, a white man, proper "respect.") So when Ann Park, executive director of the Korean Community Center (KCC) of the East Bay, an organization whose purpose is "assisting the people of our community, particularly recent immigrant, limited-English-speaking, elderly, and low-income people," invited me to attend the 1992 annual dinner, I didn't know what to expect, in light of the Los Angeles riots.

I met Ann when I invited her to join a PEN media-boycott meeting held in Oakland, called to launch the second annual PEN Oakland boycott of network news. I had read her remarks, printed in the *San Francisco Chronicle,* that were delivered when representatives of twenty-one Korean American groups met in San Francisco to challenge media images that showed blacks as "looters" and Korean Americans as "gun-toting" vigilantes.

The dinner was held at the Claremont Hotel, a beautiful, spectacular, rambling Queen Anne number overlooking Berkeley that was built to entertain European aristocrats. While we were fetching our name tags, Ann Park greeted us and there didn't seem to be annoyance from the others in line that we outsiders had come to the dinner.

As soon as Carla Blank and I sat down, some of our fellow diners came over to greet us. Two were Ken and Ann Yabusaki, of the Japanese American Citizens League; Ken said that he didn't like La Jolla, California, because it lacked diversity. Professor Elaine Kim, of the University of California at Berkeley, also stopped by. It was Ms. Kim who put her finger on the post–Los Angeles situation of race relations in this country when she said that the black-white paradigm of race is obsolete. The keynote speaker, Angela E. Oh, came to our table to greet a friend. She welcomed us and asked who invited us. I congratulated her on her appearances on the Phil Donahue and Ted Koppel shows, during which she articulated the mood of the Korean community in the aftermath of the riot. She told Donahue that the media were exploiting the tragedy of two embattled communities, and she refused to engage in the blame-the-blacks-for-everything line that was promoted by the media. The think-tank line blamed the riots on dysfunctional black families, when most of those arrested for looting were Hispanic, and when the majority of poor Hispanic children live in two-parent households. Long since forgotten was the white participation in the riots, which was described not only by on-the-street observers but by the mayor of Los Angeles and the *Wall Street Journal*. While blacks and Hispanics attacked Korean stores in south central Los Angeles, whites participated in the looting and burning of stores in Koreatown. Also forgotten has been the fact that thousands of black businesses were burned and that, contrary to those who blamed the devastation of Korean businesses on blacks harboring racist attitudes toward Koreans (which was the way ex–Reagan speech writer Mona Charon put it—a woman who gets commissioned airtime to make ignorant comments about blacks), a poll result showed that the majority of blacks opposed the riots.

Angela Oh had avoided the trap of being used by the media to insult blacks, but after her speech I wondered whether she had changed her mind. She recommended that I read the report of the state legislature's Special Committee on the Los Angeles Crisis, on which she served as counsel.

The dinner music was nice: Mendelssohn, Bach, and Brahms. The dinner itself was excellent: "tossed baby lettuce with tomato wedges and baked walnuts, over poached salmon with lemon carp sauce, rice with pine nuts and orange rinds, fresh vegetables, chocolate macadamia nut torte, red wine." I had two desserts. I learned that some things are universal. The dinner was supposed to begin at 7:00 P.M. It began at 7:20 P.M. Somebody at my table said KP time. At that point in the evening, I could not have imagined that I would leave the dinner shaken and depressed.

The speeches got off to a good start. Oakland mayor Elihu Harris, perhaps the fastest-talking politician in the country, spoke of the need for the Oakland multiethnic community to be devoted to harmony and consensus. He cited Oakland's lack of violence in the aftermath of the Los Angeles riots as proof that Oakland was achieving this goal. Ann Park was introduced to great applause. She spoke of the Korean American community as being composed of "liquor store keepers, social workers, garment workers, roofing contractors, maintenance workers, engineers, housewives, and doctors."

She said that the KCC was expanding its services to include "a race relations program, community advocacy, and youth substance abuse prevention." Among those who received awards during the presentation was Peter Hong, a graduate student and the author of an essay about life as the son of a liquor store owner in a black neighborhood.

After these preliminaries, Ms. Oh, the keynoter, was introduced and her accomplishments listed. She was born and raised in Los Angeles and graduated from UC Davis Law School. As an attorney, she specializes in state and federal justice. She is the president of the Women's Organization Reaching Koreans, and the president-elect of the Korean American Bar Association of Southern California.

She spoke of 1992 as not being a good year for Koreans in the country or around the globe. She described the Los Angeles riots as a tidal wave that had left, in its wake, not only physical but psychic damage to the Koreans, damage that would take many generations to heal. She compared what happened to Koreans in Los Angeles with the internment of the Japanese during World War II.

Though most Koreans have been here only twenty years, Ms. Oh said, they've had to take on the burden for three hundred years of racism that has been inflicted upon African Americans and to pay for the impoverishment of the country's have-nots. Ms. Oh spoke with power and conviction as she described herself as a woman whose anger has become serene. At first, she said, she did not believe that the Korean businesses had been targeted, but after investigation, she decided that they had been. The Korean businesses suffered $750 million worth of damage, and 3,000 businesses were destroyed. Some of the insurance claims will never be paid, because of bogus insurance companies, some of which are operating out of the Bahamas. Ms. Oh spoke of the Los Angeles riots as the most recent tragedy in the history of tragedy for Korean people. On the Donahue show she said that the Koreans didn't have to be lectured about oppression, since they'd suffered two thousand years of oppression. She spoke bitterly of the Japanese occupation of Korea, during which an attempt was made to annihilate Korean culture. She mentioned the 100,000 Korean women who were forced into prostitution by the Japanese, but in the name of Asian American solidarity, she said, these old feuds should be abandoned. She said that the Korean American community lacked political clout because the vast majority of Korean Americans who had arrived within the past twenty years were not citizens and hence could not vote. As though her remarks were not grim enough, Ms. Oh ended her speech with a warning of a new riot.

She said that the millions of dollars that have been poured into Los Angeles in the wake of the riots haven't created new jobs, and that Peter Ueberroth had expressed his unhappiness about the situation. She said that the events of April 24 to May 4, which was the way she referred to the riots during her speech (on other occasions, she referred to the riots as "the crisis"), demonstrated the amount of firepower on the streets, and she predicted that if the blacks who were accused of assaulting the truck driver are convicted and the four policemen acquitted of violating Rodney King's civil rights, then, in her words, "all hell will break loose."

Ms. Oh, who has become a symbol of a younger generation of articulate, activist Korean American leadership, also criticized the Korean American community. When she declared herself a feminist, some of the guys in the audience turned to each other and smirked. She described herself as every Korean mother's nightmare. She urged the Korean American community to become more inclusive and to take interest in the communities in which they operated their businesses.

The Los Angeles riots were a catastrophe, and like most catastrophes, mindless. Thousands of black and Asian American businesses were destroyed by a minority of blacks, whites, and Hispanics, who have been described by some talented tenth intellectuals and academics, safely ensconced on college campuses, as "warriors" participating in an "uprising."

What kind of warrior is it who would take his or her rage out on a mom-and-pop store, on people who worked under near-slave-labor conditions in order to eke out an existence in a country that is often hostile to them? Of course, I know that there's another side to the story. A Chinese American dinner companion wondered why Chinese Americans have been able to operate in black ghettos for decades without problems. Another Chinese American novelist told me that Koreans are just "uptight." But does rudeness or uptightness warrant the devastation the Korean American community received during the riots? What if we were to firebomb every store or business whose clerks were rude to us? The United States would be a continuous inferno. Are African American intellectuals so hard up for heroes that they have to heroize the hoodlums and thugs who ransacked stores? Is the test of a warrior these days engaging in a shoot-out with the operators of a mom-and-pop store? I knew that the affair was tragic, but I didn't know the extent of the tragedy until I attended this dinner. The dinner ended with a performance done in the Korean style.

As we were leaving, our dining companions asked me what I thought of the performance. I said it reminded me of rap. They nodded their heads.

The hurt and the agony that the Korean Americans exhibited at this meeting, despite their strained attempts to have a good time, affected me. I would discuss it during the coming months whenever I had a chance, on the radio and before black audiences, including before some black schoolchildren in Oakland who had never heard of the ordeal Koreans have experienced in history. They listened with rapt attention.

As I walked toward my car after dinner, Ms. Oh's final words echoed in my mind. She said that we are able to launch vehicles into the vast regions of space and to uncover civilizations from thousands of years ago, but we still can't seem to get along.

PART 2

Profiles / Reviews

Elaine Brown
Activist

Afrocentric nationalism has been taking a real pounding from professional op-ed writers, talented tenthers, and magazines published by some of the most rigid and brazen of ethnic chauvinists. Whatever one may think of Afrocentrism, it will take many years and billions of dollars in appropriations for its leaders to do the kind of damage to the national psyche that has been done by the Eurocentrics—certainly a misnomer, since, based upon my travels to some of the oldest universities in Europe, I haven't found a tenth of the kind of resistance to a varied educational curriculum that I've found in the United States. In fact, while our educational curricula and the media continue to be breeding grounds for hate crimes, American multicultural studies are in vogue in Spain, Germany, France, and England.

It's because of the Eurocentric control of the public school curriculum that the United States produces generation after generation of white bigots and black, yellow, and brown intellectuals who spend half of their adult lives seeking their "identity." Their lack of knowledge of African American, Latino, and Asian American history condemns them to repeat the mistakes of the past.

Both my and Elaine Brown's generation, though of humble circumstances, received bourgeois educations that omitted or even disparaged the study of non-European cultures. Intellectuals of my generation believed that the issues we faced as young writers in New York during the 1960s were unique, until we read Harold Cruse's *The Crisis of the Negro Intellectual*, which educated us about the issues that separated our predecessors: integration versus separation; the cultural nationalism of philosopher Alain Locke versus the international socialism of poet Claude McKay; a feud that caused a conflict between Maulana Karenga's U.S., a Los Angeles group devoted to cultural nationalism whose main legacy is the holiday Kwannza, and the revolutionary socialist group the Black Panthers. Unlike the literary feud between Locke and McKay, the one between the Los Angeles Panthers, led by a former gang leader, and U.S. resulted in armed conflict. Ms. Brown's eyewitness account of a shoot-out that led to the deaths of two Panthers is chilling.

Deprived of a multicultural education, Elaine Brown was introduced to the Communist philosophy by Jay Kennedy, a Jewish Hollywood scriptwriter (*I'll Cry Tomorrow*) whom she met while working as a cocktail waitress at the Pink Pussycat. She'd come to Los Angeles from Philadelphia to pursue a songwriting career. Kennedy, a member of Frank Sinatra's circle and onetime manager of Harry Belafonte, bragged to her about his influence in the civil rights movement and provided her with a reading list of black male authors. (One wonders how the reading of conservative Zora Neale Hurston would have shaped her thinking.) She became Mr. Kennedy's mistress and Pygmalion.

He lectured her about the evils of capitalism as they travelled about in limousines and rendezvoused at places like the Beverly Hills Hotel or in Frank Sinatra's home. Little did Ms. Brown know that the black community had abandoned the Communist party in droves during the late 1930s, when its Popular Front changed its focus from domestic issues affecting blacks to rescuing the Soviet Union after the Nazi-Soviet pact. The Communist party's abandonment of blacks provides the backdrop for Ralph Ellison's *Invisible Man*.

Ms. Brown was also unaware that in the 1930s, Claude McKay encountered racism in both the American and the English Communist parties and became bitterly anti-Communist as a result. He ended his life as a Catholic because he found a bishop who could empathize with his blackness more so than his Communist party allies, who saw the struggle between classes as society's basic contradiction.

Though Ms. Brown was hurt when she finally realized that Mr. Kennedy wasn't about to abandon his wife and capitalistic lifestyle to marry her, he and other white male benefactors and contributors to the party are treated gently by Ms. Brown, while black men like Bobby Seale and Maulana Karenga are described as buffoons and brutes.

It has been my experience that the most fervent critic of black misogyny is a liberal feminist who is silent about the misogyny of men who are members of her own ethnic background. One of them must have had a hand in writing the press release that accompanies Elaine Brown's *A Taste of Power*. It claims that the Black Panther party was destroyed by its own misogyny. The problem with this kind of narrow political correctness is that it lets powerful institutions and individuals off the hook. This line has been used in early reviews and comments about the book in feminist strongholds like the *New York Times Book Review* and NPR. Chicago Panther Fred Hampton wasn't murdered as a result of black misogyny; he was murdered by the police. (Kenneth O'Reilly, in his useful *Racial Matters*, describes the policy of the FBI toward the Panthers as "The Only Good Panther Is a Dead Panther.")

The fact that the Panthers organized against Los Angeles and Oakland warlords and their technicals, who were (and still are) parading as officers of the law and terrorizing the black ghettos, made them the targets of physical and psychological aggression from local and federal police forces. The treatment of Elaine Brown after she and her partners were stopped by a Los Angeles technical is typical. The policeman assaulted her with the kind of language blacks hear from the police every day: "You think you're doin' something for your people. That's a fuckin' joke. Niggers don't want nothin'. I know niggers. I kicked niggers' asses all over Hell's Kitchen. A Sicilian can kick the shit out of a nigger, and a spic. I hate niggers. How do you feel about that?" (The irony of this speech is that in Europe, it's the Sicilians who are referred to as "niggers.")

Of course, I'm aware that there are thousands of decent police throughout the country, but there are still just enough deputized, trigger-happy outlaws to make day-to-day life in black communities hazardous, communities where the assaults on black citizens range from what Philadelphia historian James Spady refers to as "microaggression" to Rodney King–type beatings and even murder. Blaming black men for their problems is becoming as big a market as soft drinks, and the press pitch for this book is obviously geared to reaping a share of the profits. To do so, the publisher and the feminist reviewers must portray Elaine Brown as an oppressed black woman, victimized by black male "evil" (Alice Walker's term). Ms. Brown wanders through her book complaining about having to cook for men and about the subservience of women to men—which is strange, because during her career as a Panther, she held important party posts.

If Ms. Brown is a feminist, then so is Ma Barker. In one scene, Ms. Brown and her companions burst into the office of George Jackson's lawyer and slap her around because she refuses to release Jackson's poetry. In another, she joins the male Panthers in an assault on Ike and Tina Turner and their band. In one of the most bloodcurdling scenes, Ms. Brown, who has been appointed party chairman after Huey Newton flees to Cuba to avoid being charged with the murder of a prostitute (in this book, Ms. Brown claims that Newton was innocent, and was framed by gangsters whose "after hours joints" the Panthers were shaking down), presides over the beating and torture of one of her former lovers, an act of revenge for the beating he had once given her. (Ms.

Brown, like other white and black middle-class women of the 1960s movement, seems to have had a knack for picking cads as bedmates.)

The Panthers' harassment by the Oakland police resulted in an incident during which a white police officer was killed, and Huey Newton shot in the stomach. This made Newton a marked man. The description of his treatment by vindictive prison officials is not recommended reading for the squeamish. Carlton Inniss, a member of the team of lawyers that defended Newton during the murder trial, said that Newton entered prison an idealist and left prison, almost two years later, a different personality, "hedonistic," subject to mood swings, and seeking "cheap highs." Inniss blames this change on the mind-altering drugs with which Newton was assaulted in prison. Newton's advocating the overthrow of the government invited various government agencies to hound him until he was murdered on a West Oakland street on August 22, 1989.

Panthers Newton, Eldridge Cleaver, Bobby Seale, David Hillard, and Ericka Huggins appear in vivid scenes throughout *A Taste of Power*. Ms. Brown seems to have kept detailed notes about the events and personalities that have made the Black Panther party an American legend. It's the kind of fascinating book that the general reader—not just feminists—will find hard to put down.

Ms. Brown is not only a good writer, but a former party insider, who traces its history from the days when it was only an idea in the head of Huey Newton, while he was visiting Bobby Seale's house and eating his mother's food, to the last days when Huey Newton, addicted to cocaine and alcohol, hosted international celebrities, as well as street people, in his Oakland penthouse. A scene during which Newton and Minister Louis Farrakhan have a showdown is riveting.

A Taste of Power depicts Huey Newton as a genius given to drug-induced psychotic episodes, vainly attempting to apply the theories of his white patrons and of revolutionary movements elsewhere to the domestic reality. As an interracial person, he was hardened by the taunts he'd received during his childhood. His yellow skin made him a target (his grandfather was Jewish). He always boasted about having defied the soul breakers of the criminal justice system. Obviously, he was wrong. It's only when Bobby Seale decided to run for mayor and shocked the establishment with his strong showing—he garners 45 percent of the vote—that the Panthers got real and began to initiate the policies that would result in the black middle class receiving political power in Oakland. They helped to elect a mayor, a congressman, supervisors, and council members. They changed Oakland from a feudalistic fiefdom, controlled by a few families, to the twenty-first-century multicultural city that it is becoming. They brought power to the people.

Ms. Brown was instrumental in this switch of tactics and successfully engineered the Panthers into becoming players in Oakland and national politics. For choosing Ms. Brown as party chairman, Newton was criticized by the male party members, upon his return from Cuba. Here as well, as in other places in the book, the male Panthers demonstrate that, when it came to the treatment of women, they could be just as asinine as yellow, white, and brown American males, no more and no less.

An Oakland judge, Lionel Wilson, became Huey Newton's Sun Yat-sen, and was elected Oakland's first black mayor. Ironically, he was later defeated for favoring downtown development over neighborhood issues and for failing to solve Oakland's crack epidemic. The Panthers' noticing that the initial drug deliveries to poor neighborhoods were made by whites, some of whom were driving Rolls-Royces, challenges another media myth: that the American crack plague is the result of black male behavior instead of, for example, a need to aid anti-Communist allies by using the inner cities as fund-raising drug bazaars for groups like the Contras.

Another scene questions another myth. After she made love to Hollywood producer and Panther patron Bert Schneider in a motel, and he gave her $12,000 to pay a year's rent for Huey Newton's penthouse, he referred to himself as her "trick." This is the fantasy promoted by Tom Wolfe in *Mau Mauing the Flak Catchers,* and *Bonfire of the Vanities,* and in John Guare's *Six Degrees of Separation.* Blacks, these writers claim, con liberals into donating money to dubious causes. They have it wrong. It was the Panthers who were the tricks.

White counterculture writers and former Panther allies made millions of dollars by writing books and producing films that placed themselves at the center of an era that was inspired by black culture and politics. It took a German letter writer to remind a *New York Times* book reviewer that Gilbert Moses, Marion Barry, and Julian Bond were also students after, in the course of a review of a counterculture book, a critic had remarked that Tom Hayden was the greatest student leader of the 1960s.

And wasn't a chance to see their political fantasies enacted worth the donations that wealthy white leftists made to the Panthers and other black "revolutionary" groups? With some films in the works about the Panthers, Hollywood will soon recoup its investment many times over. The life of Huey Newton, a complicated, volatile individual capable of both compassion and viciousness, reads like a movie script (playwright Ed Bullins has already written a play about Newton).

Ms. Brown's entertaining book has soon-to-be-a-motion-picture written all over it. In Walt Harrington's *Crossings,* Dolores Robinson, a Beverly Hills personal talent manager, discusses the various Hollywood Panther projects. In the works are a Wesley Snipes–Joel Silver Panther project, a Suzanne DePasse Panther project, a Charles Burnett Panther project, and a Meryl Streep Panther project. Panther-mania will probably generate more consumer revenue than Malcolm-mania, which has become a multimillion-dollar business. There will be Panther cups, T-shirts, jackets, and berets; Huey Newton dolls; and so forth.

I wouldn't even be surprised if a future head of the FBI, the organization that persecuted the Panthers and promoted deadly feuds among its members, will remember the Panthers fondly. After all, the man responsible for the execution of Jesus Christ, Pontius Pilate, died a Christian.

Ultimately, the Panthers were caught in a crossfire between the white Left and the white Right. A suburban family quarrel. Eventually, the feuding relatives made up so that by the middle of the Reagan era, the *New York Review of Books,* which was printing illustrations of Molotov cocktails in the 1960s, was sounding to the right of the *National Review,* and former Students for a Democratic Society (SDS) members are boosting their ratings on the networks, where they are now establishment correspondents, by playing to white irrational fears of black crime. J. Edgar Hoover, a man who had persecuted black leaders, entertainers, and other celebrities since 1919, must be smiling in hell.

There is much in Elaine Brown to admire. She rose from the poverty of 2051 York Street, "buried in the heat of the black section of North Philadelphia," to become an international celebrity by sheer will, drive, brains, talent, bravado, and a discipline she learned from her mother and her grandmother. She took all that a vindictive government (which has harassed black leaders and dissidents since President Buchanan tried to jail Frederick Douglass) could throw at her, as well as abuse from men, both black and white, and she's still standing. While many of the male members of the Panthers were destroyed, Ms. Brown survived. She married a retired French industrialist and now lives in a 132-room château in France. Hers, as they say, is an American story.

1993

Eldridge Cleaver
Writer

Though the young African American hip-hop intellectuals picture Malcolm X as an apostle of armed resistance—their favorite poster is that of a rifle-bearing Malcolm, peering out from behind curtains, preparing to do battle with his enemies—the revolutions that both Malcolm X and Martin Luther King, Jr., precipitated were textbook Sun Tzu. They produced change—King in the law, Malcolm in consciousness—without throwing a punch (at whites), or firing a shot. And though they are regarded as opposites, it was Malcolm's threats that were partially responsible for the establishment's agreeing to some of King's demands.

Malcolm made wolfing and jive into an art form, and though his battles were fought on television (Marshall McLuhan referred to him as "the electronic man") and his weapons were words, he was a symbol of black manhood; "our shining prince" was the way Ossie Davis put it, in a eulogy delivered at Malcolm's funeral. Black men were in need of such a prince, manhood being very much on the minds of black men during the sixties. Their frustration was heightened when some black children were blown to bits during church services in Birmingham, Alabama; King, Jr.'s macho critics thought that he had "punked out" when he used children in one of his nonviolent demonstrations.

Black nationalist poet Askia Muhammed Toure wondered aloud, "But who will protect the women's quarters?" the desperate cry of men whose women were being poked with cattle prods and beaten to the ground by white thugs in uniform. I wrote a long noisy rambunctious poem entitled "Fanfare for an Avenging Angel," dedicated to Malcolm, and, after reading it, Malcolm told me, charitably, that it reminded him of works by "Virgil and Dante."

That's how we saw Malcolm X. He would make them pay. Pay for the humiliations we suffered in a racist country. Young black intellectuals were out for revenge. They were in a Kikukyu warrior mode. On the west coast, a young black prisoner was using the Spanish dungeon of the sort that used to hold slaves as his personal library. Eldridge Cleaver was also impressed with Malcolm X and took Malcolm X's position over that of Elijah Muhammad, whose generation called whites devils, because they had come out of the southern racist hell where the whites had shown themselves to be capable of the most fiendish acts.

As in the case of his hero, Malcolm X, Eldridge Cleaver went to school in jail, reading, writing, meditating, and practicing his intellectual style on mentors, who were obviously no match for his probing, hungry intellect. In his book *Soul on Ice,* he confessed to a former career as a rapist and admitted to relationships with white women (still the cardinal taboo in the eyes of white and black nationalists).

He assured his readers, especially the eastern Left, which had the power to make celebrities of those who supported its issues, that he was a recovering racist, a former black muslim, who read and admired Norman Mailer's *The White Negro* (the usual bit of Noble Savage gibberish), but the recurrent theme in the book is that of an eternal struggle between the black supermasculine menial and the white omnipotent administrator—a struggle that continues in various forms, to this day. While white males were on the receiving end of criticism by black writers during the sixties and early seventies, some white male writers and media commentators have since gotten even by bonding with the black feminist movement and criticizing the treatment of black women by black men.

In this war, women are regarded as bargaining chips and loot for both sides, the black ones, Amazons, the white ones, gullible Barbie dolls. A white guard objected to Cleaver having pictures of a white woman on his cell wall. This guard, like many white men, regarded all white women as their property, while black men feel that black women belong to them. Both groups were upset when the women declared that they owned their own bodies, their souls, and their minds. In *Soul on Ice* the women are either Madonnas or whores. In some gushy, heart-wringing letters, Cleaver professed his love for his lawyer, Beverly Axelrod, and her responses, printed in the book, were equally cloying.

Cleaver was first pushed as a celebrity by the New York Old Left and its branches in Northern California and Los Angeles. They had given up on the worker (at the time depicted by Robert Crumb and other underground cartoonists as a bigoted, flag-waving, Budweiser-guzzling hard hat and incipient Reagan Democrat) and in his place substituted the black prisoner as proxy in their fight against capitalism. In *The New York Times Magazine,* in an article that was preceded by a quote of mine that if Thomas Jefferson were around he'd be reading Eldridge Cleaver, Old Lefter Harvey Swados referred to Cleaver as the quintessential American. And he is, in the sense that Tom Sawyer, Huckleberry Finn, Ellison's Rinehart, Gerald Vizenor's Bearheart, and the creatures in those African-Native American animal tales who use guile, wit, and flattery to accomplish their ends are quintessential Americans. (In a classic tale a snake says to a benefactor, who expresses dismay after being bitten by the creature it has rescued, "You knew I was a snake.")

I was in Leonard Bernstein's apartment the week before he gave a party for the Black Panthers (a party made notorious by Thomas Wolfe, in whose latest book, *The Bonfire of the Vanities,* blacks are likened to rats) and Bernstein, pointing to Cleaver's book on the coffee table, asked me had I read him. I hadn't read him at the time, but figured that the New York Left was going to make use of Cleaver and the Panthers, for whom he became Minister of Information. I said so publicly. I was hip to the eastern intelligentsia which was dabbling in Marxism at the time and knew of the intelligentsia's "contradictions." Leonard Bernstein, who was sympathetic to the Panthers' cause, was having trouble with black musicians like Arthur Davis, who accused the conductor of discriminating against black musicians.

After the collapse of the Black Panther party, Cleaver, like Doug Street in Wendell Harris's extraordinary film *Chameleon Street*, went through different changes. In *Soul on Ice* he refers to himself as though he were different people: "I was very familiar with the Eldridge who came to prison, but that Eldridge no longer exists. And the one I am now is a stranger to me." He went into exile and lived in Cuba, Algeria, and France (where it was rumored that he shared a mistress with a prime minister), returned to become a fundamentalist minister, campaigned for the Republican senatorial nomination, designed clothes that highlighted the penis, and began a church devoted to the male reproductive organs and the preservation of sperm. Recently, he was criticized for poaching curbside recyclables, on behalf of his "Church of the Great Taker," that were intended for the nonprofit Berkeley Ecology Center. Once in a while he appears in the local newspapers, in trouble with the law over some petty charge, or for assisting an elderly white woman from being evicted from her house. Sometimes the local media uses him for comic relief.

He wrote a second book, *Soul on Fire*, which in many ways was as absorbing as *Soul on Ice*. But, like Till Eulenspiegel, he had worked his tricks too many times; the book was ignored and his description of his conversion to Christianity, mocked (he said that he joined the fundamentalists because they had brought him from exile, and if the Panthers had brought him home he would have sided with them).

Each group of Cleaver's supporters claimed that it had been taken by the head of the Church of the Great Taker, but it could be argued that they did quite a bit of betraying themselves. Besides, if they had read *Soul on Ice* instead of marveling at the fact that a black prisoner could hold such a gifted mind they would have learned that Cleaver's most persistent intellectual quality is doubt. And doubters aren't followers and are distrustful of structures, which is what perhaps inspired Amiri Baraka to describe Eldridge Cleaver as a "bohemian anarchist," a highfalutin name for the trickster.

His supporters used him, but he used them too. And who could blame a black man for using his wits to get out of one of these Nazi-like pits, often guarded by depraved sadists, where this society had cast him to rot and die at the age of twenty-two? Today, thousands of young black men like Cleaver languish in the country's prisons while the inside traders receive light sentences for nearly wrecking the economic system, while the Justice Department spends millions of dollars to trap a black mayor on a misdemeanor charge, while the BCCI money-laundering enterprise, perhaps the biggest drug scandal in history, is ignored, and in a society where most of the S&Lers won't even come to trial.

Had Cleaver remained in prison without the publicity that ultimately led to his release, he'd probably be dead.

By the end of the sixties the Left and the Right, like lovers, began to trot toward each other so that at the beginning of the eighties they were in bed together. Cleaver hurt James Baldwin (so did I) who was deemed politically incorrect by the young lions who were so paranoid about their manhood. Baldwin was also considered a sellout, and "radical chic" was the expression introduced by the late Seymour Krim to chastise Baldwin for permitting *The Fire Next Time* to be published in the *New Yorker*, the epitome of uptown pretensions and snobbery. Baldwin pretended that he didn't care. Baldwin used to tell me that he didn't mind my criticisms of him because, "Ishmael, you're a

writer, but that Cleaver. . . ." Cleaver and Baldwin underesti-
mated each other. Far from being a clown, Cleaver is a writer,
too, and though Baldwin comes in for some vicious criticism
from Cleaver, it is obvious that *Soul on Ice* is influenced by Baldwin's flamboyantly eloquent taxidermist's style, just as Baldwin's *If Beale Street Could Talk* reminds one of Eldridge Cleaver.

But Baldwin proved to be more reliable than Norman Mailer,
who is championed in this book. Baldwin went to his grave pro-
testing the injustices committed against the underdogs of the
world by forces and institutions more powerful than them,
while by the end of the sixties Norman Mailer was saying that
he was "tired of Negroes and their rights," and there is only a
thin intellectual partition between his recent comments blaming
blacks for the drug trade and those of the new policy elite at
the *New Republic* (whose neoconservative about-face can be
gauged by the fact that an endorsement from the pre–Right
wing *New Republic* appears on the paperback edition of *Soul on
Ice*. The publisher, Martin Peretz, who seems to spend all of his
waking hours making up fibs about the "underclass," formerly
had ties with SDS, wouldn't you know). Cleaver supporter, the
New York Review of Books, which, during the sixties, carried in-
structions on how to make a Molotov cocktail, now prints long,
unreadable pieces by Andrew Hacker denouncing affirmative
action and seeking to divide Asian Americans from black Americans with ignorant comments about the model minority.

The New Left, who sought to use the Black Panthers to foment
a violent revolution, by the late seventies had joined the Reagan
consensus, or had begun to wallow in a selfish consumerism.
Others became Second Thoughts, denouncing the Panthers
before neoconservative banquets of the sort that get carried on
C-Span. Sylvia Ann Hewlett describes the spirit of postrevolu-
tionary America as that of "a therapeutic mentality . . . which
focuses on the self rather than a set of external obligations."

Cleaver believed that the younger generation of whites would
be wooed away from their omnipotent administrator fathers by

African American dance and music. Whites began to dance better, but that didn't make them more humanistic. Rock and roll
made billions for white artists and became the entertainment at
white-power rallies and accompanied the black-hating lyrics of
Axil Rose. Even the creator of the Willie Horton campaign, Lee
Atwater, received a better review in the *New York Times* for his
rock and roll music than Miles Davis. *Rolling Stone,* which was
the voice of the counterculture during the sixties, went Republican and upscale, and Malcolm X, the symbol of black sixties
manhood, has been "outed" in a new book by Bruce Perry.

The groups that are the subjects of so much abuse in *Soul on
Ice,* women and gays (the Cleaver of *Soul on Ice* considers homo-
sexuality to be a disease), have placed their oppression front and
center and have even made villains of the former black male ma-
chos who fantasized a revolution (while borrowing their strategies). These groups could even be accused of trivializing the
oppression of the white and black underclass because once you
propose that all women, including Queen Elizabeth, or all gays,
including Malcolm Forbes, are oppressed, then everybody is oppressed, even the omnipotent administrator—white males with
Ph.D.s, the new oppressed, whom the media would have us believe are being set upon by a politically correct multiculturalism.

And now Hollywood, which poured money into Black Panther coffers, will get its money back with interest, with a slew of
films now in the works about the Black Panthers demonstrating
that Cleaver's scientific socialism was no match for the witchcraft of capitalism. (One of these films is being scripted by Anna
Hamilton Phelan, the writer for *Gorillas in the Mist,* the favorite
film of the gestapo wing of the LAPD.) Capitalism could even
transform a group that once advocated its overthrow into box-
office receipts and T-shirt revenue. (Whatever became of Jerry
Rubin and Cleaver's wife Kathleen Cleaver? They went to Wall
Street. Tom Hayden married Jane Fonda.)

I always wondered what would have happened if Cleaver
and Huey Newton and the Panthers hadn't been used as pawns

in a struggle between the white Right, who destroyed them, and the white Left, who piled an agenda on them that went way beyond their original community concerns, and who viewed them as cannon fodder. (They wanted "a nigger to pull the trigger" as one Panther put it.) Thanks to the Panthers, the downtown Oakland political establishment is black but that doesn't seem to prohibit the police from continuing to beat the shit out of black people in Oakland (and as elsewhere in the case of these black ceremonial governments, the cash is controlled by whites). They also elected a Congressman.

Huey Newton was shot dead in the gutter and was bitterly denounced, before his body was even cold, by a post–New Left Berkeley "alternative" newspaper whose editorial line mirrors the confusion of the Left—one week printing a long piece sympathetic to still-imprisoned Panther Geronimo Pratt, another week printing an article favorable to University of California anthropologist Vincent Sarvich, a member of the new oppressed, who maintains that women and blacks are intellectually deficient because of their small brain size (the same argument that Hitler's "scientists" used to advance against the professor's ancestors).

In this political and cultural environment Cleaver seems a has-been and the villains in his book, Lyndon Johnson (promoter of the Great Society) and Barry Goldwater (who challenged the CIA's mining of the Nicaraguan harbor)—in comparison to the sinister crowd in power now—seem like populists from the quaint old days of the American Weimar.

But I suspect that history is not finished with Eldridge Cleaver. If he never does another thing in his life, he wrote this book. It's not just a book about the sixties like those books and films written by his former white allies that prove that the authors were white nationalists all along because they omit, or give scant attention to, the role of blacks, who created the political and cultural matrix for that decade. The conclusion of one recent film, Mark Kitchell's *Berkeley in the Sixties,* most of whose narrators are white women, seems to be that the significance of the political and cultural upheaval of the sixties was that it led to the formation of the middle class feminist movement.

The reissue of Eldridge Cleaver's *Soul on Ice* will challenge the current bleaching out of the black influence on the cultural and political climate of the sixties. This book is a classic because it is not merely a book about that decade, regarded as demonic by some and by others as the most thrilling and humanistic of this century. *Soul on Ice is* the sixties. The smell of protest, anger, tear gas, and the sound of skull-cracking billy clubs, helicopters, and revolution are present in its pages.

The old cover's image of the lilies juxtaposed with the young prisoner's rugged face and unkempt hair is apt.

Out of the manure that American society can often be for black men, the growth and beauty of their genius cannot be repressed. Cannot be denied.

GWENDOLYN BROOKS
Poet

Some of the most memorable poetry that springs from the heart has been created by people who couldn't spell their names, while others, like Ezra Pound, Melvin Tolson, Robert Hayden, Wallace Stevens, T. S. Eliot, and Lorenzo Thomas, dazzle our intellects through their wordplay and their knowledge. Some poets connect to the inside of our rhythms with their mastery of sound—Eugene Redmond, Quincy Troupe, and Jayne Cortez. Other poets seem to be in direct communication with the gods—Sonia Sanchez. A class by herself.

Then there are the geniuses who are hard to classify—Amiri Baraka, Bob Kaufman, Ntozake Shange. Gwendolyn Brooks is that rare poet whose genius is accessible. She is one who stimulates both our hearts and our intellects. With her great technical virtuosity that ranges from rhyme royals to Old English stanzas, to the blues, ballads, and jazz, with her inventive experiments with every variety of rhyme, she could have stopped taking risks long ago. But instead of catering to the literary court, she sent her poems to the basketball courts, to the beauty parlors, to the churches, and to the projects. She is the craftsperson who can handle iambic pentameter as well as colored pentameter.

She follows in that tradition of Chicago writers who place their pens in the service of the common people: Richard Wright,

Nelson Algren, James T. Farrell, Haki Madhubuti, Carl Sand-
burg, the late Hoyt Fuller, and honorary Chicagoan Mari Evans.

In her poems, a domestic—a "Bronzewille Woman in a Red
Hat"—receives as much respect as Madam Walker, a millionaire
whose tallest monument cuts grandly into the air at Lincoln
Cemetery. A hunchback girl dreams of a heaven where everything is straight, and a poem about an ugly child, Lincoln West,
who realizes his beauty only after an overheard racist remark,
demonstrates Ms. Brooks's wonderful gift for irony. Her survey
of characters in the black towns and cities of America, characters
we're all familiar with, is broad and variegated.

Some of them eat kidney pie at "Maxion's" and "Grenadine
de Boeuf" at "Maison Henri"; others eat at "Joe's Eats," where
you get your fish or chicken on meat platters with coleslaw,
macaroni, candied sweets, coffee, and apple pie. "You go out
full." Her pages are full of black heroes, black patriots, black
retaliators—a man goes berserk after his home is attacked by
bigots, and a crazy woman refuses to sing in the spring. Even her
god is a human god. Not the feudalistic tyrants of Ife and Olym-
pus, not the brooding, insecure god of the Old Testament, prepared to wipe out whole tribes at the least offense, but a god
who gets lonely.

She knows the voices and the styles of the people, but her observations are not limited to them. When outsiders intrude,
where others with less skill would bludgeon these philanthro-
pists Ms. Brooks is very gentle in her ribbing of these women
from Glencoe and Lake Forest—"sweet tender clad fit fiftyish
a-glow"—who invade the ghettos, seeking to assuage their con-
sciences by doing good works.

Like the best of artists—Langston Hughes, Miles Davis,
Garth Fagan, Joe Overstreet, Betye Saar, Max Roach, Adrienne
Kennedy—Ms. Brooks is always contemporary and is always
experimenting with new styles. But while she is fresh, she is not
given to trendiness. At a time when all it takes to get on the
cover of *Newsweek* is a foul, X-rated speech defaming a black

man's character, Ms. Brooks writes tributes to Willie Kosetile, Haki Madhubuti, Paul Robeson, Walter Brashford, John O. Killens, and Langston Hughes.

At a time when feuds between racial nationalists are tearing the heart out of our intellectual community, Ms. Brooks prints a generous poem about a good craftsman, the poet of the birch trees, Robert Frost. She is not swayed by the politically correct moment. Though she is devoted to the movement for black cultural sovereignty, she demands that others be as genuine as she. She will not tolerate the fools who cry, "Africa!" only to go home and watch "Gunsmoke," "Gilligan's Island," and the NFL.

Her poetry, like all great poetry, rises above the controversies of the day. Whether you're prochoice or antiabortion, feminist or masculinist, you have to agree that "The Mother" is the greatest poem about the subject of abortion ever written.

I remember traveling to New Orleans in 1978 to witness another great artist exhibit his talents. After the Muhammad Ali–Leon Spinks fight, I tried to get into the champ's dressing room, but it was so crowded with celebrities that I couldn't. I noticed an old black boxing trainer sitting alone, in a corner. I walked over and asked him why he thought the champ had won. He said, "Because class will tell."

Writing poetry is the hard manual labor of the imagination. It is a high-risk profession, with a history strewn with those who've struggled with alcoholism and drug addiction and suicide. The muse of poetry is the cold, demanding figure.

Ms. Brooks has survived the trip to the interior of the soul that all poets must make and has come back from that unmapped interior to tell us about it.

The gods on both sides of the Atlantic and the Pacific will bless her with many more years of great writing, for ultimately, that black trainer in New Orleans was right: Class will tell.

Paul Robeson
Actor

The life of a black celebrity is perilous enough, but a black celebrity who becomes a spokesperson is asking for pure hell. Not only has the outspokenness of those regarded as "radicals" gotten them into trouble, but Gary Giddens's new book, *Satchmo*, reveals that even Louis Armstrong came into conflict with the American secret police for his criticisms of Eisenhower's handling of segregation in the South. Had Paul Robeson fulfilled the role for which American society prepared him—that of a patriotic token, lecturing the "underclass" of his time about its "slovenly" habits and exhibiting, by his efforts, that with hard work and determination, one could achieve anything in this land of opportunity—he'd probably still be around, delighting audiences with his spirituals and playing Othello. Martin Baum L. Duberman's *Paul Robeson* portrays Robeson as someone who chose to use his celebrity status as a platform for speaking out against the injustices of the oppressed all over the world, and especially of blacks at home. For his efforts, he was hounded by his enemies into physical and mental breakdown, and in one of those Orwellian ironies that black life in America accumulates, this man who was persecuted from the early 1940s until his death in 1976 was diagnosed as having a persecution complex.

In 1950, at the height of America's cold war hysteria, the State

Department lifted his passport, closing an iron curtain on his opportunity to earn a living abroad. Not only did J. Edgar Hoover's FBI become part of the Robeson family, it seems, devoting more resources to the investigation of one black singer, actor, and intellectual during the 1940s and 1950s, than to investigating organized crime, but even the Communist party sent an informant, posing as a bodyguard, to spy on Robeson. Though Robeson was sympathetic to some Communist causes, he never joined the party, and he was never brought under its discipline. He once refused its order that he be silent.

His father, the Reverend William Drew Robeson, who in 1850, at the age of fifteen, escaped from slavery, was forced out of his New Jersey ministry and into poverty. He was punished by the white elders of the presbytery for his tendency to "speak out against social injustice," and in later years, when Robeson himself was subjected to vitriolic abuse from the press and the government, a family friend would comment, "They did it to his father."

Paul Robeson graduated from Rutgers University, where he excelled as an athlete, and in 1921 he married Eslanda Cordozo Goode, whose great-grandfather was Issac Nunez Cordozo, a member of a Spanish-Jewish family, and whose grandfather, Francis Lewis Cordozo, was described by Henry Ward Beecher as "the most highly educated Negro in America."

Duberman's excessive and voyeuristic details about Robeson's "multiplicity of romantic and sexual encounters" degrade an otherwise useful, fine, and well-researched biography. Robeson and his wife remained companions until her death from cancer in 1965. A serious rift between the two occurred after the publication of her book, in which she alluded to his affairs and described him as lazy. (Throughout his biography, whenever there's a dispute between Robeson and his wife about a fact, Duberman sides with Essie Robeson.)

A C student at Columbia Law School, Robeson stumbled into an acting career in 1920, appearing in some dreadful thing called

Taboo, in which, typically, Afro-American religion was subjected to the usual ignorant stereotyping. *Taboo* was written by what Duberman describes as a "fashionable young white socialite" named Mary Hoyt Wiborg, daughter of a wealthy financier, Frank Wiborg. (Throughout his life, Robeson would roam around freely among different classes, from the Australian aborigines, whose treatment he bitterly criticized during his stay in Australia, to the denizens of the English court.) Robeson would, throughout his career, be criticized for playing such trashy roles. He appeared in *Showboat, Emperor Jones, Sanders of the River* (which Jomo Kenyatta, one of the performers, praised), and *Tales of Manhattan*. Robeson hated these film roles and was evidently duped sometimes by the usual promise of control over the script, or perhaps he saw himself as paving the way for a succeeding generation of black film actors, who he felt would have it better (to no avail, since some of today's black actors take roles that make Robeson's role in *Emperor Jones* seem majestic by comparison).

At any rate, by the 1930s he bitterly denounced both *Sanders of the River* and *Emperor Jones*. Though Duberman provides testimony from some of the many he interviewed that Robeson regretted his lack of acting and singing training, the nation's newspaper critics gave him high praise for his performance abilities. Yet even the role of Othello was demeaning, Shakespeare's Moor being a little more dignified than Emperor Jones, but still a gullible half-cannibal who constantly berates himself for his inferiority to the Venetians, and who takes no offense when they call him racist names.

Robeson evidently had more freedom when he performed in movies by black filmmaker Oscar Micheaux and in an experimental film entitled *Borderline*. One of *Borderline*'s producers was a founder of modern poetry and a feminist, Hilda Doolittle. In the film, Robeson appeared with his wife, Essie.

His concert career was as controversial as his film and stage careers. Zora Neale Hurston accused him of corrupting the original intent of the folk songs' creators and of pandering to white audiences. Others argued that he limited his range by singing the songs of the black proletariat and urged him to attempt "serious" European music. The ever culturally conservative black middle class was offended by both his songs and his politics. Some of the most scorching criticisms of his left-leaning views emanated from the black press, but the black press didn't have the power to persecute him as relentlessly as the white press did. It was the white press that stirred up violent passions against him for appearing in Eugene O'Neill's *All God's Chillun* opposite a white actress, and it was the white press that created the atmosphere for an ugly civil disturbance occurring in 1947 in Peekskill, New York, where Robeson had gone to perform for a benefit. And it was an American wire service that distorted a key political speech Robeson made in Paris—a disinformation smear that caused Robeson's enemies to declare open season on him and NBC to ban Robeson from its airwaves.

It could be said that Robeson was a victim of the experiential difference between blacks and whites. According to a recent NAACP poll, this gap still exists. The black experience as articulated by writers and intellectuals is arrogantly dismissed as "paranoid," or prone to imputing conspiracies which aren't there, when noticed at all. Based upon his often humiliating experiences—especially in the area of public accommodations—and his observations about black life in the United States, Robeson's version of American political reality was different from those of powerful white men in the government, who considered him ornery for pointing out that the human rights violations they hypocritically condemned abroad also existed at home. At the White House, Robeson once got into a heated argument with Harry Truman about such contradictions. Truman responded to Robeson's plea for antilynching legislation by ending the interview. Truman later included Robeson in a "gang" that, he claimed, he'd defeated. Eleanor Roosevelt's view of Robeson was similar to Truman's.

Duberman's book indicates that Robeson could have made it

easier for himself had he recanted his support for the Soviet Union, something he refused to do. His support for the Soviet Union has always baffled some. Robeson was warned by Emma Goldman in the 1930s that the Russian Revolution had its cruel side, and even after the purges, the Nazi-Soviet pact, the invasion of Hungary, and the revelations about genocide committed by Stalin, Robeson remained loyal, shrugging off every criticism of a country he regarded as a color-blind, ideal worker's paradise. He must have known, after partying with Khrushchev and his friends in their private lodges, that some Communists lived much better than others. He was himself a cultural nationalist but apparently took little note of the fact that the Soviets had attempted to eradicate the cultures of Latvia, Estonia, and Lithuania. One wonders how Robeson would have reacted to *glasnost, perestroika,* the appeal for Western capital, the experiments with private enterprise, and the mass murders committed by Soviet forces in Afghanistan.

In ill health, Paul Robeson was permitted to return to the United States, thanks to a 1958 Supreme Court decision for which William O. Douglas wrote the majority opinion, declaring that "the Passport Division had no right to demand that an applicant sign an affidavit concerning membership in the Communist Party." During the last years of his life, Robeson was honored by a generation of civil rights workers whose coming his career had anticipated.

The mixed attitudes with which his country viewed the career of Paul Robeson—a man both praised and damned in his native land, and a man who had the courage to articulate in public ideas what most confine to their thoughts—didn't end at his death. Last year, "A Celebration of Paul Robeson" was held in New York. Among the sponsors were American Express, General Electric, ITT, Philip Morris, Mrs. Vincent Astor, and the Rockefeller Group.

1989

Bill Gunn
Director

What are the dry facts? In a bio sheet sent to me in 1979, Bill Gunn referred to himself as a writer/director. His play *Marcus in the High Grass* was produced in 1958 at the Theatre Guild in Westport. His second, *Johannas,* was produced in New York and Helsinki. *Black Picture Show* was produced at Lincoln Center in 1975 and, according to the sheet, a play called *Rhinestone* was to be produced for Broadway in 1978 and 1979. His novels were *All the Rest Have Died,* published by Delacorte Press in 1964, and *Rhinestone Sharecropping,* which Steve Cannon and I published, along with his play *Black Picture Show.* In addition to a dramatic version of *Rhinestone Sharecropping,* his play *The Forbidden City* opened on the day following his death. This master of irony would have found this to be the ultimate irony.

He wrote the screenplays for *Stop, The Landlord, Angel Levine, Friends, Fame Game, Don't the Moon Look Lonesome,* and *The Greatest: The Muhammad Ali Story.* His teleplays included *Johannas, Sojourner Truth,* and *Change at 125th Street.*

It's an impressive career. But his credits and his numerous awards, which include an Emmy, and the honor accorded to *Ganja and Hess,* one of the most beautiful and unusual films ever produced in the United States, and to *Personal Problems,* an experimental soap opera, don't tell the story. The heroic story of an exquisite writer maintaining a quiet and elegant stoicism while being battered by the crass forces of bottom-line commercialism and racism. These forces and institutions are the subjects of biting comments in his *Black Picture Show* and *Rhinestone Sharecropping*, where Bill Gunn exposes, with the wit of a Bosch or the Rembrandt of Dutchmasters, the pernicious influences which poison and pollute our national imagination. The Hollywood that gave us Montgomery Clift and James Dean, his tortured and brooding friends—the Hollywood that gave us great technicians like James Wong Howe and Hugh Robertson—also gave us *Birth of a Nation, The Color Purple,* and the sinister characters, the producers and image makers who talk shop in *Rhinestone.* Unlike some of the young black filmmakers of today, who talk the same way, Bill was too risky, too moody, too much of a genius, too savvy, and too clever for the Hollywood moguls. They didn't find him bankable: "you write something people can understand. None-a-that intellectual junk that ain't worth a quarter, much less a million dollars," Sam Dodd, *Rhinestone's* protagonist, is warned by one of the seamy Hollywood merchants he encounters in the film capital, where his adventures are similar to those of a Kafkaesque hero.

Gunn used the stage and the page to rail against these Movie Industry forces, not in the manner of the diatribe, but in the style of the samba and the bossa nova. With subtlety and with wit. He was too deft for the obvious. Too complicated. Too odd. ". . . if you expect to hold another assignment in this business you better learn to control your temper," Sam Dodd is advised by the same character. Gunn revealed the depraved managers of the Dream Factory, and its front-office tokens.

Pulitzer Prize winner Charles Gordone remembers Bill Gunn as being among those few black actors to read for parts in New York in the 1950s. At the time, James Dean was appearing in André Gide's *The Immoralist,* and another friend, Sal Mineo, was on Broadway as Yul Brynner's son in *The King and I.* Gunn was one of the first black actors to experiment with The Method and, as Charles Gordone recalls, he was a good actor and a sensitive one. He was slated to be the next major black male star but there was always trouble. He got the reputation for being difficult, the adjective they use for the uppity black man. He could kill with eloquence. He has J.D. say in *Black Picture Show* that "the poem is a sword." Bill Gunn's pen was his. He couldn't be bought. Throughout his work, Gunn used the image of castration when discussing the black male's position in American society. In *Rhinestone Sharecropping*, an athlete gets his nuts crushed. Each day the black man is subjected to symbolic castration. They get signified on and called out by their enemies in the media and elsewhere. If black male writers want to win establishment approval they'd better write fictional and dramatic versions of tabloid editorials about the "underclass," a code name for what is considered black male aberrant behavior, in stay-in-your-place forms. No experimentation. No cryptic images like the white man in the mask who recurs in *Ganja and Hess*. The focus on the Louis Armstrong doll in the production of the *Personal Problems'* version shot by Bill Stephens of People's Communications. The clown who appears when Charles Brown and his mistress are about to make love. No mixing of Bach's Jesus Joy of Man's Desiring with Bessie Smith. No poetic dialogues and monologues which on the surface seem incoherent. The black actor or director who gets ahead in Hollywood, using Gunn's imagery, is not in possession of his genitals. The seat of power.

You can tell what they want from blacks by the images they reward and put their dollars behind. In 1940, Hollywood gave Hattie McDaniel an Oscar for her role as a Mammy in *Gone With the Wind*. In 1990, Morgan Freeman was nominated for his role as a chauffeur in *Driving Miss Daisy*. Maybe ten years from now another member of America's permanent household staff will pick up a little man, the Oscar who comes alive and taunts a black actor in Amiri Baraka's brilliant *The Sidney Poet Heroical*. Symbolic castration. *The Color Purple* sends out one message. *Driving Miss Daisy*, another. Bill Gunn refused to submit his vir-

114

ile talent to the chopping block. Refused to stay in his place, and after being blackballed from the industry went out and bad-mouthed his persecutors. He, Cecil Brown, and Amiri Baraka are the black male poets of the Hollywood Plantation where there is white money and black money. "I will receive thirty thousand dollars and a small percentage. I am not flattered be-cause the budget is eight million and the running rate for white writers of my caliber, or less, is at least two hundred and fifty thousand or more," Sam Dodd says in *Rhinestone Sharecropping.* After Bill Gunn was fired from working on a film, a white writer was brought in. Though the finished product differed only slightly from Gunn's version, the white writer got the credit.

In Hollywood he was a prince among the philistines. In *Rhine-stone Sharecropping,* which like *Black Picture Show* and possibly *Ganja and Hess* are semi-autobiographical works, he voices his dissatisfaction about his treatment over two films. *The Greatest.* And *Stop,* which he felt was butchered by the producers. In Hol-lywood Bill Gunn was vamped. "I notified my union that I wished to put the matter into arbitration. They sent me a copy of the new script by the new writer. Out of a hundred and twenty, there were thirty-five pages that weren't mine. The rest were ex-actly as I wrote them. I made a legal objection to my union, to not being in the credits, trying to keep my one percent," says the character in *Rhinestone Sharecropping.* No wonder the central image in his classic *Ganja and Hess* was vampirism. Gunn was a sharecropper whose talent was vamped.

He was the solitary genius who caught hell from both whites and blacks in the industry. I remember taking *Personal Problems* to PBS in Washington, for possible showing on the network and being accosted by the sarcastic remarks of a black woman, the program director, as we viewed the tape. She referred to Gunn and the late Kathleen Collins Prettyman as members of what she characterized as the Hudson River school of cinematography, because of their cinematic style—a style that took its time to lin-ger over a flower, a body of water, some interesting light, a walk through the woods, a camera that moseyed over elegant dinner scenes, or paused on a piece of sculpture. His beloved Hudson River Valley was his location for peace. Where Johnnie Mae of *Personal Problems* rendezvouses with her lover, Raymon, stealing some moments from the urban nightmare in which she and her husband, Charles Brown, live. But the Hudson River Valley is the haunted grounds of ancient Dutch legend. Of headless horsemen, and ghostly little men. It is the scene of one of what might be the country's most intellectual and sophisticated horror films, *Ganja and Hess*.

Personal Problems, this avant-garde soap opera, was never shown on PBS, which devoted hours of time to black crack stories and produced a maimed version of Richard Wright's *Native Son* and a docudrama which made vigilante gunman Bernard Goetz a hero. Gunn admired the European filmmakers, and a critic described *Personal Problems* as a soap opera as Godard would have done it. But he was not the Europhile that his critics said he was. Bill Gunn was eclectic and multicultural. His black aristocrats in *Ganja and Hess* and *Black Picture Show* were those ignored in the popular depiction of blacks by commercial whites, and blacks. Mythical welfare queens and blacks who always seem to be poised for a jump shot. Blacks whose dialogue is limited to Hey, Home. Nobody could do Gunn's blacks. Blacks who know about old furniture, azaleas, and who can order their wine in French. Blacks who seem to be saying that even after you have the assets and the class doubts will nag at you. At the end of Martin Luther King, Jr.'s dream is the cheerful hotel registration clerk, and the counter seat at Burger King. His people wanted dignity. Gunn's characters already have status, drive Rolls Royces and sportscars, and though they may be a few months behind in their MasterCard payments, they will never have to return to the real sharecropping. Picking cotton, or working in a factory. When they clean up after whites, it's only metaphorically. At the end of Bill Gunn's vision is ennui. Hell is Eternal Boredom. Alienation. Notice how the alienated vampire anthropologist has to go into the ghetto to get fresh blood. Has to receive blood from bloods. Has to be recharged. The successful Doctor who can only receive eternal peace through communion with a community. *Personal Problems* brought Gunn to the community. If Oprah Winfrey now says that she wants to do a television series depicting blacks as ordinary people, and not as popular mass-media stereotypes of the kind that she presented in last year's pilot for *The Women of Brewster Place*, then *Personal Problems* beat Ms. Winfrey and the millions of dollars behind her by a decade.

After completing this production, which was shot between 1979 and 1982, Gunn said, now I know that I can do my own movies. *Personal Problems* was before its time. There was no commercial backing for this eccentric version of the soap opera which permitted black producers, a black director, black actors, and black writers and actresses to have control over their work. A black composer, Carman Moore, had the freedom to write whatever music he desired without fear of censorship. And though it was a black production, there were whites who appeared as actors and actresses and as members of the crew.

Bill Gunn achieved complete freedom to direct *Personal Problems* and though it was never adopted for showing by any network, Volume I premiered at the Centre Georges Pompidou in Paris, November 1980, and in 1986 the completed work was honored by the Japan Foundation, which enabled the tape to be shown in six southern cities.

It was at video centers throughout the nation and was enthusiastically received by critics and the public when it was picked up by two local PBS affiliates, KQED television in San Francisco and WNYC television in New York City, through the efforts of Robert Gore and Jane Muramoto. This soap opera about a nurse's aide, Johnnie Mae Brown, played by Verta Mae Grosvenor, and her husband, Charles Brown, a New York City transit worker, played by Walter Cotton, provided a new direction for black artists on television and had widespread appeal. Even white audiences in Kentucky, Georgia, and Louisiana were able to identify with the problems of the people in the film. I know those people, an elderly white woman said to me.

Bill Gunn was dedicated to *Personal Problems* and like most of the participants worked within a budget that was based upon grants from the National Endowment for the Arts and the New York State Council on the Arts. Walter Cotton, who produced *Personal Problems* for Steve and me, remembers working with Gunn. "He was a morale builder and would reassure the crew and the actors with his humor when they encountered the usual problems associated with a small-budget production. He was easygoing and enthusiastic about his work. He inspired loyalty."

Though he was our friend and colleague he was not among us. He was remote, and alone as is the character in his Gothic film, and his favorite photo seemed to be that of Bill Gunn in boots and black cloak, like a German baron in a medieval castle. He hated telephones. I never really got to know him because I was always in a hurry. But I remember the cool and gentle voice on the telephone when I did reach him. He wanted to do another film with us, but we couldn't raise the money and were denied funds by a number of grant panels composed of our "peers." Until his death he was controversial, and was even labeled a misogynist by a newspaper that receives part of its revenue from skin ads, the kind of hypocrites that Gunn would have viewed with his usual poker face. He never forgot that he was a black man in a society that's uncomfortable with black men, whether they appear in a Mapplethorpe exhibition or run for President. He was a gifted black man who was called paranoid, which means that one has a heightened sense of awareness, and evidence of that heightened sense is in all of his plays, films and novels. Somebody said that the sweetest sounds come from hell and that's where his characters come from and that's where black men get their experience and pay their dues. Ganja says, everybody is some kind of freak. Everybody I know is into something, and before he dies the vampire's male assistant utters a speech that could have been Bill's. "The only perversion that can be comfortably condemned is the perversion of others. I will persist and survive. Without your society's sanctions. I will not be tortured. I will not be punished. I will not be guilty."

If John O. Killens was the soldier of darkness, James Baldwin the prophet of darkness, then Bill Gunn was the prince of darkness. And now that we are undergoing an assessment of his career with the kind of attention that eluded him during his life, we are beginning to see what producer Walter Cotton saw when working with Gunn. "He was an original. He was one-of-a-kind."

1990

Frederick Douglass
Politician

Born to an African mother and a European father, Frederick Douglass was, by any standard, one of the extraordinary men of the 19th Century and the most powerful black man of his age.

William McFeely's compelling biography covers the career of Douglass from his early years at a Tuckahoe, Maryland, plantation, which he spent with his grandmother, "a strong, copper-dark woman, intelligent and physically powerful," to his death in 1895.

Some of this is familiar territory, covered in Douglass' three autobiographies. One can hear Douglass reciting the details of his life: melodramatically satirizing the slave master's use of the Scriptures to justify the "pernicious" institution; witnessing the cruelty of slave master toward slave (he saw his brother beaten until blood flowed from his ears); besting Edward Covey, a man he called "the nigger breaker," in a duel.

Unlike many of his black contemporaries, Douglass was able to escape slavery by becoming a spokesperson for the abolitionist movement. It began when he was sent to live as a house servant with the Baltimore family of Hugh and Sophia Auld. (Separated as an infant from his slave mother, Douglass never knew his white father.)

Defying state law, Sophia introduced him to literacy, a key to his freedom. His early Baltimore years provide history with one of its most moving images, that of a twelve-year-old slave child purchasing Caleb Bingham's "Colombian Orator," a book whose speeches (including Cicero, Cato and William Pitt) Douglass would recall in later years as an anti-slavery orator.

Upon the death of his master, Douglass was returned to the Maryland plantation as a field hand at age sixteen. Five years later, however, masquerading as a sailor, he fled to New Bedford, Mass., where he worked as a common laborer, successfully eluding slave hunters by taking the name "Douglass," based on a character in Sir Walter Scott's poem "The Lady of the Lake."

Like other fugitive slave intellectuals, Douglass criticized Christian churches for their "hypocrisy," but it was in the African Methodist Episcopal Church that he developed the oratorical style that would make him an international celebrity. A speech opposing the colonization of African Americans, delivered at a church meeting on March 12, 1839, gained the attention of abolitionist William Lloyd Garrison's *Liberator* newspaper, and on August 16, 1841, after being scouted by William C. Coffin, Douglass was brought into the anti-slavery business.

Douglass became a sought-after performer for the anti-slavery agitation, but soon fell into trouble with the abolitionists. Marcus Garvey, a man whom some regard as the father of black nationalism, remarked that it usually is whites who select black political and cultural leaders, but when these "leaders" defy their sponsors, they are dismissed as ungrateful (as Douglass was) or replaced by another "leader."

Like the white feminists or neoconservatives of today, who have their own black spokespeople, the abolitionists demanded obedience to a party line. Douglass was their star, and those who were critical of the mouth for hire at that time were dismissed by their sponsors as envious, or unreasonable. But unlike some spokespeople today, Douglass was no puppet for his sponsors. He was regarded as arrogant by antislavery groups at the time and viewed with suspicion.

Douglass' antislavery lectures and oratorical style were constantly monitored by the abolitionists. Recalling those today who dismiss black independent thinkers as "paranoid" or given to "race-based denial," one abolitionist scorned Douglass for being "haughty, self-possessed and prone to take offense." Douglass also was attacked when he struck up friendships with white women and criticized when he decided to marry one after the death of his black wife, Anne.

In an essay about how New Yorkers reacted when they saw him walking down the street with two white women in 1849, Douglass viewed racism as a mental-health problem: "Colorphobia," a kind of mental leprosy. With this shrewd observation, Douglass anticipated the efforts of contemporary black psychiatrists to have the medical establishment declare racism a mental-health problem.

Though his insolence and his support of the Constitution annoyed the abolitionists, what finally estranged him from his former allies was his decision to publish his own newspaper (*The North Star*) rather than depend upon white editors for space in which to air his views.

In contrast to radical black leaders such as Henry Garnett, who called for rebellion against the slave masters, Douglass was a centrist. And yet, while he was a relentless campaigner for the Republican party, the party rewarded him only with political appointments no one else wanted. As marshal of the District of Columbia under President Rutherford Hayes, he was humiliated when one of the job's duties—greeting visitors to the White House and introducing them to the president—was eliminated. Working for whites was one of the many compromises that Douglass the centrist had to make, for Hayes' administration ended federal protection for the rights of the newly emancipated black people.

Douglass, however, didn't always play compromiser. He was cheated out of his position as ambassador to Haiti, for example, because he refused to be a tool for the expansionist policy of the

United States under President Benjamin Harrison. His abuse by the Republican party after having placed so much faith in it reminds one of Jesse Jackson's attempt to reform the Democratic party.

Any black man who speaks frankly from a black male point of view will be regarded as "controversial." While some saw Douglass as perhaps one of the great orators and statesmen of the 19th Century, he was also seen as a "long yellow devil." He was regarded as "dangerous" and once, when Thomas Auld, his master, broke up a church class that Douglass was conducting, he was accused of wanting to become another Nat Turner, the self-taught visionary who led a slave rebellion that people still talk about in Virginia.

A black audience booed and hissed at Douglass when he criticized the "exodusters," blacks who wanted to abandon the south for the west. People objected to his buying of his freedom, claiming that in so doing, he endorsed the slave system. He was criticized for neglecting his family in favor of his political career. He was criticized for visiting Auld after he became a free man. He was criticized for not being black enough (English audiences expected their anti-slavery performers to be dark-skinned, and Douglass was a mulatto). He escaped hanging twice. His house was destroyed by arsonists. He was physically attacked and threatened throughout his life.

After John Brown's bold and daring capture of the federal arsenal at Harper's Ferry, Douglass was implicated in the conspiracy. Brown, in fact, was Douglass's house guest and apparently discussed the plot with Douglass. Douglass found himself pursued by Gov. Wise of Virginia and President James Buchanan, who wanted to capture the most "arrogant" black man in America. Douglass had to flee the country.

McFeely offers a sympathetic portrait of Brown, a Christian who—like Jesus Christ, the scourge of the temple moneylenders—believed that sometimes force had to be employed to eradicate an evil. It is a comment on the political underpinnings of the school curriculum that in the textbooks our children read, Brown is dismissed as a maniac, while Robert E. Lee, who fought to uphold a slave society and under whose command free Pennsylvania blacks were returned to slavery and blacks who fought on the Union's side were executed and buried in mass graves, is regarded as a hero.

Shelby Foote, narrating the PBS series "The Civil War," viewed by historian Leon Litwack and others as being pro-Confederacy, even described Maj. Gen. Nathan Bedford Forrest as a hero. Forrest massacred more than one hundred black men, women and children at Fort Pillow. (During an interview with columnist Noah W. Griffin, published in the *San Francisco Examiner* on October 14, 1990, Foote referred to the black Civil War soldiers as "niggers.")

Douglass made mistakes. He became president of a bank that was involved in shady dealings. He supported a tyrannical regime in Haiti. His courage and brilliance, however, never were questioned. Many of his ideas were ahead of their time.

Douglass, for instance, addressed the need for a multi-ethnic curriculum in the nineteenth century. Like those who advocate multicultural education today, he observed that "A Benjamin Franklin, in the eyes of scientific Europe, redeemed the mental mediocrity of our young white Republic, but the genius and learning of Benjamin Banneker of . . . Maryland, the wisdom of Toussaint, are not permitted to do the same service for the colored race to which they belong." And like our contemporary African-American intellectuals, he criticized the claim that the Egyptians were Caucasian: "I see a much stronger resemblance to the Negro than to the Europeans. They are not the genuine crisp-headed Negro, but they are very much like the mulatto and would be taken for such in the United States."

McFeely's biography is welcomed as the period of American history during which our institutions were dominated by Europeans and European thought comes to a close; a period during which the native population nearly was exterminated, blacks were held in chains and forced to perform slave labor, land was seized from the Mexicans, nuclear weapons were employed against Asians, and Japanese Americans were "interned."

This engaging and well-written work of literature suggests that the Age of Douglass was this nation's greatest epoch. People of humble origin transcended themselves. Former slaves rose to greatness and spoke with the eloquence of angels. Abraham Lincoln, our greatest President, ascended from a log cabin to sainthood. European Americans produced their most magnificent Christian, John Brown (whose life certainly deserves a more balanced treatment than that of the dismissive 1940 movie *Santa Fe Trail*).

We were given two great songs: "The Battle Hymn of the Republic" and "Amazing Grace."

What a time. What a book.

1991

Ambrose Bierce
Writer

Son of a farmer, Ambrose Gwinett Bierce was born in 1842 at Meigs County, Ohio. While a soldier, he fought in some of the key Civil War battles and participated in General Sherman's March to the Sea.

He was a prolific short story writer and essayist. His journalism appeared in Hearst newspapers, the *San Francisco Examiner* and the *New York Journal*.

He died in 1914 under mysterious circumstances. M. E. Gremander, author of *Ambrose Bierce*, speculates that he was killed in Mexico, during the battle of Ojinaga.

In order to cure his asthma, he lived in Oakland in 1888. The Victorian Oakland, California, where Ambrose Bierce lived, still exists. Mansions and public sculpture from that bustling Oakland of merchant princes and railroad tycoons, sailors, and cattlemen, stands in contrast to new Oakland's functional earthquake proof buildings with their Hemingwayesque lines. To the modern reader, Ambrose Bierce's prose style may seem as gabled as those restored buildings in what is being called Old Oakland: "Without a movement, without a sound, in the profound silence and the languor of the late afternoon, some invisible messenger of fate touched with unsealing finger the eyes of his consciousness—whispered into the ear of his spirit the mysterious awakening word which no human lips ever have spoken, no human memory ever has recalled" (*The Complete Short Stories of Ambrose Bierce*, 359). But though the design may seem busy, Ambrose Bierce, in a series of short stories entitled "Soldiers," wrote about the horrors of war with insight and technical mastery. Unlike our current think-tank bureaucratic military experts, Bierce, a student at Kentucky Military Institute, knew what he was talking about.

As a participant in some of the Civil War's bloodiest campaigns, First Lt. Bierce saw the war close-up, from bush to cliff, from corpse to corpse, and writes about war with meticulous detail: "the white face turned upward, the hands thrown out and clutched full of grass, the clothing deranged, the long dark hair in tangles and full of clotted blood." Death is the companion of war ("It is the business of the soldier to kill"). And death, like war, has its advantages, its surprises: "Death has taken an unfair advantage; he has struck with an unfamiliar weapon; he has executed a new and disquieting stratagem. We did not know that he had so ghastly resources, possibilities of terror so dismal" (372).

In Bierce's war there is always the unexpected. And in one of the more absurd wars (unwilling to disobey a General's orders, Captain Ransome, of "One Kind of Officer," fires upon his own men)—a war that divided families—the enemy could be one's own blood. In "A Horseman in the Sky," Captain Carter Druse, of the Union Forces, shoots a Confederate enemy: his father. "The Affair at Coulter's Notch" ends with one of Bierce's typically impetuous young soldiers (a whole battery to himself), Captain Coulter, holding his dead child and wife. His wife was a "red-hot Secessionist." But no matter what the blood ties are, the enemy is not like us. The enemy is an alien. "The soldier never becomes wholly familiar with the conception of his foes as men like himself; he cannot divest himself of the feeling that they are another order of beings, differently conditioned, in an environment not altogether of the earth" (284).

"You are bombing us as though we were from out of space,"

said a diplomat, recently, whose country was being destroyed by American B-52s.

Those who are heroes to some are fools to Bierce. A young officer, who risks death to scout the enemy's position, is cheered on by his troops. While they admire his bravery, Bierce takes him apart: "His saddle blanket is scarlet. What a fool! No one who has ever been in action but remembers how naturally every rifle turns toward the man on a white horse; no one but has observed how a bit of red enrages the bull of battle" (285).

Bierce strips men of their claims that they are fighting for noble abstract goals. A recent Public Broadcasting System documentary about the Civil War endorsed the idyllic claim that the Confederacy and its leader, Robert E. Lee, who has been given Arthurian status by some historians, fought the war to defend their homeland, or for some other romantic reason. First Lt. Bierce, the writer, is to the point: "Being a slave owner and like other slave owners a politician he was naturally an original secessionist and ardently devoted to the Southern cause," Bierce writes of Peyton Farquhar, who gets himself hanged for committing a terrorist act against the Union (307).

Throughout Bierce's work there is always a gentleman who is capable of the grisliest savagery. Bierce saw through the veneer of good breeding of the slaveowners who permitted their children to ride Negroes for fun. These characters, who always seem to be wary of offending their fellows—"I realized the brutality of my remark, but not clearly seeing my way to an apology, said nothing," one gentleman says—give little thought to shooting or hanging people. "The liberal military code makes provision for hanging many kinds of persons, and gentlemen are not excluded" (306). Indeed, the most frequent description of these men and women who commit unspeakable acts is that they are cultivated, civilized, well-bred. (The harshest word for a character in the book, "detestable," is reserved for a "well bred" woman whose letter, challenging an officer's bravery, is responsible for the death of one hundred men.)

Nothing has changed. Members of "the civilized world"

demonize and attribute horrible deeds to "the enemy" while they bomb defenseless populations and destroy the ancient capitals of culture with their "surgical strikes." In Ambrose Bierce's time, removing corpses from the field was called "tidying up." Today, dead people are "collateral damage." If Truth is the first casualty of war, then language is the second. Bierce says that war is a business in which "the lives of men counted as nothing against the chance of defining a road or sketching a bridge" (369), echoing the sentiment of a pilot returning from his tasks in the Persian Gulf: "I don't want to see the enemy. To me, the enemy is a blip on my radar screen and all I want is to make that blip go away. I don't want to know my enemy."

For Bierce, humanity is capable of bestial acts and in one of Bierce's most famous stories, "The Eyes of the Panther," a woman is transformed into a panther. Men are beasts and Happiness is a woman who eludes them. Tantalizes them. The Hermit in Bierce's "Haita, the Shepherd," says that he has only known Happiness twice. They cannot escape their essential animal state, their "rathood," as Bierce might say, an expression used in "One of the Missing," the brilliant story about Jerome Searing, another one of Bierce's characters who has to risk his neck in order to improve the position of his comrades. He ends up being threatened by the very rifle he has loaded for the purpose of killing the enemy and in one of those twists of fate of which Bierce is so fond, his corpse is discovered but not recognized by his brother.

What Bierce refers to as "The Power" is a trickster given to such cruel coincidences. Learning of his wife's infidelity, Captain Armisted in "An Affair of Outposts" enters the service (because none in his family has committed suicide) only to protect a Governor who is his wife's lover.

> But it was decreed from the beginning of time that Private Searing was not to murder anybody that bright summer morning, nor was the Confederate retreat to be announced by him. For countless ages events had been so matching them-

selves together in that wondrous mosaic to some parts of which, dimly discernible, we give the name of history, that the acts which he had in will would have marred the harmony of the pattern.

Some twenty-five years previously the Power charged with the execution of the work according to the design had provided against that mischance by causing the birth of a certain male child in a little village at the foot of the Carpathian Mountains, had carefully reared it, supervised its education, directed its desires into a military channel, and in due time made it an officer of artillery. By the concurrence of an infinite number of favoring influences and their preponderance over an infinite number of opposing ones, this officer of artillery had been made to commit a breach of discipline and fly from his native country to avoid punishment. He had been directed to New Orleans (instead of New York), where a recruiting officer awaited him on the wharf. He was enlisted and promoted, and things were so ordered that he now commanded a Confederate battery some two miles along the line from where Jerome Searing, the Federal scout, stood cocking his rifle. Nothing had been neglected—at every step in the progress of both these men's lives, and in the lives of their contemporaries and ancestors, the right thing had been done to bring about the desired result. Had anything in all this vast concatenation been overlooked, Private Searing might have fired on the retreating Confederates that morning, and would perhaps have missed. As it fell out, a Confederate captain of artillery, having nothing better to do while awaiting his turn to pull out and be off, amused himself by sighting a field piece obliquely to his right at what he took to be some Federal officers on the crest of a hill, and discharged it. ("One of the Missing," 266–67)

Dwight Eisenhower said that every war is going to astonish you, and Ambrose Bierce would agree except that, for him, what startles humans doesn't startle "The Power," which is in charge of that "wondrous mosaic, we give the name of history." But Ambrose Bierce, a determinist, an absurdist, questions the judgment of "The Power." "Would one exception have marred too much the pitiless perfection of the divine, eternal plan?" he asks after the death of a reckless soldier who sacrifices himself in order to scout the enemy's position. "The Power" pushes men about as though they were toy soldiers and uses the law of probabilities to enforce its will. So "brave" is George Thurston that when ordered to "Throw down that sword and surrender, you damned Yank!" he tells a whole company of Confederate soldiers who have leveled their rifles at his breast, "I will not" (370). Thurston is killed while swinging in a child's swing.

But unlike today when a commander can entertain a group of laughing reporters by boasting about a direct pinpoint hit at the enemy, even amid the carnage of the Civil War the combatants found some way to acknowledge the valor of their opponents. Remorseful over the execution of Dramer Brune, a Confederate spy, who once saved his life, a Union officer, Captain Parrol Hartroy, commits suicide in "The Story of a Conscience." Lieutenant Herman Brayle's daring so impresses his comrades as well as his enemies in "Killed at Resaca" that the Confederates and the Union troops interrupt their battle to honor his corpse. "A generous enemy honored the fallen brave" (376).

The Civil War was the last hot war fought on American soil. In this century, Americans have never suffered the disasters that Europeans have experienced. In Berlin's War Museum I read the demographics. Starving European families living in the streets. The drastic decline in the male population. The raping of women by the invading enemy army. The burning of great cities. Visiting a cemetery, I was struck by the irony of bullet holes appearing near the grave sites of some of the most "civilized men" in the canon, including Georg Hegel's. Maybe that's why the Europeans seem to appreciate African American culture; the culture of the Blues. They've been there.

Some have compared the joy with which some view the performance of hi-tech weapons with that of a child fascinated by his Nintendo game. "The Technoeuphoria!" a grinning anchor woman exclaimed as a missile hit a hydroelectric plant as though there were no humans inside. A commentator compared the most recent villain in War's Fairy Tale plot to a child, threatening his playmates with a gun so that he can get at the chocolates.

Though "An Occurrence at Owl Creek Bridge" is the best known of this collection, the most chilling is "Chickamauga," named for the scene of one of the Union's most devastating defeats. A child wanders through the corpses of the Union dead wielding a wooden sword, playing at war. It was fun until the child stumbled upon his dead mother. "The child moved his little hands, making wild, uncertain gestures. He uttered a series of inarticulate and indescribable cries—something between the chattering of an ape and the gobbling of a turkey—a startling, soulless, unholy sound, the language of a devil" (318). The war had hit close to home.

Bierce hated war. "Ah, those many, many needless dead!" he wrote. The Governor's lines in "An Affair of Outposts" could have been Bierce's. " 'Ugh!' he grunted, shuddering—'this is beastly! Where is the charm of it all? Where are the elevated sentiments, the devotion, the heroism . . .' " (346). An army for Bierce is a "great brute," with "dumb consciousness."

His pen is like the best state-of-the-art film camera, and one wonders whether that ghoulish carnival of death, World War I, would have been avoided if Bierce's sharp images of war could have been broadcast with the satellite technology of today.

In the preface to the first edition of *Tales of Soldiers and Civilians* by one of our most uncelebrated American writers, who on the basis of this work certainly ranks with the best of our nineteenth-century writers, Bierce once wrote: "Denied existence by the chief publishing houses of the country, this book owes itself to Mr. E. L. G. Steele, merchant of this city." The date is September 4, 1891.

One could see why Bierce would be out of favor. By today's standards he is didactic, over sentimental, and his plot lines are often baffling, but when Presidents of the United States list their favorite western writers, I wish that Bierce's would appear among the names.

REGiNALd LEWiS
Businessman

Elsewhere in this collection, I include details about what I refer to as "the black-pathology industry," among whose ranks are hired intellectual hit-persons for various corporate-financed think tanks, journalists, policy persons, and a media-selected talented tenth (a black mandarin class composed of black intellectuals from Harvard, Princeton, and so on)—all of whom supplement their incomes by fingering blacks, especially black males, for causing this society's social problems: illegitimacy, crime, drugs, child abandonment, welfare, anti-Semitism, homophobia, misogyny, and anti-Asian sentiment, even though whites beat and murder Asian Americans year-round. Such incidents, according to Asian American intellectuals, are ignored by the media, whose job seems to be maligning blacks and coddling whites. Daily the media furnishes its viewers with myths about black life.

Unfortunately, myths influence public perceptions, and so blacks have to pay, in subtle ways, for the distortions that come down daily about black life from places like CNN and NBC network news. And when the facts are rigged about blacks being the sole perpetrators of unwed parenthood, crime, and the drug war, blacks don't have the means to fight these electronic

Goliaths, the way one Goliath, General Motors, brought down the head of another Goliath, NBC News.

I was waiting for these networks to comment about the death of Reginald Lewis—the richest black man in America and the head of a multinational corporation, Beatrice International—who died in February. His death, however, was virtually ignored. I found this strange, because blacks are always getting a scolding from places like the *New Republic* and the *New York Times* op-ed page about their lack of the work ethic. Yet when a man who epitomized stable Protestant ethics died, the network news shows typically handed black children buffoonish entertainers and athletes as role models, while ignoring Reginald Lewis, who gave millions of dollars to cultural and educational enterprises.

The *Wall Street Journal* is another place where some of the white male suburbanites who dominate the discussion of the problems of the inner cities are always lecturing blacks, sometimes in a very nasty tone, about their lack of responsibility. A few months before his death, Reginald Lewis was pilloried in the *Wall Street Journal* for ingenious business practices for which white entrepreneurs are usually praised. The writer of this article was, in so many words, calling Mr. Lewis "uppity."

After his death, his company was lectured by the *Times* for not revealing the fact that Mr. Lewis had a brain tumor. I mean, here was a man who was a perfect model for all that the media pretend they want blacks to be, and yet he was criticized and nagged even after his death by the very same media.

Reginald Lewis is a hero, not only for scaling the heights of the business world—going where no black man had ever gone before (it must have been lonely)—but also for showing abundant generosity toward Americans both black and white, and for revealing a very important truth: that the powerful white Americans who control the equipment upon which most Americans rely for information don't want blacks to lose and don't want blacks to win. Another reason Chester Himes was right-on when he said that to live in a racist society is to live in a situation of comic absurdity—and, I might add, a situation of irony and paradox.

1993

Langston Hughes
Writer

After Lena Horne attended Langston Hughes's jazz blues funeral, she commented that she didn't know whether to laugh or cry. She confessed to pianist Randy Weston, "There I was, tapping my toes and humming while y'all played."

Before Hughes entered the hospital for the surgery that would cost him his life, he told Ivan von Auw, a friend, that he was laughing to keep from dying. Wherever Langston Hughes is, he must be having a long last laugh because of history's April Fool's joke on some of his critics.

Now that Russia has MasterCard and China has private banks, Hughes's anti-Communist persecutors look as silly as their predecessors, the Puritan fathers, who hanged a woman for running an after-hours joint where people drank cider and played shuffleboard. Hughes, like many other black intellectuals, naively believed that the Russians were color blind.

His fundamentalist critics, who dogged him for some irreverent poetry that by today's standards seems mild, are either forgotten or, like Aimee Semple McPherson, disgraced. High Modernism, an imitation-European movement that rewarded the tokens who faithfully mimicked its standards, and whose icons were anti-Semites and racists like T. S. Eliot, is out of fashion.

Also forgotten are the elitist critics, the prima donna collaborators, the theater moneymen, and the trendy editors and anthologists who gave Hughes such a hard time.

The 1960s militants who considered Hughes to be passé have gotten tenure and serve brandy and cigars after dinner, the way it's done on "Masterpiece Theatre." Some have joined the Republican party.

Like any black male writer who truthfully records his perceptions, Hughes got into difficulty with the Left, the Right, and the middle. He was chastised by blacks and whites, and though he fearlessly spoke out and wrote against injustice and the humiliating Jim Crow to which he was subjected, he occasionally succumbed to his critics. In 1954, he repudiated his radical poetry before the McCarthy Committee.

The fact that Hughes, while a guest at the Kennedy White House, was being harassed by J. Edgar Hoover demonstrates the ambivalent attitude American society held toward him.

Hughes's range, like that of Charlie Parker, Max Roach, and Miles Davis, was so broad that he was able to take old forms like gospel and give them new interpretations, and like those musicians, he was always mindful of new forms: bebop, rock and roll. He was writing jazz poetry thirty years before it became avant-garde. He was one of the first Black Power poets. He was also a black feminist and a multicultural poet before these styles became trends in American literature. His poem "Cafe: 3 A.M.," about a vice-squad entrapment, anticipates the poetry of gay liberation. He was a versatile editor, anthologist, translator, novelist, playwright, songwriter, and journalist. By the time of his death—which occurred under bizarre circumstances—Hughes had gained an international reputation. He was credited by Leopold Sedar Senghor for having influenced the Negritude movement, and unlike some other entrenched tokens, he was generous with his time, aiding writers as diverse as Chester Himes, Melvin Tolson, James Baldwin, and even an enemy, Zora

Neale Hurston. He was responsible for my first novel being published and would always return my calls, or drop me a postcard from time to time. He was generous like that, receiving visitors from all over the world in his Harlem home, and to his credit, unlike some of the more successful black writers, who abandoned the ghetto yet earned a living by turning out what could be called fictional and nonfictional tourist traps, he remained there.

He criticized some writers who depicted only the pathological side of black society (he was accused of doing the same thing); he knew better. And unlike those neoconservatives who believe that the problems of the inner city are the result of what they call black culture or behavior, Langston Hughes traced the decline of Harlem to the introduction of heroin by organized crime; this was done deliberately and with the aid of law enforcement officials, who still share the profits. Though some black-pathology hustlers might claim that the problems of the inner city are not imposed from outside, the high crime rates and AIDS are related to the importation of the drugs from the outside. The Kerry Committee even implicates the current government.

Hughes encountered some of the same problems that the contemporary generation of black male writers encounters. The media, whose current pillorying of black males is more intense than ever—movie, television, radio—still exclude their points of view. Hughes, one of the most prolific writers of this century, was constantly broke and not accorded the same royalties as white writers. In 1953, he confided to his collaborator and friend Arna Bontemps that he'd spent another year of starvation. Occasionally, his poverty was relieved by a hit; "Street Scene," the result of a difficult collaboration with Elmer Rice and Arnold Kurt Weil, brought him $30,000 one year.

Arnold Rampersad's biography, *The Life of Langston Hughes,* offers glimpses of those Harlem Renaissance poets and writers who have now become legend—Claude McKay, Carl Van Vechten, the underrated Countee Cullen, Zora Neale Hurston, and Duke Ellington. Rampersad, unlike those black critics who write in an impenetrable prose in an attempt to out-jargon the jargonists, writes clearly and intelligently so that Hughes's contribution to American letters will be available to the general reader.

In the middle of the next century, when the literary establishment will reflect the multicultural makeup of this country and not be dominated by assimilationists with similar tastes, from similar backgrounds, and of similar pretensions, Langston Hughes will be to the twentieth century what Walt Whitman was to the nineteenth. I can hear him chuckling as I write this.

1988

John Edgar Wideman
Writer

MOVE was an anarchistic, back-to-nature, nouveau-Rousseau, new-age movement that rattled the Philadelphia establishment under two mayors. "Letting their kids run around naked, sassing the police, and getting their heads busted, cussing out the neighborhood on loudspeakers. . . . Sooner or later those nuts had to go," says Timbo, the most interesting character in John Edgar Wideman's new novel, *Philadelphia Fire,* inspired by the 1985 police bombing of MOVE headquarters that killed eleven.

They were nasty, noisy and bizarre. And though they had supporters among the black intelligentsia and the radical fringe, they wouldn't have lasted more than a month in the black neighborhood of plain folk in Oakland, California, where I live. Something would have been done to root them out. Some of their Osage Avenue neighbors felt the same way and were prepared for vigilante action before the fatal encounter between the MOVE members and the Philadelphia police.

But whatever one feels about these crazies, they have raised questions that won't go away.

I remember my anger at seeing a black MOVE member being kicked and stomped by Mayor Frank Rizzo's police in 1978. In that instance, television revealed to the "dominant culture" the kind of mini-Selmas that happen to black people each day. (The contrasts between the treatment of MOVE by Rizzo and his successor, W. Wilson Goode, receive a few lines in *Philadelphia Fire* in the form of a vaudevillian routine between "black mayor" and "white mayor.")

Not that members of the "dominant culture" pay any attention to black people's treatment. They sold their souls to the devil when they gave Ronald Reagan a mandate to put blacks back in their place, or out into the streets (where a lot of Reagan voters ended up, too); forgave Iran-contra, and ignored their government's tacit approval of, if not cooperation with, the dumping of tons of cocaine into the United States by the nation's anti-communist allies—a policy that has added to the woes of these desperate emergency-room patients called cities, which black mayors are supposed to resuscitate.

MOVE, in its life and death, proved that things happen to blacks that don't happen to whites. Do you think that Dick Thornburgh would still be attorney general if he had pimped a destitute white woman to love-sting an elected official, in the same way a black woman was used to lure Marion Barry? Do you think that members of MOVE would have been bombed from the air had they been members of an armed, white anarchist group? Or that the Philadelphia fire department would have permitted a white neighborhood to be destroyed?

As Margaret Jones, one of the book's characters, says: "Why'd they have to kill them two times, three times, four times? Bullets, bombs, water, fire. Shot, blowed up, burnt, drowned. Nothing in those sacks but ash and a guilty conscience."

Press reports say that Mayor Goode went along with police plans to drop an explosive on MOVE headquarters, and if he did, he has to carry in his head for the rest of his life the screams of the children who died.

The unnamed mayor of Wideman's book is referred to as an "Oreo."

But black mayors such as Goode, Marion Barry, David Dinkins and Coleman Young are asked to do the impossible. They're like the man who gets dunked at the fair. All you have to do is lob a baseball. You don't even have to have good aim. Easy targets.

They're asked to preside over these ruins that have been abandoned by the money. Philadelphia's credit rating is among the worst of all American cities. It is a city in a state of near-bankruptcy.

Black mayors incur the resentment of white ethnics, the urban underclass that op-ed writers never discuss. Black mayors are the "crossovers" caught between the aspirations of the neighborhoods and downtown developers, between white nationalists and black nationalists. They have to negotiate with a federal government that has abandoned the cities and to deal with hostile state legislatures.

Was Goode totally responsible for the MOVE disaster? The FBI furnished a key explosive used in the bomb. And paranoid blacks believe that the FBI has long treated black America as a national security threat, targeting black leaders from Marcus Garvey to Elijah Muhammad, with the despicable entrapment of Marion Barry the most recent example. Most likely, Goode was caught up in one of those ceaseless counterinsurgency games that are constantly played against black America by a department that has been accused of racism by Hispanic and black FBI agents.

The voices in Wideman's *Philadelphia Fire* touch upon these questions, but never develop them, nor are there many details about MOVE's history, its members, its philosophy, or the fire and the aftermath. The book devotes more pages to basketball (some of the most artful writing you're bound to encounter about the sport) and the sexual adventures of the principal narrator, Cudjoe, than to the Philadelphia fire, details of which are provided by Margaret Jones and Timbo, the mayor's cultural aide.

To tell his story, Wideman has chosen devices associated with a hybrid genre that some critics call "metafiction"—in this case a cut-up narrative, which includes fictional and autobiographical details. And faithful to this form, the material sometimes seems arbitrary and quirky.

A page is used up describing a woman's left breast. This seems a little decadent when you realize that the book has been pushed as dealing with the police assault on MOVE (a marketing mistake). Some details seem to be overdone. Wideman writes of a computer that "swallows every bit of evidence—telexed phoned mailed modemed cabled punched faxed—from across the globe, evidence it will digest and excrete in graphs, plots, statistical tables, colored projections, Mercator maps, holograms, laser-printed bulletins, updates, summaries reports . . . pieces of information, sources of information proliferate crossbreed, cyberneticize."

It is a fiction that can't decide whether it's a collection of short stories or a novel. Even as late as page 46, it hasn't decided. "Maybe this is a detective story," Cudjoe muses.

If there is any plot, it has to do with Cudjoe, an expatriate described as a "beachcomber . . . and artiste," who takes multiple forms in the book. Sometimes the confusion of Cudjoes makes it difficult to tell where one begins and another ends.

Cudjoe is a narrator we've run into before in Wideman's fiction—one excessively devoted to himself, so much so that other characters are pushed from the page. This character believes that his fuzzy interior monologues are profound, and sometimes they are.

While working as a bartender on the Greek island of Mykonos, Cudjoe reads about the MOVE fire and becomes obsessed with a MOVE child who escaped. His attempts to find the child seem lackadaisical, but Wideman, being true to the form he has chosen, isn't looking for plots.

Some of the most effective passages are obviously about John Wideman. One of the principal characters, also named John Wideman, has a son in jail, just like the author. Unlike the computer-language segment, this writing is passionate and comes from the heart. A writing of lament.

Wideman's gift is that of an eye in the middle. He commutes between different worlds, between different classes like a reporter covering a story in a foreign country. He doesn't know his way around as well as the inhabitants, but can pick up details that the inhabitants, immersed in the scene, can't discern.

His is a mulatto writing, neither black nor white. His double-consciousness has always been his chief asset. He is a member of the establishment, but doesn't know it as well as Louis Auchincloss does. He's been near the projects, but can't cover them as well as a generation of young writers who have been influenced by George Clinton and rap music. (When these writers' revolutionary novels and plays begin to appear, around the mid-'90s, the establishment will long for the quiet days of the black arts revolt in the '60s.)

Reading this book was like attending a Miles Davis concert, where the artist turns his back on the audience. I felt that Wideman had turned his back on me. The book is reader unfriendly, but look who's talking. As a writer, I thought the performance was terrific.

Wideman, who has always been his own man, has gone out on a limb with *Philadelphia Fire*. The critics have been down on metafiction since the beginning of the Reagan era. Unlike critics in the other arts, many establishment literary critics insist that every book be written in the same way that art students in the Louvre faithfully copy the works of the "masters," stroke for stroke.

Very few writers have Wideman's gifts and range. His artistic courage is rare these days, and it will be interesting to see where this new direction takes him.

MOVE leader John Africa's story, however, has yet to be told. I can see him in the future being compared with John Brown and

Joe Hill, and other people viewed as crazies by those uncomfortable with the truth. A prison inmate who sends a letter to John Wideman, reprinted in *Philadelphia Fire,* is right. John Africa is very much alive. Since the MOVE fire, the John Africas have multiplied.

We see them, black, white, young, old, male and female, crowding the cities, sleeping on grates and in parks, pushing those grocery carts, evidence of how the United States of the '80s and '90s regards its least fortunate. They smell bad and have bad manners. They seem to be grinning at us as they roam the streets, muttering to themselves, perhaps because they know that millions of us may soon be joining them.

One thing is certain about these John Africas. You can't bomb them all.

1993

ZORA NEALE HURSTON
Writer

A line from Countee Cullen's famous poem "Heritage" typi-
fies the attitudes of many "educated" white and black Americans toward African and neo-African religion. For them, these
are exotic faiths whose gods, "quaint, . . . outlandish," and "heathen," are "naught" to them. It took the restless intellect of Zora
Neale Hurston to make neo-African religion, and its gods, more
than "naught." The result was *Tell My Horse,* a major work of the
Voodoo bibliography, which includes books written in Spanish,
Yoruba, French, Portuguese, and Creole, as well as English. That
the majority of these works have yet to be translated makes Ms.
Hurston's work a treasure for the English reader who is curious
about the subject. Though Voodoo had been driven underground by the time *Tell My Horse* was published, there has been
a resurgence recently, due to the arrival in the United States of
many of its followers from South and Central America and the
Caribbean. Since white American readers are suspicious of the
scholarship of those they deem to be aliens—they seem to need
one of their own to translate—the efforts of such scholars as Robert Thompson and Michael Ventura, and of musicians like Kip
Hanrahan and David Byrne, have been invaluable in defusing
some of the hysteria with which neo-African religion has been
regarded in the United States, a Protestant country. The contem-

porary misunderstanding of Voodoo was recently shown by the harsh criticism that African priests and Americans like the Reverend George A. Stallings, Jr., received from the Catholic hierarchy as a result of their incorporation of the African style with Western Catholic rites, even though such blending of styles has been long established in the Caribbean, Central and South America, and Haiti (where it is said that the people are 95 percent Catholic and 100 percent Voodoo). It is with this background that Zora Neale Hurston's pioneer work can be appreciated, though one can understand why a writer, tackling such a taboo subject, would have appeared odd to the intellectually slothful of her time. If Ms. Hurston has any successor at all, it is Toni Cade Bambara, whose work *The Salt Eaters* is clearly ahead of its time.

But *Tell My Horse,* the result of Ms. Hurston's travels to Jamaica and Haiti, is more than a Voodoo work. She writes intelligently about the botany, sociology, anthropology, geology, and politics of these nations in a style that is devoid of pompous jargon and accessible to the general reader. It is an entertaining book.

Hurston's gift for storytelling is immense, whether she is writing about the hunting of a wild boar by the Maroons at Accompong ("men who had thrown off the bands of slavery by their courage and ingenuity") or an account of the extraordinary steps Jamaicans take to appease a "duppy," lest it return from the grave and do harm to the living. In one of the book's very good interviews, an informant tells Ms. Hurston that "the duppy is the most powerful part of any man. Everybody has evil in them, and when a man is alive, the heart and the brain control him and he will not abandon himself to many evil things. But when the duppy leaves the body, it no longer has anything to restrain it and it will do more terrible things than any man ever dreamed of. It is not good for a duppy to stay among living folk."

Part travelogue, *Tell My Horse* invokes the beauty of Jamaica and Haiti and the sacred zones where African gods continue to dwell—the "good" ones, the Rada group, and the "bad" ones, the Petros. The enemies of Voodoo have exploited rumors associating the Sect Rouge—a Petro sect—with human sacrifice in order to defame Voodoo, less a religion than the common language of slaves from different African tribes, thrown together in the Americas for commercial reasons. This common language was feared because it not only united the Africans but made it easier for them to forge alliances with those Native Americans whose customs were similar. Voodoo has been the inspiration for the major slave revolts in this hemisphere, including the one that ousted the French from Haiti. But just as Christianity has been used by tyrants as a means for persecuting their opponents, Voodoo has been similarly abused. Though its critics associate it with the Right, Voodoo is absorptive enough to include Left, Right, and middle. Rene Depestre, who uses Voodoo allusions in his work, is a professed Marxist.

Zora Neale Hurston, a conservative, praised the American occupation of Haiti, an occupation that's remembered with hatred and bitterness and that was denounced by James Weldon Johnson. She admired the ruthless Santo Domingan dictator Trujillo, under whose regime more than 35,000 Haitians were slaughtered, an atrocity that gave rise to the term *genocide*.

Ms. Hurston's account of the neo-African religion practiced in Haiti is fascinating. She gives a thorough description of the main *loas*, their needs, their desires, and their powers. The details about art and dance are informative, though she describes the dance as "barbaric." But the most interesting discussion in *Tell My Horse* concerns possession, that strange phenomenon during which a mortal is taken over by a god. Dr. Louis Mars (mentioned in Ms. Hurston's book), in his work *The Crisis of Possession in VooDoo*, translated by the late Kathleen Collins Prettyman, is one of the few scholars, after Hurston, to have explored this mystery.

Whether a result of feminist revenge—disproportionately

meted out to black male writers—or an attempt to market books by black women at the expense of those by black male writers, contemporary myths about black literature proliferate, the most flagrant of which is that there exists an "explosion" in black women's literature. Certainly, the few who've peddled the sort of black-male-bashing that's become characteristic of the age of Reagan have been rewarded, but the fate of most black writers, male or female, is the same: Nonavailability of their books, reviews that are often influenced by racist ideology or exhibit a double standard, and difficulty in getting their points of view aired, even about issues that concern them, are just some of the problems that hamper their careers. Most would agree with Countee Cullen's assessment that a black writer in a country in which blacks are treated as aliens is a "curious thing." As though Wright, Baldwin, or Hughes were members of the racist American literary establishment, we are told that black male writers were included in the American canon until recently, when they were "eclipsed" by black women writers. The facts are that Baldwin, Wright, and Hughes were never included in anybody's canon, and were even placed under surveillance by the American government. New biographies reveal that both Wright and Hughes were not well-off at the end of their lives.

A critic, writing for the *Boston Review,* even proposed that black female writers have received less favorable reviews than black male writers, when reviews accorded to books by Baraka, Baldwin, Himes, Wright, Williams, and Hughes have been pronounced in their viciousness and violence.

As part of this campaign to promote some black women writers as good, because, it is argued, black male writers are not so good, Zora Neale Hurston has been packaged as a radical feminist and martyr to black male chauvinism, as though any black male writer or editor has had the power to impede the career of a black female writer. All I can think about when hearing Zora Neale Hurston's name associated with this cynical effort is the song "Please Don't Talk about Me When I'm Gone." Was Zora

Neale Hurston a radical feminist, as her contemporary supporters claim? The men in *Tell My Horse* reflect the range of types
that can be found in world culture, and in both sexes.

The human family has room for a President Jean Vilbrun Guil-
laume Sam, a "greedy, detestable criminal," as well as his son,
known by the peasants of his time as "fine" and "intelligent." In
Their Eyes Were Watching God, despite their flaws, the men are
productive and talented, as opposed to the relentlessly unflattering portraits of black men appearing in some of the black feminist literature of the Reagan period. Ms. Hurston describes,
without sermonizing, the Jamaican practice of cultivating black
geishas for the delight of prospective grooms, and comments in
passing on the practice of polygamy. When commenting about
the status of women in the United States, she sounds more like
Phyllis Schlafly than bell hooks, or Michele Wallace: "The majority of men in all the States are pretty much agreed that just for
being born a girl-baby you ought to have laws and privileges
and pay perquisites. And so far as being allowed to voice opinions is concerned, why, they consider that you are born with the
law in your mouth, and that is not a bad arrangement either. The
majority of the solid citizens strain their ears trying to find out
what it is that their womenfolk want so they strain around and
try to get it for them, and that is a very good idea and the right
way to look at things." Many of today's feminists would consider such thinking to be "retrograde." Zora Neale Hurston has
also gained a reputation as a racial chauvinist. She reserves some
of her harshest opinions for black nationalists (Race Men),
whom she dismisses as "windbags" and "demogogues."

The Zora Neale Hurston of *Tell My Horse* is skeptical, cynical,
funny, ironic, brilliant, and innovative. With its mixture of techniques and genres, this book, originally published in 1936, is
bound to be the postmodernist book of 1990. But her greatest ac-
complishment is in revealing the profound beauty and appeal of
a faith older than Christianity, Buddhism, and Islam, a faith that
has survived in spite of its horrendously bad reputation and the
persecution of its followers.

A growing number of psychiatrists and physicians are beginning to trace the mental and physical health problems of many blacks—the lack of self-esteem—to the symbolic annihilation to which their culture is subjected by the white-pride school curricula and media. Perhaps another cause of this depression is the severance of any link to the images of their ancient religion. One wonders how the millions of Catholics and Protestants who came to these shores, or the followers of Buddhism and Confucianism, would have fared had these faiths been driven underground, depriving them of spiritual nourishment, or had their religions been exposed to the kind of pillorying that neo-African religion receives in the media and from the motion picture industry. Typical of the treatment accorded Voodoo was NBC anchorman Tom Brokaw's sensationalized announcement that the drug murders occurring in Mexico during 1988 were the result of Voodoo rites; it was revealed later that the so-called drug cult had been inspired by a Hollywood "Voodoo" film entitled *The Believers*.

What if "possession," this amazing phenomenon, were as available to the millions of anxiety-ridden Americans as the billions of toxic stress-reducing pills that are shoveled across the drugstore counters or the illegal substances that are consumed by Americans, making ours a nation of junkies? When serious scholars begin to unravel the mysteries recorded in *Tell My Horse*, Zora Neale Hurston's reputation will be based on more than the ideological grandstanding of some of her contemporary fans, out to get even with the entire male species, or so it seems. She was not an ideologue, but a humanist, not a buffoon, but a scientist. Her tragedy is that she did not live to witness her vindication.

1990

CHESTER HIMES
Writer

Life in the United States was hard for a man like Chester Himes, a proud, nonconformist rebel and mulatto whose mother, often mistaken for white, demanded respect even to the point of armed combat. There's that great scene in his book *The Third Generation* in which his mother, passenger in a car whose student driver is threatened by a white farmer, pulls a gun on the farmer.

James Baldwin, another proud and temperamental genius, said that if he hadn't left the United States he would have killed someone. The same could be said of Chester Himes, the intellectual and gangster who left the United States for Europe in the 1950s. He achieved fame abroad with his Harlem detective series, which are remarkable for their macabre comic sense and wicked and nasty wit so brilliantly captured in Bill Duke's *A Rage in Harlem*.

The black male characters in these stories either rage against the assaults upon their dignity and self-worth by American society or channel this rage, the strategy used by the dignified Dick Small, the deferential headwaiter in the story "Headwaiter," a virtuoso performance that shows Himes's gift for scene, speech and characterization was evident as early as 1937.

Most of the men in the book spend their time "on the muscle," that is, in a constant state of anxiety and depression. In *All God's Chillun Got Pride,* Keith Richards has a "tightfaced scowl . . . high shouldered air of disdain . . . a hot, challenging stare . . . uncalled-for and out-of-place defiance, and a lack of civility and rudeness." As a result of his pride, his career ends in the Army's guardhouse.

Another character's pride almost results in his murder by the landlady of a prostitute he's sharing with a rich white john named Mr. Shelton. When the wealthy Mr. Shelton visits his paramour unexpectedly, Joe Wolf hides in the closet, where he is discovered by Shelton. Shelton refuses to notice him.

"All of a sudden it hit him that Mr. Shelton had opened the door deliberately, knowing he was there, and after having satisfied himself that he was right, had refused to acknowledge Joe's existence. Why he had not only refused to recognize him as a rival, not even as an intruder, why the son of a bitch looked at him as if he was another garment he had bought for her."

Insulted and humiliated, Wolf attacks the prostitute until the landlady "Miss Lou burst into the room pointing a long-barreled .38." Wolfe has to run for his life and swallow his "innate pride, his manhood, his honor."

James (Happy) Trent, an ex-convict, returns to civilian life, only to find his mother and brother experiencing hard times. An old ragged overcoat cast off by his brother symbolizes his failure and misery. He steals a new coat and is murdered by a policeman while trying to escape.

The condition of these brooding, troubled characters is so bleak that they spend a good deal of the time dreaming. Some of these stories were written while Himes was serving time in prison.

In *The Meanest Cop in the World,* Jack fantasizes that he is a college freshman in love with a co-ed named Violet, "a brunette with a tinge of gold in the bronze of her skin and nice curves beneath her simple little dress," whose demeanor causes a "flip-flop" in his heart. He awakens in jail. "Suddenly Jack realized that he wasn't in love with a pretty girl called Violet, that he didn't even know such a girl, that he was just convict number 100012 in a dark, chilly cell."

Another character slips into a daydream after he reads of a Mississippi trial of two white men accused of murdering a "Negro youth for making a pass at a white woman." His dream locates him at the scene of the trial where, using a variety of weapons, he slaughters every "peckerwood" in sight.

American ethnic literature might be divided between the missionary tradition, that which espouses assimilation and preaches adherence to what one newspaper critic of black behavior calls "white mainstream values" (whatever that might mean), and the satirical comic "trickster" tradition that undercuts and even mocks the writing of assimilation.

Charles Fanning, in his "The Irish Voice in America," argues that the satirical tradition is the one employed by the underdog: "The power of words is a great offensive weapon, a potent and public act of comic aggression that fortifies one against one's enemies." The "serious" and "earnest" writing in this collection often falls flat, especially the love stories in which, typically, a man is involved with a woman of a higher class than his own. Himes, however, is highly successful when he uses "comic aggression" to puncture the social and political daydreams of his times.

The daydream that if blacks prove their valor by sacrificing themselves for whites or by fighting against their enemies, American society would embrace them as dark brothers is treated in "Two Soldiers," about a black private who displays his bravery on the battlefield on behalf of Joshua Crabtree, who goes "berserk" at the very sight of a black man in uniform. " 'Set me down, white brother, and save you'self,' George whispered through blood-flecked lips." As in "Glory" and "Home of the Brave," only then does the white character recognize the black's humanity. Calvin Hernton is right in his excellent introduction when he asserts that some of these stories, though written in the '30s and '40s, address contemporary issues.

Feminist revisionist theory, promoted in such plays as "The Straw Woman," that white women in the South suffered as much as the blacks who were often lynched and maimed, is a daydream exploded by Himes's story "A Penny for Your Thoughts": A white woman assaults a man who is trying to calm a mob bent on lynching a black man accused of rape. " 'Why, you nigger-lovin' bastard, what's Texas comin' to when a white woman . . .' She drew back and slapped him across the mouth with the barrel of her gun." To add to the irony, the intended victim is a black veteran.

Himes's America is alive and well, and racism, that ugly social parasite, has found a host in parts other than the South, and festers in the speeches of politicians who know they can gain votes by "running against the nigger" as politicians used to say in the old South.

After an hour's flight during which I was red-lining sections of this book, one of those "aberrational" events that happen to the black men, including those in Himes's book, frequently, happened to me.

While approaching the parking lot accompanied by a black professor and a white student who'd come to pick me up for an engagement at the California Institute of the Arts, I was stopped by three white men who identified themselves as Burbank Airport Narcotics Security. The one who did all of the talking was obviously high on testosterone. He wanted to know why I exited from the terminal instead of choosing the exit in front of the baggage claim, as my fellow passengers had. (I hadn't checked any bags.)

I could imagine Chester Himes, for whom living in a racist society was a situation of absurdity, doubling over from laughter. I thought of a dozen smart answers that I could have given to such a stupid question. But I know my America like a book. The wrong answer would have given me the same fate as a character named Black Boy in "The Night's for Cryin' ":

"The cops took him down to the station and beat his head into an open, bloody wound from his bulging eyes clear to the base of his skull."

As evidence that the same experiential gap between blacks and whites that existed when Himes wrote these stories exists now, a white friend to whom I related this incident said I should have taken down the officer's badge number.

1991

JESS MOWRY
Writer

Jess Mowry was born near Starling, Mississippi, in 1960. He and his father were abandoned by his mother when Mowry was three months old. They moved to Oakland, where Mowry grew up, living on the east and west sides, "down near the water." He wouldn't tell me the street names of the neighborhoods; these and other details of Mr. Mowry's life are kept private. The author refused to grant me a face-to-face interview.

Ninety percent of his education, he says, was based upon reading books at home. His father, Jessup, a scrap-metal worker, was an avid reader and introduced him to H. P. Lovecraft, Mowry's favorite writer, William Saroyan, and John Steinbeck. He read *Cannery Row* when he was seven.

As a gifted black child, he experienced difficulties in school from the unsympathetic teachers, and as in the case of many poor inner-city children, he switched from school to school. He recalls one teacher who resented the fact that he could read ahead of the other children and who greeted such precocity with sarcasm.

The main purpose of public schools, Mr. Mowry maintains, is to keep the kids off the street for a few hours during the day. The "kids" who people Mowry's books share this attitude.

His father was also responsible for Mowry's moral education, teaching him that blacks had to be better than (not superior to—Mowry is an egalitarian) whites and that blacks had to learn how to forgive. The elder Mowry, 230 pounds and six-foot-three, would rather talk than fight and was good at using his verbal skills to disarm an opponent. Mowry says that his father used to talk like a militant but has long since mellowed.

He remembers coming home drunk at age eight, and his father holding him out the window by his ankles in order to teach him a lesson. Mr. Mowry believes that families that lack a father suffer. He "jumped over the spear," with his wife, Marquita, sixteen years ago. They have four children, ages six, ten, twelve, and fifteen. One of the principal characters in *Way Past Cool*, Ty, bodyguard to Deek, a sixteen-year-old drug dealer, is modeled after Mowry, he says. Ty's main squeeze, named Markita, "boxes burgers" in a fast-foods restaurant.

Mowry began writing as a result of ties with what might be called an extended family of "kids" with whom he came in contact during a storefront storytelling workshop. The workshop has since been partially financed by Mowry from his book earnings. His award-winning novel *Rats on the Roof* emerged from Mowry's discovery that there was a dearth of books with which young blacks could identify. He began making up street stories for the consumption of his workshop members; eventually, he wrote them down. His three books, *Rats on the Roof, Children of the Night*, and the recent novel *Way Past Cool*, were the result. This gives Mowry's novels the effect of rapping on the page. He likes rap because, he says, it's a medium kids can relate to. Rap is not the only form of popular culture that Mowry draws upon to form his books. He likes "Star Trek" and horror movies, especially the Bela Lugosi classics. Like some of the postmodernists, he even grafts images from B-movies like *The Screaming Skull* into his movie/comic book–like novels. He is also inspired by science fiction writers like Robert Heinlein and Larry Niven. His novels are replete with allusions to Ninja Turtles and to the antihero of the *Psycho* series.

Mowry grew up during the 1960s and experimented with psychedelia. The disillusionment over the Haight-Ashbury hippie period coming to an end is reflected in some of the speeches of the young characters in his new Farrar Straus Giroux novel, *Way Past Cool*. He believes that the black middle class has deserted the black inner cities. (Though some studies claim that it hasn't, Mowry is suspicious of studies and reports compiled by college professors. He mentioned a professor who hung out with the homeless for three weeks, only to conclude that there was no homelessness problem.) *Way Past Cool* includes some remarks about one of those whom Mowry feels has deserted the inner city. M. C. Hammer and his $6 million home in the suburbs of Oakland is criticized, but Mowry would be the first to acknowledge that M. C. Hammer contributed very generously to the Oakland Christmas drive for needy kids, and though Mowry contributed $6,000, the mayor of Oakland didn't thank him as profusely as he did Hammer. (Mowry also contributes to other charities; one is Brick Fire, an organization that helps poor Mississippi children.)

A year or so ago, one of the permanent members of what I refer to as my Phonetree University, novelist Al Young, who is also from Mississippi, called and said that he was excited about a young writer named Jess Mowry and was going to nominate his book *Rats on the Roof* for a prestigious PEN/Miles literary award, named for the late poet and University of California at Berkeley professor Josephine Miles. This award is bestowed by the Oakland chapter of PEN International, which is headed by Floyd Salas, author of the Grove classic *Tatoo the Wicked Cross*. Poet Jack Foley is program director for the awards.

As a member of PEN Oakland, I was designated to read from *Rats on the Roof* at the ceremony at Yoshi's restaurant in Berkeley, and it was then that I began to share Al Young's confusion about the ethnic background of the author, as well as Al's enthusiasm for the book. While reading *Way Past Cool* during a trip to Paris, where I was traveling to attend a conference convened to celebrate the careers of Richard Wright, James Baldwin, and Chester Himes, my confusion was compounded.

Henry Louis Gates, Jr., one of the critics attending the conference, had written an essay in the *Times* about how difficult it sometimes is to identify the racial or ethnic background of an author. He was referring to the controversy about a book about Native American life that was actually written by an ex-Klansman but apparently fooled everybody (except for Native American scholar and novelist Gerald Vizenor, who smelled a fraud; he said Native Americans just don't write that kind of "romantic" book).

The question that came to my mind while examining Mowry's prose was, How could a white writer have access to all of the inside language of Oakland's "kid" culture, which, as Mowry says, keeps changing, but at the same time pen some dialogue that sounded like Uncle Remus dialect. Mowry said that the plantation dialect was employed because his agent complained about his characters sounding alike. The "kids" from Bakersfield who appear in *Way Past Cool* speak in archaic stage dialect so as to distinguish them from the hip Oaklanders.

Mowry cleared up my confusion on another point: Jess Mowry's mother is white, blond, and blue-eyed. As a Creole, Mr. Mowry has access to a perspective that defies category. A sort of extra sense. Most Afro-Americans have a mixed heritage—European, African, and Native American—but the mixing occurred generations ago. His mixed background has influenced his worldview and his experience. His is the point of view of those caught in the middle.

The thirty-two-year-old is five-feet-eleven and has curly hair. His "dusky" color changes with the light—"I don't take to color photos," he says. Though he identifies with blacks, he has had to endure the kind of ostracism that children of mixed parentage often experience. He has been beaten by blacks for being different but is not "black" enough for some whites. He is right when he says that many blacks are as opposed to the race mixing as the

Klan—even those who might be enlightened and progressive about every other issue, and even those who have become designated role models by the media (a trap Mowry is cunning enough to avoid). His comparison of a black cop to a gorilla leaning over in search of a banana could have emerged from a misty part of his mixed heritage or, more likely, from a beating he suffered at the hands of a policeman when, at age thirteen, he told a cop to go fuck himself.

Studies indicate that children of mixed background are often the mediators between blacks and whites. When Mowry talks about Malcolm X, he mentions the post-Mecca Malcolm who, after meeting many white-skinned Muslims, refused to see all whites as blue-eyed devils. This explains the references to the interracial prototypical gang the Little Rascals.

Mowry agrees with Martin Sanchez Jankowski, author of *Islands in the Street,* that gangs aren't always malevolent. The core gang in *Way Past Cool* provide protection for one another and for those within their territory who are assaulted or harassed by outsiders; nevertheless, some of their protection falls on the lethal side: A junkie who disturbs the peace of some tenement dwellers is set afire.

Currently, U.S. society has been encouraged by its political and subsidized mass-media intelligentsia to view U.S. life as a continual "morning in America" paradise, where the only social problems occur in the inner cities. Psychologists call this denial. The media often behave as the mad scientist's assistant in spreading this myth. CNN responded to a study that expressed alarm about the problems of American teenage life—problems that ranged from obesity to alcoholism—by rushing to Oakland and hurrying some kids on camera to talk about violence. All of the children were black. (Mowry's novel reserves some of jts harshest criticism for the television news industry.)

Most telling of all was Bush cabinet member Louis Sullivan describing, during a speech in Oakland, a culture of violence that's taken hold in the inner city, shortly after his boss, President Bush, had ordered the devastation of a small country in a manner the United Nations described as "apocalyptic."

A Senate study cited in the June 19, 1991, edition of *USA Today* reported that most rural states had greater increases in violent crime over the past year than New York City. Nevertheless, the myth, supported by the media, that violence is exclusively a black urban problem continues to flourish, even though a 1990 study about violence, printed in the *New York Times*, found whites to be the only American racial group most likely to attack members of all groups—blacks, gays, lesbians, Asian Americans, Hispanics, Jewish Americans, and so on.

Jess Mowry knows what all black writers know: that their work may be enjoyed for the wrong reasons. He speaks for all of us when he says that in a white society, "you never know what you say or what you do that people are going to pick up." He knows that the success of some black women writers stems from their marketing an image of black males with which a racist society is comfortable. He knows that some of those who want to award him book contracts and put his fiction on the screen might be attracted to the violent parts of *Way Past Cool*, the parts that depict black youth as the number one menace to society, the line promoted by the *New York Times* each day. A white woman representing a big publishing company said she would publish Mowry if he'd remove the sex and dirty words. She said he could keep the violence.

Unlike the quick-buck journalists, academics, and syndicated columnists who blame all of American society's ills on blacks' personal behavior, Mowry is aware of this hypocrisy. He knows that the high incarceration rate of black youth stems not from their committing more crimes, but from the fact that they are four times more likely to be sentenced than white kids who commit the same crimes. He knows that the large number of black youth who are jailed for drug crimes (in a society where 80 percent of the drug consumers are white and where whites operate the most lucrative components of the drug market) wouldn't be

there if they were white—the best argument I know for the legalization of drugs.

The difference between Mowry and those who are marketing
black pathology for money or political power is that Mr. Mowry
is sincere and authentic. He is an absolutely charming and dis-
arming and shy young man, with manners good enough to refer
to his elders as "Sir." He is writing about what he knows and
covers the 1 percent of black youth who are causing such problems in the fictional neighborhood of his books—as well as those
who shoot up my Oakland neighborhood from time to time—in
a manner far superior to that of a mega-media instant expert,
like the well-known columnist who has sick attitudes about
black people and became an expert on the inner city by virtue of
having traveled with the police one night. Mowry understands
these kids, what makes them tick, and why they behave as they
do. Moreover, his characters are based upon real people.

Another thing he has going for him is his humility. I doubt
very much whether the fame that has come to him and that gives
him the feeling of having been "born again" will change him.
He's not moving out of Oakland and will probably continue to
take his family out to Burger King and McDonald's.

With a more attentive editor, and more contact with black
writers, Mr. Mowry could very well become the successor to the
mighty novelist—product of a black father and of a mother so
"white" that she could pass—Chester Himes, one of the writers
we celebrated during that trip to Paris.

But Mr. Mowry's contribution doesn't end with his writing.
He has presented the educational establishment with a direct
challenge. With his own meager funds, he has gotten those kids
deemed "incorrigible"—children who've been forgotten by the
system—to read books, to become interested in intellectual activity: a feat that not only some inner-city schools but also suburban and private schools have failed to accomplish. Workshops
for the "kids" might go a long way toward solving the illiteracy
problem in the United States, a major problem if only because, as

we approach the end of the century, the United States will have to rely on a work force composed of the "kids" Mowry writes about. While the educational system hems and haws about whether the literature Mowry uses in his workshops truly constitutes literature, more of our brightest youth drop out of schools and are alienated from their curricula, a curricula that, according to a study conducted at SUNY Albany, largely excludes the works of minorities and women.

The brilliant wordplay of rap music and the prose of Jess Mowry, the Homer of inner-city youth, indicate a full-blown word renaissance among black youth. These youth have inspired white and brown youth as well. The questions for educators are, Why is it happening in the streets and not in the schools, and why is a grammar school dropout more successful than they have been in motivating inner-city youth to take as much interest in language as they do in basketball, with a budget that amounts to less than the lunch tips of a conference and commission convened to investigate why Johnny can't read?

1992

Reginald Martin,
Toni Cade Bambara
Writers

I once struggled to review a novel by one of Africa's leading writers, and though the book was written in English, the allegory was so dense that, for me, it was like translating Sanskrit. The sections I was able to understand dealt with the corruption of a brutal and repressive regime. I concluded that the writer, who'd been jailed by the regime, chose this style to avoid losing his head. This is not a new literary device. Shakespeare's Hamlet signifies upon—that is, criticizes indirectly—his villainous stepfather, by presenting a play in which he catches the conscience of the king. A more modern example was the staging of a version of Sophocles's *Antigone* as a symbol of the French spirit under Nazi occupation.

Confronted by a society in which people were viewed as equipment, and not human beings, where their literacy was prohibited and their protest often brutally suppressed, the Afro-American slaves used storytelling as a way of articulating their situation. In these stories, tricksters, often animal characters, or conjure men and women outwitted superior forces, and the abiding commandment seemed to be to do unto others before they did unto you. Even in this unchristian world where you were given one warning and no second chance, reprieve, or opportunity for redemption, a world of haunts and the supernatu-

165

ral of amoral monsters, a place where illness and death had metaphysical causes—there existed an almost Yoruban kind of protocol. A character who greeted you cordially one minute might be devouring you during the next. "If a Yoruba wants to kill you, he will smile at you" is the way my teacher Adebesi Amolaran puts it. "If an Iboe wants to kill you, he will tell you first." The signs are known only to the initiates, and communication is couched in a turgid ambiguity. To those who were satirized in these stories, they must have sounded like a foreign language, just as contemporary Black English—which serves some of the same functions as this ancient oral literature—is viewed by many as a foreign language.

These stories reveal that exasperating the oppressors, or just plain getting on their skins and needling them, was just as effective a tool toward gaining one's freedom as rebellion and protest. With the advent of the abolitionist movement, a new kind of literature emerged. Written by fugitive slaves who were protected by northern sponsors, this literature inveighed against the southern system and denounced the cruelties of those who held Afro-Americans in bondage, in a style that, though eloquent, carried an unequivocal message. Unlike the pre-Christian world of folklore—the Hoodoo stories, based upon a religion whose reality swarms with invisible entities, that slaves brought to this hemisphere—the abolitionist literature used biblical morality as a basis for its arguments against slavery (though the Bible could just as easily be used as a justification for slavery). Its authors became celebrities who were much in demand on the lecture circuit, both here and abroad.

Two young writers and scholars, Dr. Reginald Martin, associate professor of composition and director of the Professional Writing Programs at Memphis State University, and Toni Cade Bambara, formerly an eight-year resident of Atlanta and now a member of two writing workshops, Pomoja and the Southern Collective of Afro-American Writers, are beneficiaries of the folkloric and abolitionist traditions, as well as avant-garde literary strategies. Their work shows that black writers have achieved a freedom of expression that was unheard of not only in the Old South of the oral tradition, but in Richard Wright's South, or even in the South of the late 1950s (I remember entering a library in Chattanooga, Tennesee, at about that time, and being given a hard time by the librarian).

Their novels also show that, though the lives of contemporary middle-class black New Southerners have changed from those of their ancestors, some of the old fears surface from time to time, like finding a brontosaurus grazing on the lawn of your condominium: "Every southern black feared the urban Southern night, even in 1988," says Zip, the narrator of Martin's unpublished novel *Everybody Knows What Time It Is,* winner of the 1987 Deep South Writer's Prize for best novel.

Toni Cade Bambara is a feminist, but one cannot accuse this enormously talented writer of being a literary hustler of the sort who write books that characterize black male chauvinism solely to sell these properties to producers of misogynistic movies like *Indiana Jones* and *Rocky.* Bambara tells the story of Velma Henry, a professional worrywart and an overactivist who never met a radical cause she didn't like. As her boyfriend puts it, she has "overloaded her circuits" with such issues as ecology, natural foods, and nuclear disarmament. She seems to have managed the mimeograph machine in every activist storefront in memory: "She could barely remember anything about home, for home had really begun with the Mobilization for Youth theatre project, the St. Mark's poetry group, the committees of defense for Carlos Felociano, the Puerto Rican Student Union at City College, and then the Young Lords. She'd written faithfully to companeros of CAFU, a feminist action group. . . . She'd kept up communications over the years with most of the independentistas, FUPI, HU, MPI, who had direct and immediate links with groups in New York." Velma Henry's primary concerns are civil rights and women's issues, and *The Salt Eaters,* like James Baldwin's *If Beale Street Could Talk,* is what could be called a post-revolutionary book; it captures the despair that set in after the revolutionary fires of the 1960s had been extinguished: "Malcolm gone, King gone, Fannie Lou gone, Angela quiet, the movement splintered, enclaves unconnected." Much of this confusion, according to *The Salt Eaters*, resulted from organizations being sacrificed on "the altar of male ego." The women of *Salt Eaters* hope to rebind this unity by holding a spring festival in Claybourne, "somewhere in the south."

Velma becomes so stressed-out by the men in the book and their silly antics that she becomes "totally out of it"; in one scene, Velma, the soldier in the civil rights army, scolds some of its male pleasure seekers: "You all continue lollygagging at De'Giorgio's, renting limousines and pussyfooting around town profiling in your three-piece suits and imported pajamas while the people sweat it out through hard times."

Velma submits to the healing techniques of Afro-Indian America, under the supervision of Minnie Ransom, Hoodoo woman, a figure from the folkloric oral tradition that has enjoyed a resurgence in recent black literature. By the time Velma arrives at Minnie Ransom's Southwest Infirmary, which has a reputation in "radical medical circles," "her veins are open, her face bloated, and she was tearing at her clothes, clawing at her hair, wailing to beat the band, asking for some pills."

Much of the book is devoted to this healing process and seems to suggest that for a black woman in a racist, sexist society, strength can be found in binding with other women in organizations and secret societies: "the mud sisters," "daughters of the yam," and "the Seven Sisters."

Though as a black male, I was uncomfortable with Ms. Bambara's boymen, welfare pimps, and types who feel as though all political solutions derive from the pelvis, I know that there are such men, and the portrayals ring true. The book seems amazingly balanced, and the writing skills are formidable; at some points the writing takes off from the page and becomes a jazz solo: "stumbling through the thorns and briars, following the rada rada bug booming of the drums or the weh weh wedo riff of reed flutes." Though Velma is healed at the end of the book, one gets the feeling that it won't be long before she's back at the mimeograph machine; the moral of the book seems to be that as soon as one oppressor lets up, another one takes his place, and while the foes in the abolitionist novel and those of folklore were as easy to identify as the devils in morality plays, the modern villain may be the father of your child.

Though Ms. Bambara's novel employs allusions to the feared and misunderstood Afro-American religion, the novel's tone is that of the Christian abolitionist tradition of "serious" writing. In contrast, Reginald Martin's brilliant work is comic, bawdy, and full of irony and absurdity; it reads like the extended tall tale of folklore and includes trickster comedy involving excretory and reproductive functions. Its concept of God and religion is also West African: "Zip was pretty sure that if there were a God, he was the head of the largest oil company in the world; he wore a spotted, clone tie, drove a Rolls, and he was out on the lake, resting, on the Seventh Day, no phone on the boat. This explained why He never answered all that praying and shouting." The Yoruba god Olorun is a capitalist whose name the descendants of his followers have forgotten. Malcolm X always described blacks as being lost in the wilderness of North America.

In a plastic card society, Zip and Seidah, the novel's main characters, have more than enough material goods with which to entertain themselves. They are aware that they are doing better than their ancestors in the New South: "The grandchildren of these maids and butlers sometimes figured out ways to turn their labors into profit, but it was almost always at the destructive expense of less profit-inclined and less worldly blacks. Yes, the grandchildren of the maids and butlers were certainly in the black." But while Ms. Bambara's characters build upon tradition, Martin's characters are concerned with now. His angst-ridden, Camus-reading character Zip concludes that "the past is dead. Only the present and the future's important." In keeping with its folkloric style, Zip, the former motel worker, through a reversal of fortune becomes a successful pop star: "Occasionally, Zip pondered these existential questions, as the Nigerian-rubbered whitewalls hummed beneath his customed phantom Rolls Royce; occasionally he murmured some phrases to Siedah, as he passed her yet another glass of Pouilly Fuisse '64, that perhaps love is more important than money in the washed-out system under which he and she now prospered, as the Rolls hummed through Beverly and Hollywood Hills toward their state-of-the-art music studio or toward their Malibu beach house with the micro-film library of 50,000 titles."

Both Bambara's and Martin's characters are intellectual, hip, comfortable, or even well-off; they're worldly, aware of tradition, and able to explain their condition, but they're still troubled. Martin's characters are aware of class divisions, and the fact that many blacks have been left behind. And while Ms. Bambara's characters mull over this contradiction—with the sort of missionary-mindedness that the German Jews of early New York felt toward their less fortunate Russian Jewish brethren on New York's Lower East Side—Martin's hedonistic and selfish characters don't lose much sleep over the matter.

What both novels seem to suggest is that Americans, both black and white, are approaching the end of this century with a great deal of anxiety, a kind of period that in the past has been accompanied by political and cultural cataclysms. While the adversaries of the past—Nazism, Alabama state troopers, Simon Legree—were clear-cut, like shadow-play figures jerking across the stage of history, those of modern times are difficult to identify or are so abstract they even elude definition. Most of the damage to African American progress over the past twenty years has been done by propaganda spread by corporate-sponsored think tanks.

Though the often hyenalike media ridiculed him, Jimmy Carter—who may be viewed by future historians as a philosopher-leader, while Reagan's disgraceful regime will make Hard-ing's look respectable—put his finger on it when he spoke about a malaise. We have material goods and pleasures, but we're still not satisfied. Political victories have been won, but the political problems seem infinite. Velma Henry tries to lessen her anxiety by jumping from cause to cause and seeking salvation in feminist bonding. Martin's characters consume and consume, but all seem to feel that they're not quite in control of their lives: the feeling, as one of Martin's characters puts it, of being in a "puppet-show" but trying to convince ourselves that we're "autonomous," when we're really "automatons." It is this feeling, shared by black and white Americans, that neopopulists Jesse Jackson, Pat Robertson, George Wallace, David Duke, Ross Perot, and Carter himself successfully tapped when they pointed to sinister forces as being the sources of our sense of powerlessness: international banking, the rich, the foundations, and Washington. Ms. Bambara's and Mr. Martin's novels demonstrate that the problem is deeper than that. They not only tell us about the modern, upscale black middle class of New Southerners but give us a glimpse into the troubled American soul as well, and they don't have to mince their words as the slaves did or flee to northern sanctuaries to write the truth, as did the abolitionist writers. In fact, the answer to the nostalgia question, What happened to the Old South? might be, It moved to New York, Boston, Philadelphia, and Los Angeles.

Miraculous Fiction
Writers

Though Latin American writers work under some of the most repressive regimes, of all of the fiction writers in the Americas, their fiction seems to be the most "made up." Maybe the noninventive "competent novels"—Ray Federman's description of those produced by a white literary diva—that flood the American market can be traced to white Protestantism's association of novels with lying. While South American writers lie big, most contemporary North American writers tell safe and self-indulgent fibs. Currently, the hip mainstream thing seems to be to exploit superstitions regarding unpopular groups or to mimic the voice of "the underclass." Sam Donaldson called Tom Wolfe's anti-Semitic, antiblack *Bonfire of the Vanities* the "defining work" of the 1980s, and Jay McInerney, a good writer gone to hell, has tried to imitate Wolfe with his *Brightness Falls*. Wolfe believes that the vocabulary of blacks is confined to *yo* and *homey*, while McInerney believes that blacks still use words like *Oreo*.

The Yoruba American experience (Yoruba American because the ancestors of most blacks in the Americas were brought from Yorubaland in Nigeria) seems to be available to all—white novelists, scriptwriters, academics—yet David Duke's supporters in the so-called Department of Education maintain that black culture is marginal and ethnic. Assistant Secretary of Education

Diane Ravitch, a truly remarkable mind, proposes that to teach a course in black culture is to engage in "ethnic cheerleading."

Colombian novelist Manuel Zapata Olivella's work demonstrates the international scope of Yoruba culture. Olivella was born in 1920 in the town of Lorica, on the Caribbean coast of Colombia. Olivella's novel *Chango, el gran putas* takes its name from the Yoruba god of lightning and thunder. Manuel Zapata Olivella's *A Saint Is Born in Chima* keeps your attention because, in his fiction, one never knows what's going to happen next.

The novel is composed of a series of miracles and spectacles about the supernatural powers of Domingo Vidal, a crippled person, whose legend begins when his escape from a fire is seen by peasants as proof of his holiness. The lives of those close to him are transformed. Some of the mystery rubs off on his sister, who becomes a sort of manager for the cripple, manufacturing miracles and recruiting customers: "Balaude, looking emaciated, is swimming in her great black robe. She makes gestures, strikes blows with her staff, smiles and weeps. Her eyes shine wildly in their sunken sockets. She is praying and repeating her brother's name uncontrollably." The Saint even gets his own public relations person, Jerimías, whose role brings him into conflict with the church, represented by Padre Berrocal. Jerimías, according to the novel, "always had a yen to be a preacher, and the half-Latin phrases learned from the priest while officiating at the mass flow easily from his lips." The church reacts to this encroachment upon its corner on the superstition market by blasting Jerimías as a heretic. Berrocal sets out to undo Domingo and his followers.

Manuel Zapata Olivella uses devices that contemporary American critics would dismiss as corny. Death and the Devil roam through the novel like carnival figures, and even animals—an alligator and a bull—assume human personalities. Death, who is lured by "stirring fandango music," snatches Domingo from his earthly presence, and, of course, he, like St. Nicholas, becomes a greater threat to the church dead than alive.

In a macabre scene, Padre Berrocal orders the Saint's corpse to be hacked, only to suffer the wrath of the violated, dead Domingo: "In his bed, squint-eyed, Padre Berrocal lies paralyzed."

Along the way, Mr. Olivella seems to be arguing that one man's superstition is another person's science, and so while the scientists attribute Domingo's condition to ankylosing rheumatism, the herb doctors believe him to be bewitched. But the townspeople's superstitions exhibited here are benign and not without charm and color. They are the exotic gossip that makes life interesting for the ordinary person and serve the same function as soap operas, which relieve the population from the insufferable boredom of modern life. Miracles serve that function in *A Saint Is Born in Chima*. Wonders are performed daily. The excitement is contagious, and everyone wants to be the object of a miracle. Even routine daily events take on an unexpected aura of mystery. The old people, accustomed to the shadows of a favorite corner, come out of their houses asking for Domingo, eager to recover the joy of living that has escaped their lives. Other charismatics might build a cult around Derrida or Anita Hill, who was referred to as an "Icon" by a professor writing in the *New York Times*.

Olivella quotes Castiglioni, author of *El mundo magico*, who believed that "myths are a necessary product of the infantile mentality as well as the mentality of primitive people." Infantile mentality? This contradicts the current situation in the United States, where myths about blacks and other unpopular groups are promoted by the media, academic, intellectual, and policy elite. They are even promoted by members of the avant-garde.

Since 1989, after being asked to respond to Pete Hamill's *Esquire* article about "the tangle of pathologies" existing in the black community, I have collected boxes of similar inflammatory articles and op-ed pieces—authored mostly by white male academics, think-tank functionaries, and media analysts and by gender-first, middle-class feminists—about blacks and Latinos that serve the same function as Jeremías: "He preaches, fans the fires of fanaticism, misrepresents facts." Contemporary American Jeremíases spread lies about affirmative action, quotas, welfare, black violence, Great Society programs, and multiculturalism and get their views published in the promoters of such superstition, the *New York Times*, the *New York Review of Books*, the *New Republic*, *New York* magazine, and the television networks. Though they invoke the "new," in reality they are the wags of the American medieval village, the staff of the Witchfinder General. We're the witches and warlocks.

Lethal racist fanaticism even appears in progressive magazines like *Utne Reader* and in outlets that view themselves as holding a position at the cutting edge of culture. Feminist Jeremíases (Jemimas) sell ugly myths about black men to spellbound, superstitious suburban and academic audiences.

Author Stephanie Golden makes a brilliant observation when she says the myth that housing for the homeless reduces property values in middle-class neighborhoods involves the same kind of magical thinking that links witchcraft to the burning of crops. Daily, the American population is bombarded with such myths, which arise not from the fevered mind of a peasant, but from the pen of people who live in Georgetown, the true contemporary Jeremías.

Tom Metzger told Christopher Hitchens that the average person on welfare is a white woman whose husband has abandoned her, when we were led to believe that fatherless homes happen only in the inner city, the circles of hell in the American paradise, whose dirty secrets are covered by a white culture of silence.

It's a sign of the times that you can get a more accurate representation of American social reality from an authentic Nazi than from a Nazi posing as an avant-gardist.

Manuel Zapata Olivella's fabulous exploration of "superstitious fanaticism" run amok in a small village helps to shed light upon that which exists in a modern "developed" society.

1992

The Fourth Ali

Boxer

In the films *Mandingo* and *Drum* former WBA Heavyweight Champion Ken Norton plays a slave boxer, moving through scenes, his flesh handled by people who have such intense feelings for him they wish to stab him or boil him in a pot. The women want to ball him, and the men want to do battle with him; some people want to do both.

The Heavyweight Champion of the World is, most of all, a grand hunk of flesh, capable of devastating physical destruction when instructed by a brain, or a group of brains. I'm not saying he's stupid. He may be brilliant, but even his brilliance is used to praise his flesh.

Edy Williams, 37-23-37, a "raven-haired" woman, jumped into the middle of the ring between rounds and took her clothes off, revealing flesh the color of the hotdogs they were serving in the press room, and a few shades lighter than the red ring ropes.

Describing herself as a "Naturalist from California," she said, "If Muhammad Ali can use his body to be a success in the ring, why can't I?" One newspaper described her show as "the most exciting event of the evening." Many were using their flesh for success outside the ring as well; it seemed that every whore and player from the Mississippi Valley and points beyond were there.

The Heavyweight Championship of the World is a sex show, a fashion show, scene of intrigue between different religions, politics, class war, a gathering of stars, ex-stars, their hangers-on and hangers-on's assistants.

It's part Mardi Gras with New Orleans jazz providing the background for the main events while the embattled Beboppers, led by former Sonny Rollins and Ornette Coleman sideman Earl Turbington, held forth in one of the restaurants facing the Hilton's French Garden bar.

Driving into town on Route 61 past the authentic Cajun music and food joints, motels with imitation French-styled balconies, car lots—heading on Canal Street toward Decatur, I heard Dick Gregory on the car radio. A saint of the prime flesh movement was naming "Carlos Mancellos," a New Orleans man, as a conspirator in J.F.K.'s assassination. Gregory was one of Ali's advisors, though an insider told me that Ali didn't pay attention to Gregory's nutritions.

Hotel Bienville, named for the founder of New Orleans, Jean Baptiste Le Moyne Sieur de Bienville, was located in a red-light district of the French Quarter. Nearby, two Greek restaurants stood in the direction of Canal Street and some small time players' bars. I checked in, changed, and then followed the huge Hilton H the way you'd follow a holy asteroid: the sign resembled a blue star on the New Orleans skyline. The Hilton is located on a 23.3 acre $250 million international river center. It has 1,200 rooms, five restaurants, three lounges, parking lots for 3,550 cars, tennis courts, and rises to 30 stories above the street. It was designed by Newhouse and Taylor Architects.

Entering the press's hospitality room I was greeted by Sybil Arum, a Japanese-Korean woman who got me a drink and introduced me to her husband, Bob Arum. They both were dressed casually; she was wearing proletariat pigtails and later someone said she was the best-looking woman in the hotel. Arum was seated next to Leslie Bonanno, a heavy, wavy-haired sheriff who is heavyweight Jerry Celestine's manager. Arum was confident that Spinks was going to win the fight. He had great admiration for Ali but it was his theory that "elements of deterioration" had set in during Ali's "exile" from 1967 to 1970. I was introduced to an ex-UPI reporter who followed Ali's career during those years, and we were about to head upstairs to the bar to discuss them when Mike Rossman's family arrived, wearing Mike Rossman T-shirts. They told me they were bringing in three planeloads to witness what turned out to be Rossman's victory over Victor Galindez for the WBA Light Heavyweight Championship of the World. After the fight, Rossman's dad said, "If he weighed fifteen more pounds, he could beat Ali."

The man from UPI talked like Jimmy Stewart and didn't want his name used. He had that glint in his eye—the glint I'd see in the eyes of the other Ali disciples, Norman Mailer, Budd Schulberg, and George Plimpton. The Ali glint belonging to the true believer.

He remembered an argument that broke out in the UPI press room when Ali fought Frazier for the Heavyweight Championship for the first time. They didn't know what to call him. They decided, finally, to call him Ali if he won the fight, Clay if he lost.

A black promoter from Charleston offered Ali an exhibition fight which was to be held on a dirt track. The UPI man and a reporter from the *Detroit Free Press* were the only ones there to cover it. The city council voted against the exhibition bout, and it was cancelled. At three o'clock that day they came to Ali to tell him there'd be no fight. Ali took it philosophically, got into a car, and headed for the airport wearing the same suit he'd worn for two years.

The punishment and cruelty visited upon Ali during those three years for refusing to step forward at the induction center have become part of the Ali Legend. It seemed that the whole nation wanted to spit in his face, or skin The Grand Flesh. Not only, to them, was he a draft dodger but also a member of a misunderstood religion which the media had hyped into a monstrous black conspiracy. The Muslims were different from many of the other black organizations of the time. They had rhetoric but they also accomplished things. They built a multimillion dollar business from mom-and-pop stores and newspapers. They were the Bad Nigger, the Smart Nigger, the Hard Nigger, and the Uppity Nigger epitomized by one organization. Ali had to pay a heavy price for his religion and for his politics. My favorite story from that period occurred when an imprisoned Ali was ordered to serve breakfast to prisoners on Death Row. One prisoner looked up and said, "My God, I must be in heaven, the Heavyweight Champion of the World is serving me breakfast."

There was a flurry in the lobby. Some of Spinks's people began showing up. Tourists were standing on the second-floor balcony staring down at the scene. Shortly, Spinks came in. With that black crest he resembled a black-silk-shirt-wearing iguana. I approached the gathering with my brand new Realistic tape recorder I'd bought at Berkeley's Radio Shack. Spinks's bodyguards made a scene. They demanded that I turn the tape recorder off. Later I understood why. A *Playboy* writer using a tape recorder had betrayed Spinks's confidence by writing that Spinks smoked some grass. Because I was standing with Leroy Diggs, Spinks's sparring partner and bodyguard, a tourist came up and asked for my autograph. It was that way the entire week. People signing autographs for each other; photographers snapping pictures of other photographers.

The next afternoon, people from both camps began to show up in the French Garden bar, a stunning environment lighted by sun rays which poured through a skylight above. Ali's brother, Rachaman Ali, his freckled-faced mother whom Ali calls "Bird," and his father, wearing a checkered sports jacket and white hat. Bundini arrived and, judging from his ringside antics, I thought he'd have an expansive sense of humor. He didn't. He was wearing a white leisure suit. Bundini always wanted to be an actor, someone told me later.

In the evening, Mayor Ernest N. Morial, New Orleans's "Black" mayor, who'd be considered white in most parts of the world, gave a reception at the Fairmont Hotel honoring Muhammad Ali and Leon Spinks. I walked into the lobby toward a big room on the first floor. There was a commotion behind the door. The first man to exit was Ali. I was standing face to face with a $100 million industry which included everything from candy bars to a forthcoming automobile capable of traveling across the desert. He was huge and awesome looking, but not the "Abysmal Brute" Jack London had pined after. "Hi, Champ," I said. I shook hands with the black man they let beat up Superman.

He was followed by his wife, Veronica ("Veronica belongs to me," he said later). A procession followed the couple to the upstairs ballroom, the whole scene illuminated by photographers' flashbulbs. I fell in behind them. When Ali reached the top of the escalator I heard a loud exchange between Ali and a figure who was coming down. It was Joe Frazier. He would sing "The Star Spangled Banner" before the fight and perform at the Isaac Hayes victory show at the Hilton Friday night.

Slave power allowed southern women to spend hours at the mirror costuming, preening, and painting their faces. In the New Orleans French Quarter you can buy any kind of doll you want. Black. White. I bought a black doll which turned inside out and became a white doll (no jokes, please!).

There was that eerie ad for Georgia Life Insurance carried on a billboard. It was a picture of a child done in the kind of oils with which Rod Serling used to introduce "Night Gallery." She was dressed in a Victorian outfit, and was heavily made-up, under the caption, "What about Her?" The southern woman was supposed to be this life-sized doll who occasionally produced a fake aristocrat while the old man went about impregnating the countryside.

Some of my very talented female writer friends have jammed up the media with their woeful tales regarding the black male's proclivity toward the Macaroni style. It took me some serious reflection to reckon with the truth in this. But if black males were that—if Emmet Till was a rogue as a demagogic feminist, so hard up for a victim, has claimed—then they certainly had a great teacher.

The doll style of the women in this ballroom, in their synthetic fabrics, bloused and belted-in at the waist, showed that even though the institution was razed, certain habits of the Old South have endured. The women were what we used to call "beautiful," and the men were youthful and virile looking. Attractive and adorned bodies gathered to witness the most wonderful body in the world. A flesh ball. The mayor was standing behind Ali's people, beaming. Don Hubbard told me that the fight would bring the city $20 million in revenue, bigger than the Mardi Gras.

Ali has so much control over his body he can turn the juice on and off. In contrast to the sombre and downcast-looking fighter I'd seen emerge from the downstairs room, with whom I was alone for about fifteen seconds, the upstairs Ali began to shuffle up and down the stage, jabbing at invisible opponents, dancing, all the while speaking rapidly. He doesn't have the brittle dry irony of Archie Moore or the eloquent Victorian style of the bookish Jack Johnson, but he is more effective because he speaks to Americans in American images, images mostly derived from comic books, television, and folklore. To be a good black poet in the '60s meant capturing the rhythms of Ali and Malcolm X on the page. His opponents were "Mummies" and "Vampires"; he was "The Man from Shock." In his bitter press conference he discussed "The Six Million Dollar Man." His prose is derived from the trickster world of Bugs Bunny and Mad Magazine. The world of Creature Features. Thus, after victory, he was able to get a whole room of grown and worldly men and women to chant with him; "Mannnnnnnn, Mannnnnnnnn. That's gone be the new thing," he said, "Mannnnnnnn."

"I don't know what to say," he said. "Where's the champ? If he stays out of jail, I'll get his tail." Ali referred to Spinks as a "nigger," then caught himself to explain that "Niggers can say niggers, but white folks can't," which is as good an answer as any to the man running for office in Alabama who requested that he have the same right to say "nigger" as "the Jews" and "the niggers."

Ali's style was a far cry from the nearly catatonic humility of Joe Louis and Floyd Patterson, but then, these are different times. Can you imagine the uproar which would have happened if Louis came up with "No Nazi Ever Called Me Nigger"?

When the question-and-answer period came, I had my hand up and so he pointed to "the young man over there." I was on his side after that.

"Mr. Ali, do you plan to run for Congress as the *Nation* magazine has suggested?"

"No, I plan to run for vice-president, that way the President won't get shot." He called himself the "Saviour of Boxing," and predicted that he'd punch Spinks out of the ring. "Spinks," he said, "will become the first spook satellite." He flirted with the ladies and praised his body.

Dick Gregory followed Ali with some familiar jokes about Spinks's arrest for driving without a license and possessing $1.98 worth of cocaine (St. Louis cocaine). Gregory strongly believes that the coke was planted on Spinks. "Why did they alert the press before he was brought into the station?"

I asked Gregory to repeat what he'd said on the radio, that the killers of J.F.K. resided in New Orleans. I figured that since the mayor and the police were on the stage the conspirators would be arrested, immediately. The laughter vanished. The mayor and Ali stood silently. Dick Gregory refused to discuss it.

During the broadcast he urged black-Italian cooperation. "If the Mafia is so big," he said, "why won't Henry Ford invite it to his next garden party?"

After Ali left, Gregory came over to the bar where I was standing. The black waiters, dressed in black bowties and green satinish jackets, weren't serving beer or wine, so I asked for what Gregory was drinking. Vodka and orange juice. UMMMMMM.

A long table covered with white linen held hors d'oeuvres

under silver tops which resembled Kaiser helmets. The South knows how to lay out the dog when it wants to. Chopin on the piano stand. Silver laid out in case somebody's coming for supper.

I got a plate, returned to my seat, and found myself being choked to death from behind. It was Hunter Thompson. Choking people, I learned later, was his way of showing affection. He was wearing dark glasses, and looked like he'd just stepped off a spaceship. They're filming his life and the crew was coming to New Orleans with his two lawyers.

The DeJan's Olympia band began to second line about the floor playing some old music. They were led by this lithe flesh wearing top hat and tails, symbolizing what to some may be a spirit imported from Haiti. The carrying of the umbrella may be an African retention. I fell in behind the band and began doing the second line around the room with them. Few joined in. As we made it about the door, Spinks appeared. His eyes seemed to roll about his head. He was wearing a droll grin. He seemed very, very happy. He took the umbrella from the band's major domo and second lined toward the stage. He stood and signed autographs for a while.

I went back to the press hospitality room and met some old timers, some trainers, and some boxing buffs.

Like there was Sam Taub. As Irving Rudd of Top Rank tells it, "Sam Taub was 92 on September 10. He was born on Mott Street on the Lower East Side and was working as an office boy when he got a job through the *New York Times* with the *Morning Telegraph*, a magazine similar to the *Police Gazette*. He worked many years for Bat Masterson, a lawman who came west to be a fight official and sports writer. It was Sam who found Masterson dead at his desk of a heart attack. I was looking through the record books and I found out that Masterson was the time-keeper for the Sullivan-Corbett fight which was held in New Orleans, September 7, 1892.

"Sam did the first radio broadcast from Madison Square Garden, in the 1920s, and the first telecast of a bout from Madison Square Garden in 1939. For many years Sam broadcast for Adam's hats and Gem razor. He has a popular show on WHN called 'The Hour of Champions.' Never took a quarter from anybody. Never put the shake on anybody.

"During the last riot in the Garden he climbed to a chair to call the rioters 'hooligans,' and had to be carried away by the police, bodily." Sam Taub told me about the time Jack Johnson worked at the Forty-second Street Library and was obsessed with these sandwiches which they were selling four or five in a bag. Taub went out and bought some for Johnson. "And when Sugar Ray appeared on 'The Hour of Champions' for the first time, I said, 'Now you watch this fellow; he's going to be the champ one day.' "

As I approached Taub to be introduced he was threatening a man who could have been forty years younger than Taub with "Take a walk, buddy!" The man moved on.

Thursday, hundreds of people were pushing into the Grand Ballroom for the official weigh-in ceremonies. Bright, unnatural lights from the television cameras. Total confusion. People were standing on chairs, craning their necks to see celebrities. It was 10:55 when Angelo Dundee arrived. He looks like a mild-mannered math teacher at a boys' high school. Jimmy Ellis, who has a teenager's bright face, and Ali's brother, Rachaman—whom I mistakenly called Rudolph Valentino Clay—following. He could have been Valentino standing against the pillar in the French Garden bar, dressed in a white suit.

The platform was so full of the press that it began to reel. Arum threatened to cancel the press conference. I see Don King.

He is followed by Ali, toothpick in mouth, and Veronica Ali. A man next to me says, "Ali is the best-known person in the world." Ali weighs in at 221 pounds, Spinks 201. I'm tempted to bid.

After the weigh-in I asked former Light Heavyweight Champion of the World Jose Torres to assess Ali's chances. Torres was pessimistic. He'd seen Ali work out and he didn't like his color. "Too grey." He thought Ali's eyes were "dead," and that he was bored. "Ali no longer enjoys fighting and despises training," Torres said. "I want Ali to win for nostalgic reasons." He liked Spinks. "The more criticism he gets the more I like him," Torres said. Leroy Diggs, Spinks's bodyguard and sparring partner, standing behind Torres, said that Spinks looked real good.

Up front, Emile Brumeau, a wizened wild turkey, the head of the Louisiana Boxing Commission, was holding a press conference. Somebody asked him if he voted to strip Ali of the crown in 1967 when he was sitting on the World Boxing Association. The Commissioner told the reporter to leave or go "to a cemetery."

Another person asked if there would be a dope test following the fight. It seemed that Ali's corner had complained about a mysterious bottle given to Spinks between the rounds of the last fight. Whatever was in it seemed to give Spinks extra vigor. He asked the Commissioner what kind of water would be allowed in the corners. He answered, "Aqua water."

I saw Don King's famous crown poking above the crowds in the aisle, moving and mashing their bodies against each other. He was blandly praising Ali but at the same time voiced hope that he would retire. He said that Ali was the most identifiable man in the world. "Strong on the inside as well as the outside." He praised Larry Holmes, "the other champion," in a short speech dotted with words like "cognizant." The most frequent adjective people use in talking about King is "flamboyant."

I went up to the second floor to inquire about my credentials. A white-haired Norman Mailer was standing in the middle of the room. I met him in 1962 at Stefan's and had gone to a couple of his parties. Gone were the pug breaks and the frantic fast-talking. He seemed at peace. We exchanged greetings.

Albert C. Barnes, writing in *The New Negro* in 1925, extolled Primitivism in Negro Art with his, "It is a sound art because it comes from a primitive nature upon which a white man's education has never been harnessed." He said it reflected "aspirations and joys during a long period of acute oppression and distress." Man in distress was existential man. Mailer popularized this idea with his "White Negro." To be Negro was to be hip. Jack Kerouac studied Negro Art, and for his dedication Bird did a tune called "Kerouac." What Mailer and Kerouac failed to realize was that the average black would have thrown Bird out of his home, or giggled at his music, or charged him with not combing his hair. It was hard enough to be a Negro but to be that and Bird too was real hard. Joe Flaherty writes in *Managing Mailer* about the freeloader blacks Mailer surrounded himself with—hustlers who turned Mailer sour on blacks in general. Kerouac and Mailer tried. As they grew older their intellectual positions regarding blacks became more obtuse than right. As obtuse as their prose styles.

Reading *The Fight* again, on the way down, I realized that what I had mistaken for racism in Mailer's writing was actually frustration—frustration that he couldn't play the dozens with Bundini and them; frustration that he couldn't be black. Maybe one day the genetic engineers in their castles rocking from lightning will invent an identity delicatessen where one can obtain identity as easily as buying a new flavored yogurt.

It's kind of sad. The trench-coated verbal and physical scrapper I used to trade jokes with at Pana Grady's salons in the Dakota. His benign eyes indicated that he had realized he could never really become a "Wise Primitive," and this had brought tranquility, like the look that comes over the face of the werewolf who finally realizes his agony is over.

I asked Mailer who was going to win. He gave me one of those answers for which he has a patent. "Ali. He's worked the death out." So had Mailer.

The black entrepreneur is caught in a bizarre crossfire. On one hand, black intellectuals view him as a sellout to the system, even though many of them have bank accounts which help sustain the system.

The 1960s social and cultural programs brought prosperity to some, and with this prosperity came the guilt feelings experienced by other aspiring immigrants toward the "brothers left behind." He is expected to kick back his gains to them, "the sub-proletariat." In Oakland, the Black Panthers, joined by white children of the prosperous middle class, picketed black merchants.

He also has to struggle against the banks and creditors who grudgingly lend him money, and against the myth of black ineptitude. He has to struggle against blacks who seem to try their damnedest to prove the myth.

He knows that if he gets too big, they'll axe him down to size.

Don Hubbard, the thirty-eight-year-old president of Louisiana Sports, sits on the arm of a couch in the second-floor lobby of the Hilton. He is confident, proud, cocky even. He blames Top Rank for the disorderly weigh-in ceremonies which had just taken place. "Only people with gold passes should have been admitted."

The Vegas fight between Spinks and Ali was the first fight he'd attended; the first time he'd heard the "moans and groans" of the sport.

Hubbard met Butch Lewis, Top Rank's former vice-president, at the fight and invited him down to New Orleans for the Superbowl. He proposed to Lewis that New Orleans would be a good scene for a rematch between Ali and Spinks. Lewis scoffed at the suggestion, reminding Hubbard that he'd never promoted a fight before and there was some strong competition, including Anheuser-Busch, groups from Las Vegas, Casino owners in South Africa, and a Miami group led by Chris Dundee, Angelo Dundee's brother.

"Spinks agreed to come to New Orleans for the YMCA and didn't show. The mayor's limousines, police escort, and everything were waiting for Leon Spinks. I looked at the five-o'clock news and Spinks was in Detroit. My wife had cooked dinner and was mad enough to jump on Spinks.

"Butch Lewis came down to save face, and raised the money for the YMCA. I started needling Butch because there was a rumor that the fight was going to South Africa. How the hell can Ali stage his last fight in South Africa? Top Rank got a whole barrage of protests from the Urban League and others, and I kept bugging Butch.

"Butch called one evening and said, 'Don, you're bugging the hell out of me. I'm coming to New Orleans at 11:30. From that time you have 48 hours to raise $3 million.' "

Hubbard said he met with the mayor to get his blessings on the international event, obtained a letter of credit for $350,000, and kept $2,650,000 in escrow. At the time I talked to Lewis, which was about twelve o'clock on the Thursday before the fight, the $3 million investment had been returned. Hubbard's partners were Sherman Copelin, a black, and two Italians, Jake DiMaggio and Phillip Ciaccio. Hubbard said he didn't know whether to call the Italians white because some Italians are white and some are Italian.

"The boxing crowd spends more money than the football crowd," he claimed; "When the Superbowl fans come, it's with clubs on chartered buses, but the fight crowd arrives in Rolls Royces, Mercedeses, private planes."

Seventy thousand boxing fans spent $6 million to see the Ali-Spinks fight at the New Orleans Superdome. New Orleans chauvinists say that the Superdome is so big you can put the Astrodome inside and still have sixty feet around. A Muslim reporter wrote an article describing it as "a white elephant."

Back in the press room I ran into Harold Conrad, who'd promoted the Liston-Patterson fights and traveled to twenty-two states seeking a license for Ali to fight during his three-and-a-half-year exile. He said that if Ali won, the only fighter he'd get money for fighting would be Larry Holmes. I had just seen Holmes encounter Angelo Dundee in the hall, when Dundee said to Holmes, "My kid thinks you're the ugliest and biggest man she's ever seen."

Conrad was completing a novel called *A Rare Bird Indeed*, which he says will be the story of a newspaperman of the 1930s and 1940s, the end of a great era when you could get a table at Lindy's and Reubens at 5:00 A.M. and everybody knew Winchell, and nightclub openings were as big as Broadway openings. Conrad, tanned and wearing a plaid sport jacket, slacks, and a thin mustache, could have been a Runyon character. He worked for Damon Runyon, a "strange man from Kansas City, who didn't have many friends and liked to be left alone." Humphrey Bogart played Conrad in *The Harder They Fall*, his last role.

My friend Sam Skinner, from San Francisco's Channel 44, and I posed for a gag picture with Larry Holmes, WBC Heavyweight Champion and one of the brightest students of the Ali style and a trickster like Ali. Holmes wanted to know where the women were. A young hostess told me that the demand for women was incessant from the Spinks people. They bragged about all the "ladies" they had coming down from St. Louis.

Skinner introduced me to a black-haired, short, and tough-looking man, Richie Giachetti, Holmes's trainer. I asked him how Holmes had made Ken Norton look so bad.

"I studied the Norton film. He can't back up, he's vulnerable to uppercuts, straight right hands; when he throws a left hook he telegraphs it; his overhand right is only effective on the ropes; he can't throw it in the middle of the ring because he drags his foot.

"So the way you fight Norton is to stay in the middle of the ring and fight and jab—jabs nullify him better than anything else. You neutralize a slugger with jabs, you back him off, you fluster him."

How would Spinks fare against Ali? "Spinks is still an amateur. In football you go through high school to college and then to the pros. Spinks went through high school—but he hasn't had enough fights to have gone through college.

"Spinks makes a lot of mistakes, but at the same time he's fighting an old fighter like when Marciano went up against Louis. Spinks would not get the recognition because he will have defeated an old man, a man who contributed so much to boxing; a living legend. Spinks has nothing to gain and everything to lose by defeating Ali."

How should Ali fight Spinks? "Go out and take the first rounds, don't give up anything, stay away from the ropes and fight in the middle of the ring; Spinks's best attack is a combo left hook followed by a right hand. Ali should sidestep him, throw short left jabs, counterpunch him, and there will be no contest.

"I'm for Ali. Got to go with Ali. But if it goes over ten rounds, Spinks will win the fight."

Spirit City had become keyed up for the fight. Boys and girls in red Stetsons and fringed jackets were bused to the Hilton to provide a marching band. The town was heavily into disco. Hilton employees, dressed in black skirts, pants, and white blouses, tossed black and white balloons in the alley next to the Hilton as they second lined to a jazz band. There was a fireworks display overhead at this New Orleans sun temple. On the second floor, celebrities moved through the English bar, or sat on the sofas. Souvenirs of the fight were for sale all over the French Quarter. They ranged from cheap and expensive dolls to T-shirts to the $100 official fight poster by LeRoy Neiman, on sale at the Bienville Exchange, where the Louisiana equestrian crowd brunch on Saturdays. Even in the airport there were waitresses dressed in glossy boxing shorts, and wearing Ali and Spinks training jerseys. The fight coincided with the Hilton's first anniversary and so it got real goopy. Baron Hilton, the son of "the man who bought the Waldorf," was greeted with a kingly reception as he walked into the lobby with a woman who wore a fur coat, even though it was about ninety degrees outside. The humidity was making life miserable. There was a huge cake near the French bar about fifteen feet high, blue and white in color. Two chefs were standing next to it. I asked how many pounds of flour went into the making of the cake. They said that the cake wasn't edible.

I had dinner Thursday night with Hughes Rudd, whose appearance in experimental anthologies alongside Barthelme and Barth is a well-kept secret. CBS's eye should be replaced with a peabrain for removing Rudd from the CBS morning news. It got us all up at 6:30 A.M. so that we wouldn't miss those long rambling anecdotes of his which were about as close to writing fiction as television will ever approach. We ate and went through a couple of bottles of Pouilly-Fuisse in Winston's Room, on the second floor of the Hilton. It was done up in the style of early Frank Lloyd Wright and included some teachers of chinoiserie which became popular in the '20s when the missionaries were looting China.

He talked about an incident during World War II when they sent him an airplane that was worth less than the crate it was shipped in. Rudd said some things about the "TV Industry" which led me to think that it ought to be sunk beneath the ocean in cans so that it won't disturb mankind for maybe two hundred years.

On the day of the fight you couldn't touch anything without getting a shock, so high was the tension. The night before I made a bet with a Reuters reporter that Ali would K.O. Spinks in three rounds. I overheard Angelo Dundee telling someone, "The Champ's going to do a number on Spinks."

In the morning José Fuentes and Jane Senno took me up to Luis Sarria's room, to the man some people referred to as the "mysterious Cuban." He was eating breakfast alone, gazing from time to time at the barges and sightseeing boats on the brown Mississippi, or watching the cartoons on television. I'd met him Wednesday night, and watched him as he stood on the periphery of the crowd, hardly speaking, contemplative, studious. He was the calmest man in the whole place. I must have asked him a hundred times whether he thought Ali would win; José or Jane would translate to Spanish, and he'd usually nod his head. José showed me a photo he'd taken of Sarria, "laying hands" on Ali's face. Sarria's face was black and his features were ancient, like those of the people who came over on the first boats.

We went to Ali's private suite, room 1729, only to learn that Ali was living in a private home in West Lakeside. He was inaccessible to all but TV and media stars. Television put up $5 million for fight coverage. There were some men sitting about the suite, silent, not talking. I was reminded of the time I was snowed in one Seattle night with the Cecil Taylor group only to hear a tape of the three-hour concert I'd just left. Nobody said a word. Drew Bundini Brown filed in with Pat Paterson and some others only to file out again. It was like a religious cult. The night before, an insider had praised Ali as Christ, Abraham, Moses. What influence would he have on international politics in the future? The newspapers were beginning to say that he was naïve about the Soviet Union. Others were saying that his entourage was protecting him from the world and that he was "easily deceived."

We went to Pat Paterson's room; he was the permanent bodyguard whom Mayor Richard Daley of Chicago had assigned to Ali. My eyes were blinded by a crowd of blazing trophies laying on a dresser, glittering like idols to the sun. I had read that there's a crunch in the dressing room after the fight and asked Pat Paterson, who was wearing a green leisure suit, my chances of getting in. He said I'd have to take my chances like everybody else.

The packed press bus headed for the Superdome at four o'clock. I felt sorry for the working press. I thought about the newspapers they worked for. The cities they had to return to. I was standing next to Ed Cannon, a Muslim reporter who was wearing a sweater which read "There Is No God Greater Than Allah." That night he was hassled on the floor by a "famous movie star." The Superdome resembled a giant concrete jaw jutting out at the end of the street. Soon we were inside the jaw. There were a lot of police. After one round a few rows of state troopers gave Ali a standing ovation. Spinks looked like the kind of guy who'd say "motherfucker, kiss my ass," as they put the handcuffs on him. The seats were of red and blue hues and extended to the roof of the building. Strobe lights blinked on and off. Processions of flag bearers headed up and down the aisle.

One blue flag carried the letters "Moron." Nobody would believe me. I asked Nick Browne of the *Soho News*, who was sitting next to me, to examine the flag through his binoculars and sure enough it said "Moron." After the chaotic weigh-in there had been a threat to call out the National Guard. Fistfights broke out on the floor during the bouts.

I decided to take my press pass and rove about the floor. Spinks's cars were on the main floor near the dressing room, all white. I went to Ali's dressing room and was stopped at the door by two whites. I moved through the crowds on the main floor who were gawking at the celebrities entering to take their seats at ringside. People were putting on a fashion show, and hardly paying attention to the bouts. Three black women dressed to the hilt in 1940s costumes walked up and down. One was wearing a gold-sequinned dress the color of her hair and skin. There was a group of men who made a ring about another man. Nobody was paying any attention to them. I walked up to see Chip Carter standing in the center of the ring.

"Who's going to win the fight?" I asked.

"Ali," he said.

"What about Spinks?"

"He's good too."

"You're really a politician."

"I hope so."

I made my way down the aisle toward ringside, past the guards who were sending people back. Up close I could see an ugly dark red wound about the eye of Victor Golindez, who was defeated by Mike Rossman for the WBA Light Heavyweight Championship. This was real blood, and some of it had sprayed on the referee's shirt. Somebody in the front row yelled "get out of the way," and I spun around and flashed on the people at ringside. It resembled one of Dadaist Lil Picard's Beauty Shop satires she used to do in the East 60s art galleries. I saw no eyes, noses, nor mouths but what appeared to be blank faces smeared with pancake make-up which seemed unnaturally dry under the lights. My mind flashed back to the Norton films, the eager and richly fed faces, despising his body but at the same time lusting after it.

I headed back toward the press box which was way up in the balcony, nearly touching the ceiling. The fighters in the ring looked like dolls from where I was seated. So I watched some of the fight on one of four giant TV screens suspended from the ceiling. As I moved toward the elevator, Veronica Ali was entering the Superdome, protected by bodyguards.

All during the fights, even the championship fights, people were entering and exiting. "They don't care about this crowd," somebody said, "what they care about is television." Over 200 million people watched the fight.

Nick Browne's remarks were more interesting than the preliminary bouts. It was the kind of grim, deadpan, jaded humor you hear traded across the bar at the Club 55. When Featherweight Champion of the World Danny (Little Red) Lopez knocked out Juan Malvarez, Browne said, "I can understand ethnicity in boxing but a guy who's part Irish, part Amerindian, and part Chicano is taking it too far."

When Rossman came on to the strains of "Hava Nagila," he quipped: 4,000 years of history and only one song.

As the main event approached fistfights began to really break out, "over bets" I was told. About six rows of state troopers spilled over one another just to stop two guys. It was like a rowdy 1890s audience which used to hurl liquor bottles at the actors, or mercilessly heckle politicians on the stump.

Sylvester Stallone, Joe Frazier, and Larry Holmes had entered the ring, Holmes receiving a few boos, but much less than the Governor of Louisiana received when he was introduced. Isaac Hayes did a disco version of "America the Beautiful," and Joe

Frazier sang "The Star Spangled Banner," grimacing as if in pain. Somebody seated beneath me said, "I ain't gonna stand." When Ali entered he was mobbed. He was alternately lifted and buried by the crowd. His party seemed to sway from side to side and as they moved him down the aisle the crowds pressed in for a souvenir of The Greatest's flesh.

"My thing was to dance, come right out and start moving, win the first, win the second, win the third, get away from the ropes, dance, do everything I know how to do. Get my body in shape so that it could do what my brains tell me. The fight's almost over, if you lose eight rounds, you lose the whole fight—so after I won about ten rounds, naturally, the opponent gets frustrated. He can't win unless he knocks me out, and I get more confident," was the way Ali described his victorious strategy at a later press conference. He fought the way the pros said he had to fight in order to win. "He cut out that rope-a-dope bullshit," as one old timer said to me.

His left jabs worried Spinks silly, and Spinks looked like a brawler, engaged in a St. Louis street fight, the most vicious east of the Mississippi. His trainer, George Benton, left his corner during the fight, in frustration at the amateurs Spinks had at ringside yelling to him "wiggle, Leon, wiggle." Arguments broke out among them over who should give Spinks advice. Spinks was twenty-five, lacked craftsmanship, was a sensational head-hunter. I remember a trainer at an exhibition fight pleading with Spinks to go for the opponent's body. Ali had followed the advice Archie Moore had given to an Old Man in the Ring. "You hone whatever skills you have left."

A reporter from the *Washington Evening Star* told me that it was Ali's most serious fight in three years. At the end of the fifteenth round there was no doubt in my mind that Ali had won, and so I headed for the dressing room without hearing the decision. Veronica Ali, Jayne Kennedy, members of the family, boxing people, and show business personalities were watching a small TV set as the decision was being announced. Stallone entered, and John Travolta was standing off to the side chatting with some people. I asked Liza Minnelli, who was standing in front of me, wearing a red dress, what she thought of the fight. She thought it was "sensational."

As soon as Ali left the ring, the crowd began swaying and moving like a papier-mache dragon, moving through the interview room to the dressing room. When Ali finally entered it was impossible to gain entrance unless you were a celebrity or an important member of the Champ's entourage. "Make way for Wyatt Earp," they said when Hugh O'Brien walked by. I spotted some of the old timers I'd met on Wednesday evening. I wanted to hear what the craftsmen had to say. James Dudley is black, grey-haired, and looks like a classical American trainer, old style. Suspenders and glasses, starchy white shirt, and a smile that makes his eyes shine.

James Dudley managed Gene Smith and Holly Mimms. When I approached him he was being congratulated. His new fighter, Welterweight Johnny Gant, had won a shot at the title.

"Ali made him miss a lot. Spinks tried to weave and bob, and weave and bob, but wasn't able to do anything. Any time Ali's left hand is working he's unbeatable, and his left hand was jabbing and hooking. Ali hit him with anything he wanted to hit him with.

"Spinks comes straight to you and any man who'll come straight to you—you hit him. You move from side to side and hit him with a right hand, hit him with hooks, hit him with anything you want to hit him with." I asked Dudley when he thought Ali had the fight won.

"In the tenth round, because I'd given Spinks only three."

"What was Spinks's biggest mistake?"

"Taking the fight," he chuckled. "Ali," he continued, "lost the last fight because he stayed on the ropes and gave away six rounds."

"How would Ali do against Larry Holmes?"

"I think he's serious about retiring. He's done everything you can do in the fight business. There ain't nothin' else you can do."

"How would Ali rate against Joe Louis?"

"Ali has the style that always gave Louis trouble. Any boxer who could move gave Louis trouble and Ali is the fastest heavy-weight of all time."

Louis, I thought, might have had a harder punch. Judging from his films, his K.O. victims take a longer time to rise than Ali's.

Congratulations were going all around as well-wishers entered the dressing-room area. Ali's brother was standing in the middle of the room chanting Muslim phrases. In English he kept repeating, "He said he's from the world of shock." Ali had told the inner circle that he would surprise everybody and he was from the world of shock. I decided that the silence among his aides that afternoon was not due to sullenness but to gloom. Ali had to cheer them up.

I caught up with Dick Gregory. Gregory said he was surprised that the fight went as long as it did. "It was a lesson for the world, a health and body lesson. If you take the physical body God has given you and purify it, there's nothing that the body won't do for you. Anything made by the universal force won't get old. That's what it was, with the right mineral balance and combination of nutrients you can make it." I overheard one of the trainers remark, "He did 6,000 calisthenics. Six thousand. No athlete has ever done that."

New studies had come out which indicated that we know less about aging than we thought. Senility was being seen as a social, not physical,* phenomenon. The idea of waning intellectual powers among the elderly was under challenge. George Balanchine, the dancer, had a body which put many a teenager's to shame. I remembered a story from an old boxing magazine, about someone running into the retired Jack Johnson. He was

---

*A new theory, announced in 1982, says that senility is physical in origin and can be cured.

eager to fight Louis, and bothered Louis so he was banned from the Brown Bomber's training camp. The story revealed that Johnson knew of Louis's weakness—dropping his left after a lead—before Schmeling spotted it on film. How would a retired Johnson have made out against Joe Louis?

But then there was something unique about Ali. Bob Arum had put his finger on it. He argued that "elements of deterioration" had set in during Ali's layoff, just as they had to Louis during his army stint, and Jack Johnson after his exile abroad. But then he spoke of Ali's regenerative capacities. He said he'd seen three Ali's—The Supreme Court victory, the victory over Frazier, the defeat of George Foreman—and that Ali might win if he had a fourth Ali in him. That night in the Superdome we'd seen a fourth Ali.

He had his skills, he had his personality, and he had the will; what else did he have at ringside? Spinks's manager, George Benton, mentioned a "mystical force guiding Ali's life." After the Zaire fight, George Foreman's corner complained that Foreman didn't fight the fight that was planned. That he seemed distracted. After Spinks lost he said that his "mind wasn't on the fight." Was an incredible amount of "other" energy in Ali's corner? His devotion to Allah is well known.

Bob Arum said that Dick Gregory warned him to call home because his son had an accident. Arum called and it was true. Was Dick Gregory laying more than physical protection on the Champion? Did Dick Gregory have "second sight"?

A Miami customs official said that with the immigration laws as they are now, half of South America will be here in the next few years. On my last trip to New York I noticed storefronts to the Goddess of the Sea, Yemanya, were springing up around the West 90s. Among the people who came were the Cubans who hold Santaria ceremonies in their Miami apartments. The Cubans brought their cults. This Cuban, Luis Serra, was protected by Chango, the perfect loa of boxing, the warrior god of fire, thunder, and lightning.

It was a "mystical" night. The Superdome audience had watched a man turn the clock back, a rare event. I noticed pigeons inside, circling the Superdome, flying above the heads of the crowd.

Spinks's six-door white Lincoln Continental was brought up by a bald man, wearing dark glasses and an earring, named Mr. T. He was surrounded by a few people including his brother Michael. Spinks waved at some people who stood on a balcony. Nobody waved back. Somebody announced that Ali was holding a press conference upstairs. He was seated, flanked by Veronica Ali and Jayne Kennedy, the actress, who resembled each other so they could be sisters.

"Immona hold it six months. I'm going to go all over the world. Do you know what I did? I was great in defeat, can you imagine how great I am now? How many endorsements, how many movies, how many commercials I will get? I was great when I lost fights. I got eight months I can hold my title . . . mannnnnn. See how big I am? Can you imagine what will happen if I walk down the street in any city?

"Do you know I danced 15 rounds with a 25-year-old boy? I'm 36 years old. Man, do you realize how great I am now? The doctor checked my temperature and my blood, and took it to the hospital, and told Dick Gregory what I needed. Do you know how my stamina was up? Do you know what he told me to do?

"Take honey and ice cream 30 minutes before the fight. Half a pint of ice cream and five or six spoonfuls of real honey. My doctor told me to eat ice cream and honey. He gave me a big hunk of honey and melted ice cream. I didn't get tired. Did you see me explode all during the fight? I said, go!

"Spinks is a gentleman; he held my hand up. Spinks will beat Larry Holmes. Spinks will be champion again. He's going to be the second man to regain it twice. He'll have to do a lot to do it three times. But Spinks will be champion again. He's young, he's in good shape, he's going to fight Larry Holmes and be the champ.

"I'm the three-time champion. I'm the only man to win it three times. The greatest champion of all time. [Audience: "Of all time."] Of all time. Was I pretty? [Man in audience: "You was pretty."] Was I moving? Was I fighting? Was I sticking? Was I a Master?

"In eight months I'll let you know, I'll either retire or fight. Hold it eight months. Why give it back as hard as I worked? I'm getting old. Somebody is going to get me. I'm lucky I came back. See, I had you thinking I was washed up. You thought I was washed up. You really didn't know how great I was. You didn't know I just didn't train for the first fight. You thought I had trained and that was my best. Wasn't I much better this time than the first time? I'm older. I'm seven months older. Wasn't it a total difference?

"Mannnnn. Mannnnnnn. Mannnnnnnnnn. Mannnnnnnnnnnn. I was the best in this fight, let me tell you. I was training six months. My legs were running, I was chopping trees, running hills, watching my food. I said I cannot go out a loser; Jack Johnson went out a loser. Sugar Ray went out a loser. Joe Louis went out a loser. Of all the great fighters only Marciano and Tunney—two white ones—went out winners and everybody's talking about how great Marciano was, and how great Tunney was.

"I said, some black man has got to be smart enough to get by all these people. I got to be that black man who gets out on top. I went training early. I put all my tools together. I tricked you. I was separated from my wife, all my friends. Mannnnnn. Mannnnnnnn. [Audience, including urbane, sophisticated sports writers: "Mannnnnnnn."] Man, I got ready a book coming out for all school children. I hang up my robes, hang up my crown, and my trunks. *A Champion Forever.* A champion forever. A champion forever. Mannnnnnnn."

A reporter asked Ali did he think we'd hear from George Foreman again.

"You'll hear of George Foreman no more. I don't think he'll ever come back. Spinks will win the title. Spinks is not finished.

He just couldn't beat me. He'll beat Larry Holmes [takes a swig of Welch's grape juice].

"I have an announcement. Kris Kristofferson and Marlon Brando have just signed to make my movie, *Freedom Road*. We have a $6 million budget. Couple of more questions then I gotta celebrate. Mannnnnn, you come over to the Hilton and we gonna ball. Mannnnnn. My victory party. All y'all playboys come on over."

Trainer James Dudley said Ali won because "Class will tell." Ali's camp did everything according to script down to even the right kind of music. In the first fight with Spinks he was introduced with a movement from a Brahms symphony. In the second fight, "The Saints Come Marchin' In." Spinks's entrance was accompanied by the macho "Marine Hymn" which boasts of an illegal invasion of Mexico. So the people were joking about Spinks's style. A friend of mine predicted that Spinks would win the fight if he weren't arrested between leaving his dressing room and entering the ring. Ali made a joke at the mayor's reception about Spinks still owing a thousand dollars on his $500 suit. Not only did Spinks lose the fight but they had trouble backing his huge white car out of the Superdome.

The political, cultural, and entertainment establishments were rooting for Ali. His victory would be seen as another sign of sixtomania now sweeping the country because, even though some of his most heroic fights occurred in the '70s, he would still remind us of the turbulent decade, of Muslims, Malcolm X, Rap Brown, The Great Society, LBJ, Vietnam, General Hershey, dashikis, afros, Black Power, MLK, RFK. He represented the New Black of the 1960s, who was the successor to the New Negro of the 1920s, glamorous, sophisticated, intelligent, international, and militant.

The stars were for Ali, but the busboys were for Spinks. They said he lost because he was "too wild." His critics claimed that he drank in "New Orleans dives," where the stateside Palestinians hang out—the people the establishment has told to get lost.

The people who've been shunted off to the cities' ruins where they live next to abandoned buildings.

They could identify with Spinks. If they put handcuffs on him for a traffic offense, then they do the same thing to them. If he was tricked into signing for a longer period in the armed forces than he thought, the same thing happens to them. For seven months, he was "The People's Champ."

Ali and his party left the stadium, with people lined up on each side to say farewell to the champion. The night before, the streets were empty, but now they were crowded, reminding one of the excitement among the night crowds in American cities during the 1930s and 1940s, or when the expositions were held in St. Louis and Washington. The black players' bars were filling up. The traffic was bumper to bumper. Hundreds were standing outside the Hilton, or standing body to body inside of the hotel. In the French Quarter, many more moved down Bourbon Street as the sounds of B.B. King and Louis Armstrong came from the restaurants and bars. Every thirty-six year-old had a smile on his face.

After returning home I learned that Butch Lewis had been fired from the Top Rank Corporation for, according to Arum, taking a $200,000 scam. Don Hubbard told me that the press conference had been called by Ali, who had remained an extra day to blast two officers of Louisiana Sports, Jake DiMaggio and Phillip Ciaccio, for filing suit against the black partners, Don Hubbard and Sherman Copelin. Ali was joined by Joe Frazier and Michael and Leon Spinks. They wanted to show support for Butch Lewis.

Ali said that those who control boxing believed that "the black man's role in the sport should be limited to boxing and carrying the bucket while the white men count the money."

He said that if he heard any more about a suit against Copelin and Hubbard, he'd go see President Carter about the matter, or bring it up during his world tour. "I don't know all the details of this suit," he said, "but I know this is a racist suit."

I called Top Rank's Bob Arum. He said that Ali had apologized to him for the press conference. He'd talked to Ali the night before and accused Copelin, Hubbard, and Lewis of "steaming Ali up" so bad that Ali "got intemperate."

"Ali is contrite," Arum said. "Jesus, when they steam him up—they almost make him drunk on rhetoric. Everybody in Chicago is concerned. Herbert Muhammed leapt to my defense. Hubbard, Copelin, and Lewis concocted the press conference to attack me, but Ali thought they were attacking the other guys [DiMiaggio and Ciaccio]. Ali was ill-used and is going to say so today. I talked to Muhammed last night."

"Why did Spinks lose?"

"I thought Spinks was going to win based on his having George Benton as trainer," Arum said. "He lost because he received no guidance from his corner. None." I asked him about the quote attributed to him by *Newsweek* that Spinks was "drunk every night." *Sports Illustrated* repeated the claim.

"I didn't see him every night, but every time I saw him he was drunk. A young fighter can drink and abuse himself and not affect his conditioning, but it has a mental effect. Spinks has great raw talent. His wife, Nova, reputedly has joined the Muslims. If he joins the Muslims they will straighten him out. If he goes on like he is now, forget about him ever fighting again. His life will end up being a personal disaster."

Arum said he'd fired Butch Lewis because "I found out he was working a scam on me amounting to $200,000." It had been reported that Lewis received the amount as kickback from the fight in the form of letters of credit. I thought it incredible that Ali didn't know the contractual details of the "Battle of New Orleans" and asked Arum why he thought this was the case.

"He's easily deceived," Arum said. Would Arum promote another Ali fight? He said that he'd do nothing to encourage Ali to fight again. There was a rumor making the rounds, the source of which he said was Dr. Ferdie Pacheco, Ali's former doctor, whose book *Fight Doctor* annoyed Ali. The rumor was repeated in *Newsweek* and *New York* magazine, whispering that Ali is showing the symptoms of brain damage. I taped a press conference that Ali gave after a grueling fifteen rounds in the ring with a twenty-five-year-old man and detected not one bit of slurring or any lapses in his usual comical brilliance. In fact, he could have been a Bible-toting Kentucky evangelist on the stump; the audience in the room belonged to him. They were spellbound by his oratory. Had he commanded, they would have permitted him to walk out of the room on their backs.

DiMaggio and Ciaccio sued Hubbard and Copelin, but later withdrew the suit saying it was the result of a misunderstanding. The "internal problems," Hubbard said, "had been resolved." "We don't want to spread our dirty linen all over the nation." But according to a report from KDIA Oakland Thursday night, September 28, the linen would be spread and the scavengers would dine. A grand jury was going to look into the promotion of the second Spinks-Ali fight.

Ali apologized just as Arum said he would. He termed his press conference "unfortunate."

"Certain people whom I regarded as my friends gave me a distorted version of events, which so enraged me that I made unthinkable, angry remarks. I never met Mr. Ciaccio or Mr. DiMaggio and hold no personal animosity. Even if they are wrong I should not have called them a name, particularly a name which offends a whole nation of people."

DiMaggio had threatened Ali with a $10 million suit unless he returned to New Orleans to "apologize" for the remarks Ali made against him.

In defending Arum, Herbert Muhammed said, "He came to me with a contract to guarantee Ali $3 million, $250,000 for training expenses, and $250,000 for any other sources of expenses, and Butch Lewis came to me working for Top Rank, and Arum's a white man. And Lewis is a white man. And Top Rank is a white organization, so I think Ali was not that informed."

Toward the end of his extraordinary Monday press conference, Ali indicated that "Blue-eyed Jesuses" and "Tarzan, King of the Jungle" were on his mind, which reminds us of Tarzan's Anglo origin and that, in many black churches, Jesus resembles Basil Rathbone. This brings us to Ali's last challenge: The Anglo-Saxon Curse on black Heavyweight Champions.

"The white hope" legend was born in the mythic Pacific White Republic of California—Atlantis—with its Anglo-Saxon ruling capital, the city by the golden gate. Early California poetry boasts of how the Anglo-Saxons were destined to conquer and rule California and become its supreme race. Jack London was the lingering myth's chief philosopher and fantasist and, for London and others, when Jack Johnson defeated Jim Jefferies, the claim of Anglo-Saxon superiority received a severe setback, and they went scrambling about to find someone to break Jack Johnson. Finally, as a historian observed, the white hope appeared in the form of legislation: the Mann Act.

The pride blacks felt in Johnson's victory led them to celebrate. They were lynched for "boasting." Other victims were accused of "strutting about." "Frenzied Negroes Exasperate the Whites," screamed headlines in the *London Daily Express*, July 6, 1910.

A curse seemed to be laid that, thereafter, black champions would retire in defeat, "the good ones," like Joe Louis and Ezzard Charles, suffering as much as the "bad guys," Sonny Liston, possibly killed. If he's a historian as I believe he is, Ali will retire, undefeated. If he's a "businessman" as he said at his press conference, he'll fight Larry Holmes for "the other" championship, and Miss Velvet Green, the phantom woman who attends his fights, her chauffeur-driven car outside the stadium, will be there at ringside, awaiting Ali's destruction. She won't be the only one.

1978

PART 3

Odds & Ends

MONEY CAN'T BUY YOU LOVE

The United Airlines pilot announced that the temperature in Oakland was eighty-five degrees. I was groggy after traveling to Washington, Philadelphia, Detroit, and Chicago within the month, but that announcement got my attention. It didn't sound right. The night before, Oakland came up during a conversation I was having with *Essence* magazine editor in chief Susan Taylor, who was sitting next to me on the dais at a tribute to poet Gwendolyn Brooks. I told her how much I admired an article her magazine had done on the city. It was one of those infrequent journalistic pieces that didn't dwell on Oakland's "negatives." Poet and publisher Haki Madhubuti, who had arranged for this tribute to take place at the University of Chicago, asked me how things were in California.

I told him that the state was running out of money and water and that the California Dream was over. (After the heavy rains of the 1992–93 winter season, the drought was declared over.) I had recently written an article for a national magazine in which I tried to balance Oakland's "positives" with its "negatives," having made the downtown "furious" over an *Image* magazine article about the Oakland crack wars. I even pushed the magazine to include a photo of Preservation Park, the circle of Victorians that was restored for the use of nonprofit and profit organizations and that I think is an example of Oakland at its best. But in the course of the piece, I mentioned that Oakland suffered from a city's version of the Kennedy Curse. I was talking about the 1989 earthquake, from which the city still hadn't recovered. It didn't occur to me at the time that the Kennedy tragedies had a tendency to come in twos.

Sometimes it appears that entities are transmitting warnings to us. We dismiss these experiences with terms like *coincidence*. The morning of that earthquake, I told dancer-choreographer Carla Blank that the night before, I had dreamed of a disaster. In the dream, there were images of fire and emergency vehicles. Since the weekend of October 10, 1992, I had been writing an article in my head and taking notes about a scene I'd witnessed in Washington, D.C. I took pictures of a mob gathering outside of the Russell Building, where inside, a black judge seemed to be taking the heat for the male domination that has happened over the centuries. The newspapers were calling the feminist reaction to the charges of alleged "sexual harassment" brought by Anita Hill against Clarence Thomas a "firestorm."

I kept turning the image of firestorm over in my mind. Regardless of whether Anita Hill was lying (the majority of Americans thought so) or whether Clarence Thomas was lying (the Northeast media establishment and its Harvard-Princeton talented tenthers believed her), I was wondering why it took this charge against a black judge for the feminist movement, which a growing number of black feminists are criticizing for its racism, to ignite this firestorm. "Where was this firestorm of rage when a black student was raped at St. John's University?" I had written in one version. I came up with something clumsy, like "This firestorm seems to conduct its heat only toward those members of society who are the most flammable—in this case, a black man." In Chicago, on Saturday night, I had written this sentence on the Hyatt Regency notepad. The image of a firestorm was on my mind as I exited from the terminal.

As I walked toward my car, I saw a huge and ugly black cloud looming over Oakland, a cloud that seemed to become larger as I drove up Highway 880.

Upon arriving home, I went upstairs to check some messages on the upstairs phone and from the deck, which provides a sweeping view of the Oakland Hills and the top of the Claremont Hotel, a building so ancient that in pictures of early Berkeley it seems to stand alone. I noticed some red spots scattered through the hills and dismissed them as windows reflecting the sun. But then the flares seemed to grow. I called down to Carla. She came up and stood alongside me and was as shocked as I. In the next half-hour, more flares went up. We spent the next hour alternating between watching television and watching the Claremont Hotel, toward which the fire seemed to be heading (it was halted within 200 feet of the hotel, and the Berkeley fire chief said that if it hadn't been stopped there, it would have reached the Bay). On Fifty-third Street, neighbors began to gather outside or stake out positions on rooftops. There came reports that people were beginning to be evacuated from the Oakland Hills.

I jested to Carla and my daughter, Tennessee, that if we had to leave, I'd grab ahold of the TV sets. But after a few more hours, I stopped making jokes. The announcement that the fire might reach Fifty-first Street and Broadway made me very nervous.

When cinders began to land on my deck and near the ground in front of the house, we began to pack some things: "important" papers, credit cards, and whatever checks and cash were lying around the house. I began to consider making reservations at the Emeryville Holiday Inn.

Earlier, Tennessee had asked whether our house would be burned. At first, I said that the chances were remote. But by 6:00 p.m., I wasn't sure. There were reports that the fire was approaching Montclair and Piedmont, and then a shocking report came in that Broadway Terrace had been devastated. Carla phoned her friend Nancy Maynard. There was no answer. She wanted to drive over to Nancy's to see whether she was all right, but I told her that she'd probably get in the way of the traffic. (Miraculously, the fire was stopped within a few feet of Bob and Nancy's house.) I called my brother, Michael LeNoir, who lives in Montclair, and there was no answer at his home either.

The television coverage was confusing me. One station switched from coverage of the fire to "Dynasty," and I couldn't tell which was in jeopardy—the Carrington mansion or a $2 million mansion located behind the Claremont Hotel. I tried to tune into KPFA, which had been carrying a marathon salute to Anita Hill. The fact that the left-wing station was bonding with a Bork-Reagan conservative made perfect sense on this surreal day.

KPFA is valuable because it usually provides the subtext for national and local crises by airing in-depth and informed commentary, rather than sound bites. The station wasn't on the air.

I knew that this fire was serious when my parents called from Buffalo to ask whether we were all right; the Oakland fire we had been witnessing had made national news. I stayed up until about 2:00 A.M., when there came a report that the progress of the fire had been contained behind some perimeters.

The next day, the media covered a controversy about whether a grass fire that erupted on Saturday could have been brought under control. This line was taken up by some of the media, but rarely did the finger-pointing callers on talk shows mention the Oakland fire and police personnel who lost their lives, or the hundreds of gallant firefighters from Berkeley and Oakland who risked their lives battling this rapacious red monster.

The class divisions had been temporarily suspended by this act of God, during which those who were still homeless from the last Oakland catastrophe and for whom every day is a catastrophe helped those who fled their mansions. In comparison to some of those Oakland Hills homes, Mount Vernon, the place I'd visited about ten days before, seemed modest. But as soon as most of the hot spots were doused, the class divisions reappeared. Some of the affluent homeless and the media seemed to be blaming a black city administration for the fire. I felt sorry for the youthful fire chief, P. Lamont Ewell. The poor guy hadn't been on the job for a month, and here he was being blamed for one of the worst fires in American history. He would possibly rank with Mrs. O'Leary as one of the all-time goats in American history.

There was also resentment in the flats over the outpouring of aid to the middle class and to the wealthy hill dwellers, aid that was denied to many of the West Oakland blacks who'd been victims of the earthquake, though many of the hill dwellers were renters of modest means. My barber, Eloisa, lost her home, and she isn't wealthy.

Some of the flatlanders seem to be gleeful over the fact that some people, whom they regarded as well-off, were "getting theirs," an attitude that Leo Bazile was right to call "sick." Only one or two KPFA and KQED callers placed the blame where it really belonged: on our age of selfishness and greed, in which people are scammed by these blow-dried, face-lifted commodities called politicians into believing that they can have civilization without paying for it. The California Barbarians, who got through Proposition 13, created the conditions for the Oakland Hills conflagration when they passed a measure that told the poor and the public school students to go stick it. These are the hoarding fatuous who have lynched our educational system, are in the process of destroying one of the world's great universities, and have closed the libraries. They're the reason we don't have the firefighters or the equipment. They're the reason we don't have enough police on the streets, so that our neighborhoods, both urban and suburban, have been taken over by crack dealers, both the Nike-wearing type and the bankers who hold their money. Though the governor was saluted by Oakland's mayor for his prompt action, I know him as the man who made a joke about welfare recipients spending their cash on six-packs, and I remember his opposition to a measure that would allow the kids in Richmond to finish their school year.

Handing these cities over to black officials without providing them with the revenue to run them and then blaming them when a catastrophe happens must be the 1990s version of gallows humor. Mayor Elihu Harris had every right to be angry, barking like Patton at stupid questions, stepping over debris. Opinion professionals said this wasn't the way that spin doctors and media consultants would have handled it. I was glad to see someone express what was on his mind. A politician with a genuine emotion. They all said he was aloof and cold, but now that he's shown that he's the guy to be on your side in a crisis, they're calling him testy and touchy.

He wasn't the only person who rose to the occasion during this crisis. In the midst of all of the bickering and friction and Monday-morning quarterbacking, and all of the talk about the class in society that has insurance and those who don't, and all of the esoteric discussions about land use and ecology, and all of the people not feeling sorry for the lawyers and doctors and professors who live in the hills, there came the moment for me that defined this tragedy in an eloquence worthy of Sophocles. That was when the sometimes stiff and guarded Marge Gibson-Haskells, her face a classic mask of grief, stepped before the microphones and said, "I lost my house. It was the house in which my child was born and where I married my husband." That was when I felt the suffering of those people, regardless of their bank balances, who had been driven from their homes. The Beatles said it all: "Money can't buy you love."

For a few moments on Sunday night, when it appeared certain that Oakland was experiencing another catastrophe, we started to think of moving elsewhere. Tennessee said she wanted to live in upstate New York near her grandparents. I said that Washington, D.C., looked very good to me. Carla agreed. But we'll probably stay in Oakland. Why? There was a line I was going to use in the magazine article that I dropped because I thought it to be corny. Something like "Oakland is like a journeyman fighter, bloodied and battered, one eye nearly shut, jaw swollen, behind on points, but still capable of a comeback during the last ten seconds of the twelfth round." I have a hunch that Oakland will not only come back, but thrive. We live in Oakland because of its fighting spirit.

1991

Reading, Writing, and Racism

Two incidents, both occurring during my first year in elementary school, would characterize the ups and downs I would experience throughout my "formal" education. One was that I wrote my name for the first time and was so delighted I ran home. The other was that I was slapped to the ground by a teacher, with no reason ever given for what by today's standards amounted to child abuse. After the latter incident, my mother withdrew me from the school. (Later, in seventh grade, I was literally punched out by a teacher. She was always accusing me of thinking I was the "whole show" during assembly programs. Like the first grade teacher who slapped me, she was white.) Even when my grades were high, I was regarded as a discipline problem.

There were other, more pleasant experiences; a black teacher, a singer who used to give me concert tickets, who looked out for me in elementary school; three white music teachers who were also very kind. In elementary school, high school and college, I performed in orchestras and bands. In high school I was a member of a string quartet. I also remember a high school teacher, a professional actress, who taught us Shakespeare with much more understanding than any college professor I ever had.

But in those days, the school curriculum was what nowadays

would be called "Eurocentric," a term I have problems with, since it lumps the points of view of cosmopolitan European scholars and intellectuals with the points of view of anti-intellectuals in the United States, such as those who oppose bilingual education and those who write op-eds and letters to the editor criticizing the "diversity" movement in education with arguments that are ignorant and spiteful. Some of our leading intellectuals are on record with the opinion that no literature exists in what they refer to as "Sub Sahara" Africa, the kind of thought that gives the mass-media-created American intelligentsia a bad rep all over the world.

I enjoyed and still enjoy the West's literature and music, but I was always curious about how people of my background fit in. The treatment of African and African American culture in our education was no different from their treatment in Tarzan movies. While in elementary school, I used to go to a flea-market type bookstore and buy pamphlets about black history written by J. A. Rogers, a black Pullman porter who spent a considerable amount of his private funds visiting world libraries to research African history and culture. But I was so brainwashed I refused to believe the information in his famous pamphlet, *One Hundred Amazing Facts about the Negro*. If Hannibal was black, for instance, wouldn't I have learned it in school? Later, while working as a thirteen-year-old printer's devil at a community newspaper where I was exposed to adult black intellectuals, I discovered that much of Rogers's information could be corroborated.

In school, most of the information about black history was confined to a description of blacks as happy-go-lucky people who were having a swell time until they were inconvenienced by their emancipation. Robert E. Lee, a traitor in anybody else's history, was held in higher esteem than Ulysses Grant, who was viewed as having brought this charming Southern experience to an end.

We were taught that being black wasn't such a terrific thing, which is why I guess Jesse Jackson remarked at Sammy Davis Jr.'s funeral that Davis believed he could do anything because without a "formal" education there hadn't been anybody to tell him he couldn't.

My discovery of black culture began in the 1960s when I was working for the same community newspaper I'd worked for as a teen-ager and met Malcolm X. He taught me that an intellectual life could be exciting, not just an activity in which one spent one's time harvesting footnotes. Later I met black nationalists in New York, an experience that broadened my knowledge of black culture.

When I came to California I became aware of the United States as a global civilization, a knowledge that has shaped my education from the late '60s to the present. In my adult years I've found that private tutors, the best in their fields, work better for me than classrooms. Throughout my life, even while attending school, I've designed my own curriculum.

But what about the children who aren't as fortunate as I was to have worked for a black newspaper during my early teens? Who weren't exposed to the Second Renaissance in black culture of the 1960s and whose parents can't afford the kinds of intellectual resources that were available to me? Maybe the reason a number of studies reveal little difference between the intellectual caliber of students who drop out of school or stay in, between those who qualify for college and those who don't, is that Hispanic, African American and Asian American children don't receive any information about where they fit into the world and into American culture. And the white students, exposed to cheap travel and television and cultural trends like world music, know the world is larger than the one they learned about in school, a depiction which, like a Dark Ages map of the world, holds that if you sail intellectually beyond something misnamed Western civilization (since only a fraction of European culture is taught in American schools), you drop entirely off the face of the earth.

A 1989 study compiled by the school of education at the State

University of New York in Albany reveals that very few books by minority authors are used in elementary or high schools. To its credit, the American Federation of Teachers resolved at a convention in July to try to change this situation. "Our children need the full picture, the whole truth, as best it is understood," they said in the resolution they adopted.

I wonder what my attitude toward my "formal" education would have been had I been exposed to the kind of education my 13-year-old, Tennessee, receives at the New Age Academy in Berkeley, where she learns, not only about Western civilization, but about African and Asian and Native American civilizations as well. I think that if I had had the opportunity to attend a school like that, my experience—characterized by intermittent pleasure, but mostly by dread and boredom—would have been different. When I was a kid, I always regretted the end of summer vacation.

1990

The Be-Bop Revival

In early March, Tom Babbitt, a drummer and one of my students, told me about some "new music" he wanted me to hear. I'm getting old and grumpy, but decided to give some of his "new music" a go. At his apartment he played some pieces by a group which sounded as though it had some influence over at Con Edison. But beneath the pretty technology I could discern the faint traces of what we, in my days, called "Be-Bop" or "Bop." I lent Babbitt my Prestige 7150, an album which included work by Miles Davis, Milt Jackson, Thelonious Monk, Percy Heath, Kenny Clarke, John Coltrane, Red Garland, Paul Chambers, Philly Joe Jones, to show that there wasn't anything "new" at all about the music Babbitt played.

A few weeks later, student Mark Wolfson, a red-haired pianist, who belongs to the U.C. Jazz Ensemble, played some ideas around "Night in Tunisia," as some students and I sat talking in the student pub, The Bear's Lair. Towards the end of March I listened with a group of Haida, and Tlingit Indians, to Kaw/Creek musician Jim Pepper, in the Shee Atika Lodge, in Sitka, Alaska, as he played an amazing fusion of Native-American and Be-Bop music. He was assisted by a black bass guitarist, his group nicknamed "the Tasmanian Devil." In April, some friends and I listened to Randy Weston, in the Hideaway, a

Berkeley restaurant, as he reminisced about his youthful Brooklyn days when he attended sessions with Thelonious Monk and Charlie Parker. "Bird's presence was always greeted with awe," Weston said. Weston left me an album called "Rhythms and Sounds Piano," which was solidly in the Be-Bop tradition.

Last week I visited a club in Harvard Square with a Chicano novelist, Puerto-Rican American poet and the executive director of the Coordinating Council of Literary Magazines. We heard a group called "Kansas City," which was composed of three young guitarists, two black and one white. They were going over some speedy Birdlike changes which to my ear sounded like "Back Home in Indiana," though there was nothing Hoosier, or corny about the work. Be-Bop, even when Diz clowned, was never corny. It was a hip, sophisticated music which suffered persecution similar to the colonial suppression of Native American and African religions. The critics didn't like it. The older musicians poked fun at it. The police seemed to want to lock up anybody caught playing it. Its exponents were ridiculed and scorned by both white and black public. John Coltrane, Tadd Dameron, Charlie Parker, Bud Powell, Paul Chambers, Fats Navarro, Richie Powell, Lee Morgan, Kenny Dorham, Cannonball Adderley, Eric Dolphy died young. A genius, Clifford Brown, was killed on the New Jersey turnpike about a year after recording a tune called "Turnpike." With the exception of the San Francisco Bohemian suicide poets, I can think of no other modern art movement with as many casualties.

I asked Martha Young, Lester's cousin, who plays at a Berkeley nightclub called Solomon Grundy's, why she played so much Be-Bop. "It's the music I grew up on," she said.

We not only grew up on Be-Bop; Be-Bop raised us. For my generation, Be-Bop came on like a light bulb going flash behind the eyes. For us, it was not only an intellectual movement, but a way of life. We walked, dressed, and rapped Be-Bop. When Norman Granz came to Buffalo the Be-Boppers bopped up and down the aisle so much, the staid Kleinhans Music Hall forbade the music after that. Be-Boppers carried new ideas across the trade routes of America. I first heard talk of Islam from Buffalo's Wade Legge, a pianist with Mingus, Gigi Gryce, and who was with Diz in Paris when they recorded "The Champ"; Babs Gonzales scatted. Legge, discovered by Milt Jackson at Buffalo's musician's local, died at twenty-nine.

The Be-Boppers weren't like the ordinary black men we knew. They were unconventional, "weird," confident; they sneered at bourgeois morality. They called themselves "Lord" and "King." They were fast. Ideas racing through their heads like Ferraris. One Bop classic was Denzil Best's "Move." And there was Billy Eckstine singing "Jelly Roll Killed My Pappy."

When we wanted to impress the high school girls we'd crow a few lines from "Moody's Mood for Love," as if we were King Pleasure. And then, there was the night when our hero, Miles Davis, showed up to perform at a dingy nightclub on William Street. I was the only one brave enough to ask for his autograph. It was September 21, 1955, and Miles, who shared the program with Eddie "Lockjaw" Davis, took time out to listen to the fight between Rocky Marciano and Archie Moore. I had just returned from Paris and told Miles how much the Europeans liked his music.

To some musicians the Europeans have always been more hospitable to Be-Bop than the Americans. That's why some of the movement went into exile: Randy Weston, Kenny Clarke, Bud Powell, Lucky Thompson, Art Farmer, Cecil Payne, Dexter Gordon, Johnny Griffin.

Perhaps the recognition is coming at home as well. I mean, if twenty years ago, somebody had told me that the president of the United States would one day join Max Roach and Dizzy Gillespie in a chorus of "Salt Peanuts," I would have said, "you're jiving." Nor would I have believed that "Georgia," the tune Kenny Clarke's group played for us in Paris, two years ago, would have become the Georgia state song.

We've talked for years, until we've become red in the face, about how geniuses of the Afro-American music tradition should be accorded the same financial security, grants, university residences, and all of the fringes that the geniuses of the Euro-American traditions receive. Wouldn't it have been swell if, like Horowitz and others, Earl Hines were economically secure enough to perform just once a year like Horowitz and others do.

And so I think that the Be-Bop revival is a wonderful thing. Tadd Dameron, the poet-composer, said that Be-Bop was like walking down a peaceful country road where on each side stood bountiful fruit trees and boughs weighed down with birds. But for some, it was a journey through hell where demons lurked to ensnare the artist. That doesn't matter anymore. What matters is that the spirit of Be-Bop has infused another generation, our children, and that's about all an art movement can ask for. To be remembered, to be cherished, to enlighten. A new generation growing up on it, being raised by it.

The Be-Boppers provided a quantum leap in American music, but they were not limited to one culture. They were international, multicultural, and worldly men, at home in Osaka as well as in Amsterdam. They often took their titles from the sciences, including astronomy. Like the science-fiction space music in the revolutionary document "Birth of the Cool." That's appropriate because Be-Bop came to us like a bright comet from another galaxy, recurrent, permanent.

1979

Savages and Liberators

Though viewed as an intellectual lightweight, former President Ronald Reagan's passionate beliefs about European destiny are no different from those of many American intellectuals, artists, academics and poets like Robert Frost of "The Gift Outright." Frost believed that the present United States was a gift to Europeans by god; their goal was to create in this land mass "A City on the Hill," which would, I imagine, have the complexion of Salt Lake City and where the muzak would pipe in songs by Nelson Eddy and Jeanette MacDonald, and where the only movie available would be *King's Row*.

Christopher Columbus, we should remember, was the expendable pawn of Queen Isabella, under whose regime the Moors and the Jews were expelled from Spain. As soon as she believed that Columbus no longer served her interests, she had him jailed and replaced. Columbus's mission was driven by her greed, and evidence that Isabella didn't trust Columbus lies in the fact that she sent her accountant, Rodrigo Sanchez de Segovia, on the voyage, so that she wouldn't be cheated out of her share of the loot. It was Segovia, not Columbus, who first sighted land and it was with Segovia, the first yuppie, that the United States' bottom line obsession began. While the natives viewed the lush natural riches as something to be shared by all

(Columbus writes: "But they will give all that they do possess for anything that is given to them"), Segovia probably envisioned the produce department of one of our present-day multinational food chains, and was probably measuring the cost of each pound of goods.

This being said, Columbus's description of the cultures that he found is quite different from the prevalent opinion that the Americas were uninhabited, or cultureless before the arrival of the Europeans. Indeed, after so many history lessons which view the arrival of the Europeans as a "civilizing" rescue mission, a view held by the majority of those in the United States' history profession, it is Columbus who presents evidence to the contrary. Compare the physical suffering, malnutrition, and disease that afflict millions of South and Central Americans with Columbus's description of the health of the Arawaks he encountered: "They were very well built with fine bodies and handsome faces." Though they are still considered savages, these indigenous people were capable of a number of skills and arts including navigation ("They came to the ship in boats which are made from tree-trunks, like a long boat all cut out of a single log. They are marvelously carved in the native style and they are so big that forty or fifty-five men came in them") and needlecraft (bringing the invaders "balls of cotton" and living in houses that were clean and "well swept" with "beds and blankets . . . like cotton nets"). They built furniture with "strangely shaped wooden seats in the form of animals with short fore- and rear-paws and tails slightly raised to support the back." They also invented hammocks. They were devoted to body aesthetics, painting and decorating themselves like the models for *Vogue* and *Harper's* and Columbus provides innumerable examples of their creation of fine art objects. After one landing, the natives gave Columbus "masks with eyes and large ears of gold and other beautiful objects which they wore round their necks." Columbus also gives the natives credit for the cultivation of food—sweet potatoes, yucca, corn, and kidney beans. This diet was supplemented by fish and game. Unlike other custodians of the Americas, the natives Columbus encountered were also good managers of the environment. Columbus describes lands that are "all delightfully green." Though it's hard for some American historians and intellectuals to imagine, the societies of Africa and the West Indies were doing all right before the Spanish and the Portuguese arrived. When the Portuguese entered Yoruba land, one of three ancestral homes of most African Americans, they found a society with a currency, a market economy, a language more complex than Japanese, a religion that still claims millions of followers not only in Africa but the Americas, a system of laws, and an art that is still exhibited and admired. Columbus was aware that such societies existed in the Americas. When he reaches Cuba, he hears of the Aztecs and Mayans.

Bent upon justifying the devastation that was begun by Spanish and Portuguese scouting expeditions into Africa, South America, and Asia, revisionist historians are scurrying about seeking blame-the-victim scenarios. The main reason for the slave trade, we are told, was the "African Chieftains," who delivered slaves to Yankee slavers. In their view, these slavers just happened to be wandering by the coast of west Africa. Some of the historians and cultural critics-at-large who hold this view are the same neoconservatives who blame the contemporary drug problem on the demand side, while attributing the African slave trade to the supply side.

Typical of the monocultural spin on the European invasion of the Americas is that offered by Professor of History at Harvard University Stephen Thernstrom. He must have a large following among American "educators" because his article "The Columbus Controversy" was printed in both *The American School Board Journal* and *American Educator,* published by the American Federation of Teachers. Further proof that the current educational system is dividing American society with a school curriculum that's based upon white pride, ethnocentric boasting rather than global culture and ideas. No wonder David Duke is the leader of the Eurocentric movement.

While admitting that the European invasion led to the deci-
mation of the native population, Thernstrom, after denigrating
the cultures of the Americas, and even blaming the Aztecs for
polluting the environment, concludes that "The European invasion five centuries ago exposed a large portion of the globe to the
influence of a questing and dynamic civilization that did much
to make the modern world what it is." Of course, if hundreds of
millions of Europeans had been slaughtered and enslaved, as
were Africans and Native Americans, in order to expose them to
"the influence of a questing and dynamic civilization," I'm sure
that Mr. Stephen Thernstrom and the publications he writes for
would have a different outlook about the arrival of Columbus.
Using Mr. Thernstrom's standard, one could say that Genghis
Khan and the Moors who invaded Europe from China and
Africa "exposed a large portion of the globe to the influence of
. . . questing and dynamic civilizations," according to Charles J.
Halperin's *Russia and the Golden Hordes* and Ivan Van Sertima's
The Golden Age of the Moors; but while Eurocentric historians look
upon these invaders as infidels and hordes, Columbus and his
people are seen as, in the words of Mr. Thernstrom, "liberators";
and though he boasts that in the United States "identity based
on blood ties has been replaced by the broader identity," by describing the European invaders as "liberators" *his* blood ties are
showing.

Though Columbus is viewed as a villain, his picture of the
lands he encountered is much more positive than that presented
by your average contemporary Eurocentric historian, which tells
you a lot about the people who construct our school curriculum.
In their minds, those who brought such colossal destruction are
viewed as "liberators," while those who extended great generosity to guests with evil intent (Columbus writes: "I asked them
for water, and after I had returned to the ship they came down to
the beach with their gourds full and gave it to us with delight")
are viewed as "savages."

Finally, is the hemisphere better off than it was five hundred
years ago? Is a society like the Inca, which fed everybody, ac-

cording to Mario Vargas Llosa, superior to a "modern" society where millions of people suffer from malnutrition and use the garbage cans for a cafeteria? Is "modern" civilization worth the threat that its poisonous by-products pose to the survival of humanity? Could it be that the human calamity caused by the arrival of Columbus was a sort of dress rehearsal of what is to come, as the ozone becomes more depleted, the earth warms, and the rain forests are destroyed?

1992

Silencing the Hordes

The phrase "the Mongol hordes" conjures images of crazed Tartar barbarians, raping and pillaging Russia in the Middle Ages. Charles J. Halperin, in his book *Russia and the Golden Horde,* presents a more balanced picture. He concludes that the effect of the Chinese invasion on Russia's development was clearly very great, contributing to its commerce and to the establishment of the Russian Orthodox church. Such contributions were denied through what Halperin refers to as the ideology of silence: refusing to admit that such an invasion even took place, or Russian historians distorting the achievements of the Chinese. These historians, in Halperin's words, were motivating European feelings of superiority. Similar techniques have been used to deny or denigrate the enormous influence of Afro-Americans on American culture.

Rock and roll, a form of musical expression created by blacks, has created a multibillion-dollar industry, yet when the all-white jury at *Rolling Stone* magazine chose the one hundred best singles by rock-and-roll artists of the past twenty-five years, Mick Jagger, a black imitator, came in first and Marvin Gaye ranked fourth.

A San Francisco novelist appearing on the *Today* show during the week of the Republican convention commented on the Irish,

German, Creole, and Cajun influence upon New Orleans culture but made no mention of the influence by Afro-Americans, without whom there would be no distinct New Orleans cuisine, architecture, music, or language. Ann Rice should read *Gumbo Ya Ya*, a 581-page book compiled by the Louisiana Writers Project and available in paperback. Langston Hughes said they'd taken his blues and gone, and now they've taken bebop. Clint Eastwood, who made a fortune in beat-up-a-black-man-and-feel-good-about-it movies, is being promoted by *Esquire* as the definitive interpreter of Charlie Parker's life. Next thing you know, Prime Minister Botha will be directing *The Nelson Mandela Story*.

Most of the books about the 1960s are written by American Princes like the ones at *Rolling Stone,* who locate themselves at the center of the American cultural and political solar system while the rest of us are viewed as so much dust and gas. It took a German writer to take issue with Paul Berman, who wrote that "Tom Hayden was the single greatest figure of the 1960s student movement." William W. Hansen of Enkenbach, West Germany, in a letter to the *Times,* cited the contributions of black students John Lewis, Julian Bond, Marion Barry, and Bob Moses.

Black-pathology careerist Nathan Glazer, writing in the *New Republic,* proposes a novel theory of geography. He believes that people who live on one side of a desert are smarter than those who live on the opposite side. He denies the existence of a literary tradition in what he refers to as Sub-Sahara Africa, when, just as the Roman and Greek pantheon of myths and legends produced Horace and Virgil, the African pantheon has produced hundreds of writers, from the early storytellers to Wole Soyinka, and in our own hemisphere, Nicholas Gullen, Langston Hughes, and others. Glazer ought to take a class in Afro-American literature from Werner Sollars, a German who teaches at Harvard, or read *Neo-African Literature,* a history of black writing, by the late Janheinz Jahn, also a German.

If left up to the mean minds that now dominate American cultural opinion, a thousand years from now Afro-Americans will be viewed as black hordes whose only contributions to civilization were crack dealers, out-of-wedlock babies, and welfare dependency. But unlike the Mongol hordes, smeared for all time by Russian historians, African American culture will not be erased from history because there are European, Asian, and African scholars who will make a different witness, and with the introduction of desktop publishing software and inexpensive video technology, black artists and scholars will be able to tell their side of the story as well.

Ms. Gore's Crusade

Where will Ms. Tipper Gore's crusade end? Will she and her colleagues demand the banning of "The Lady Is a Tramp" or "Love for Sale" as an invitation to prostitution? What about some of the great Cole Porter's drug lines?

Certainly rap, a style that's deeply rooted in the black oral tradition, includes some offensive lyrics. But in her negative and indolent surveys, Ms. Gore doesn't mention any of the rap artists like Big Daddy Kane—a favorite among children in the ghetto where I live—who urges children to stay in school and to avoid drugs and violence.

Even Ice T advocates these values in his rap record "You Played Yourself," a powerful antidrug song that also condemns extravagant consumerism.

Ms. Gore ignorantly lumps all rap music together, and in the process denigrates the creative achievements of many young people.

Does rap music lead to rape? The overwhelming majority of rapes in this country are committed by white males, who know their victims. Why doesn't Ms. Gore criticize their tastes? I'm sure that a lot of white rapists listen to country-western music.

In a culture whose multibillion-dollar media industry can't seem to sell a bag of cookies without degrading women, or pimping their flesh, Ms. Gore seems unable to locate degrading and denigrating images anywhere *but* in rap music (or heavy metal), and all she knows about rap music—this complex art form—is what she hears about on "The Oprah Winfrey Show," a program aired at a time when most Americans are at work.

Also, if Ms. Gore is so concerned about the self-esteem of blacks, why doesn't she campaign against the lopsidedly negative images of blacks promoted by the television news and entertainment shows? During the National Medical Association's ninety-fourth annual convention, Dr. John T. Chissel, a family practitioner from Boston, said that the media images of blacks contribute to feelings of self-loathing among youth, and influence the physical and psychological well-being of blacks in general. Does anybody expect a politician's wife to lead a campaign against the media?

I'm waiting for Ms. Gore and her feminist allies to address some major misogyny, like the Bush administration's cynical invocation of the safety of white womanhood in order to win an election, or to justify its "incursion" into Panama at the cost of thousands of lives, and the displacement of thousands of people. Or the pornographic pandering of a female "bait" in order to ensnare the mayor of Washington, an act that not only qualified the government as the world's biggest crack dealer, but the biggest pimp as well.

Though Ms. Gore says that people pay more attention to racism than to sexism, the military and the police seem to see their mission as protecting white women (the Stuart case in Boston, in which a white man wrongly accused a black man of his wife's murder, and the resulting gestapo aggression against Boston's black males by the police are an example).

Finally, one suspects that somebody like Ms. Gore would criticize rap music even if it were without lyrics. After a decade of the establishment pushing quiet, cautious, and safe black art and journalism of the kind that preaches self-reliance for the poor and none for the rich and the middle class, and of the establishment scapegoating black men for all of the country's social problems, along come the rappers with a style that is sassy, militant, energetic, original, and avant-garde. Some uptight folks find this difficult to deal with, just as their ideological ancestors, the Salem Puritans—who banned theater and Christmas—were so bothered by Barbadian culture that the entire village came down with what the Salem tour guides refer to as "hysteria."

To Be an American
Is to Be Fair

One night in 1948, I came home from my newspaper route, to find our project's apartment deserted. My folks had gone to Buffalo's train station to greet Harry Truman, who was always talking about fairness and the humanity of the common, everyday working person. Harry Truman had desegregated the armed forces, and for my working-class parents, epitomized the hope that, though segregation was persisting—in those days, blacks were not merely beaten by the police but lynched by mobs—the United States was moving toward a fair and equitable society. Having been born in the South, my parents had experienced the ugly side of the American personality, but Harry Truman and his predecessor, Franklin Roosevelt, gave them hope.

Four years later, I wanted to see what my young parents saw in this man, Harry Truman. In 1952, I attended Harry Truman's speech at Buffalo's Memorial Auditorium and was impressed by his plain speaking and his common touch. The speech was sparsely attended, and I had a full view of Truman from my orchestra seat to his left. He was a man of diminutive stature, he wore a bow tie, and between gulps of water, he would say the word *Republican* as though it were something you wanted to spit out.

After the speech, Truman's red convertible rolled out of the stadium. There were crowds of whites on one side of the road, and on the other side I stood beside my friend Roy Cook. We were the only people standing there. I yelled, "Hey, Harry!" and Harry Truman turned to us and, with a big smile, waved his hat.

As a result of that experience, I thought of this country as a place where every person had a chance and where you could call the leader by his first name and he'd respond in a friendly manner. I lived in a fair country.

I don't feel that way now. It's not that I think that American whites are unfair. Once in a while, you'll read a poll that indicates the existence of a residual fairness among white Americans. The majority of white Americans, for example, disagreed with the Simi Valley jury's decision to acquit the four policemen accused of beating Rodney King. In a poll taken after the riots, a majority of whites also agreed that not enough has been done to improve the lives of those living in the inner city. I even remember reading a poll that appeared about six months after the Reagan election and reported that 68 percent of Americans supported affirmative action.

With the decade of propaganda emanating from the media; from professional intellectuals out to make their black-pathology books into best-sellers; from academics posing as experts on the inner city, which for them is another planet; from white novelists who do quick-buck tours of the planet and in whose books the black characters' speeches are limited to *yo* and *homey;* from politicians who'll do anything to get elected; from black intellectuals who, belonging to the separate but unequal world of American conservatism, only get to practice their conservatism of blacks; and from bottom-line-minded neoconservative television news producers, who are fixed on such programs as affirmative action and the Great Society programs as black giveaway programs, when most of those who have benefited from these programs—Social Security, Medicaid, and Medicare—have been whites, is it any wonder that the hostility between the races is so thick, and that a majority of Americans now oppose such programs?

You'd think that the intellectual would desire to combat the myths that serve only to tear our nation apart, but the *New York Review of Books* and other "high culture" organs that hold, regardless of the facts, that the "underclass" is "mainly black" and that there are such things as "white ways" blacks should emulate are just as guilty of spreading such divisive propaganda as your most raucous talk show. As Carl Rowan put it, we have been "outpropagandized."

As I see it, the task for black and brown and yellow intellectuals is to overcome their Dukakis problem and build institutions capable of opposing this propaganda tit for tat. Institutions that will give them hell. Institutions that will turn around the unfair and ugly press relations deal that is being aimed at African Americans, the vast majority of whom are hardworking, tolerant, and decent.

1993

Black IrisHMAN

When I told the man who does my Xeroxing that I was going to attend a forum that evening at the Irish Cultural Center, he told me to be careful. "Those people get a few drinks and no telling what they might do." This got me jittery and so on the way over to 2700 Forty-fifth Street in San Francisco, I kept trying to get Bob Callahan to assure me that some Dan White–type whacko wouldn't pop me.

Callahan had been inviting me for months to meet some Irish musicians, writers, and scholars, but I'm always busy doing one thing or another and don't like to go out at night. I probably travel to New York more than I do to San Francisco.

This time something in me said go. I was greeted at the entrance to a brilliant room by Pat Goggins of the Irish Forum: "We wish to explore all avenues toward a peaceful resolution of the problem of Northern Ireland. Hence, we provide a forum for the exchange of ideas from across the spectrum of Irish, British, American, and other international viewpoints. We further intend, through our activities, to advocate an environment of peace, justice, and freedom, to pursue human fulfillment and fellowship"; and they had chosen a fine space in which to achieve their ends. The beams of the ceiling reminded me of those I'd seen at the bottom of Viking boats.

I was introduced to a number of people, including Charles Lafferty, who was arrested and without trial sent to hold up on a British prison ship for thirteen years. When he finally came before a judge, he told him that he didn't recognize the legitimacy of the British judge's court. Quite a few professional people and dignitaries were introduced before the main speaker, Tim Pat Coogan, author of *On the Blanket*, a book about the Irish Republican Army's attempt to extend their battle into the prisons the British built. They are shaped like an "H," with an administrative building connecting the two sides. They even introduced me from the speaker's stand and I was so flabbergasted that when the audience applauded, I applauded too.

Tim Pat Coogan was a pleasant, avuncular-looking plump man with seven grandchildren. He detailed in dispassionate tones the 800-year-old struggle between the Irish and the British. The Irish were fighting to rid their lands of foreigners as do nationalists all over the world. The movement included Martin Luther King, Jr., and inspired individuals and groups like Bernadette Devlin and the IRA, which use violence as a tactic. The British were domineering, with that special comic-opera pomposity for which the British are noted. Their stance has always intimidated less hearty souls like this spineless group over here with inordinate cultural power, yearning so much to be Tory.

Ireland has been viewed as the country home of the decadent feudalistic-minded British ruling class whose forebears backed old Jefferson Davis, president of the Confederate States of America, and most recently the insane super-Fascist Nazi state, some, like the Duke of Windsor, even allowing themselves to be photographed with Hitler. These British plantation owners have decided to make their last stand in Ireland.

The Irish that they deprive of civil rights, and send to the prisons to rot, have learned the importance of symbols in their struggle against the British, and so, in jail, they refuse to wear uniforms issued by the British, preferring to wear blankets instead. The British retaliate by humiliating the prisoners. Placing them in 8 × 6 cells and forcing them to abide inhuman conditions. Some prisoners had begun hunger strikes. When Pat Coogan made his speech at the Irish Cultural Center on March 20, 1981, Bobbie Sands had yet to become a household name.

The next time I saw Pat Coogan was on the "Today" show. I had a good laugh when Tom Brokaw asked Coogan why the IRA wasn't using the nonviolent tactics of the American Civil Rights movement. Coogan replied: They felt they should use the methods the American settlers used in gaining their independence.

I had a good time at the Irish Cultural Center. The food—mashed potatoes, peas, and roast beef—was excellent and the company at my table agreeable.

Warren Hinckle came up and said hello, and before we left, Tim Coogan interrupted his conversations with well-wishers in order to come down from the stage to say goodbye to us. Before we left I went to the restroom. A voice in a booth said: Black Irishman. This brings me to my grandmother, sturdy old gal. I get my orneriness and crankiness from her. I have her looks sometimes. During the last years of her life, she became disoriented, I suspect from the drugs the doctors gave her at the state hospital. Once I visited her and she snatched a dollar bill from my hand. "How am I going to pay for this hotel?" she asked. She was always concerned about paying her way. She worked like a plowman's horse all of her life, buried two brothers and a sister—her first husband was murdered, her second, a suicide. In the face of all of this, my grandmother was tough. The doctors had frequently counted her out for dead only to have her bounce back, sit up, and start demanding things. She said that she didn't want to be buried in no ghetto cemetery and so they buried her in Forest Lawn, this woman who'd spent her life cleaning the homes of the middle class, and even while doing that maintaining high standards, buried in the same place as Reagan's political ancestor, Millard Fillmore.

She read. She used to bring home back issues of *Time* and the

New Yorker from these houses she worked in. She talked often of Marcus Garvey, a 1920s leader of the biggest Black Pride movement yet (if only he'd had good accountants). Garvey was like her, overbearing, driven, and unlike some of those who espouse his ideas today, international, sending a telegram of congratulations to the founders of the Irish Free State.

I'm almost grateful that she spent her last years in a twilight. She was spared the sight of America stumbling backwards into ignorance, panic, and racism. During the year she was born, 1896, seventy-seven blacks were lynched, and at the end of the summer before she died, a black child was shot by police in Boston, a black man was beaten to death by police in Miami, and in our ancestral home, Chattanooga, Tennessee, six black women were shot by the Ku Klux Klan. The Klan killed demonstrators in Greensboro, North Carolina, and the shootings were recorded on videotape. Nobody did time for any of those crimes. Can you imagine living for eighty-four years only to find things as bad at the end of your life as they were when you began? I think that the Irish might have an idea. I think that my grandmother could get behind old Tim Sweeney who went on a seventy-two-day hunger strike. He said: "The victors will not be those who inflict the most, but those who endure the most." This takes me back to the last conversation I had with my grandmother, Emma Lewis, because after that she was unable to recognize me. It was 1975 and we were sitting in the kitchen of my mother's home.

She was home for a visit from the hospital. I asked her about her background. What was her father like? She said that his father had disowned him for marrying a black woman and she didn't see much of him because he had to leave Chattanooga after a valiant attempt to organize the pipe workers failed. He was Irish.

1982

AMERICAN POETRY:
IS THERE A CENTER?

In *Our Time*, a book edited by Allan Katzman and published in February 1972 by Dial Press, there appeared an interview of Buddhist monk Kina Murti Bhikku, described by interviewer Jakkov Kohn as "a gentleman whose deep clear eyes tend to pierce the vacuum around him." Bhikku was appealing to an audience of liberal intellectuals and artists on behalf of the Buddhist monks who were being murdered in "the tens of thousands" by the invading Chinese Communists. Bhikku accused the Communists of "annihilating Tibetan culture." The Chinese Communists, according to Bhikku, had destroyed most of the monasteries and used the remainder for "camps, barracks, and horse stables."

In order to "corrupt" the monks, the Chinese Communists—who entered Tibet in 1959—accosted them with homosexuals and prostitutes. Some, like Chogyam Trungpa, Rinpoche, made it across the Himalayas to safety. Rinpoche landed in India, and from there he went to England. According to one report, Rinpoche's unorthodox approach to Buddhism dismayed some of his English followers and so he came to America. The immigrant Buddhists appealed to the American left-wing cultural establishment because they were both oppressed and had a psychedelic angle.

May 14, 1977

There was some conflict between Robert Bly and Allen Ginsberg, backstage at the KPFA-radio benefit poetry reading held at
the Greek Theatre in Berkeley. Whispers were trickling out of
Boulder, Colorado, America's Tibet, where Rinpoche was now
enthroned, surrounded, according to the secret All-Colorado
Hamadryas News Agency, by "young foolish money" or, as
Richard Dillon said, "weaker personalities who bounce off
stronger ones."

Agitated, Bly said to me that he considered Boulder Buddhism a "con job," and that "some of those people up there are
no more Buddhist than my grandmother." William Burroughs,
mentioned with photo in the Naropa catalog, "represented the
Death Principle," Bly had said in the *Co-Evolution Quarterly*. Bly
was for the Great Mother principle.

Organizer Alan Soldofsky hustled about backstage like a
white-suited chicken. The poets were drinking wine and eating
deli sandwiches. It was a U.C. football Saturday and 4,000 people turned out for the reading. Backstage, black slavemasters
were selling books I put my guts and sweat into and which these
squatters had no part in making. They didn't want to pay me
and so I had taken my black slavemasters to court just as Dred
Scott had done his white ones.

The audience heard Ginsberg, Bly, McClure, Dorn, Bobbie
Louise Hawkins, Alta, Joanne Kyger, Lewis MacAdams, Jana
Harris, Jessica Hagedorn, Simon Ortiz, David Henderson, and
Victor Cruz.

When it came my turn to read I was told to limit it to ten minutes because "Allen wanted to come back and chant some
more." Soldofsky told me afterwards, a cigar wiggling in his
lips, hands clasped in his suspenders, "Kid, you were great. You
were only supposed to take ten, but I'm glad you took twenty."
Another day in the poetry business. It's an industry, with con-
glomerates, companies, and mom-and-pop stores. If the kind of

crowd Soldofsky was able to raise continues to attend them, poetry readings might even become big business. They shouldn't have any difficulty fitting in, since they include many of the other attitudes characteristic of a "modern urban civilization": competition, greed, sexism, and racism. Some kind of caucus was now criticizing the *American Poetry Review* for featuring the works of white males—in the eyes of the major white male book reviewers the only people among us gifted with writing talent— and demanding it be put on a rotating editorship.

When I said in the *Berkeley Barb* (December 12, 1975) that the New York School, the Beats, and the Bolinas clique constituted an AT&T of the poetry world, many people were annoyed. The self-assured East underestimates the cultural explosion now taking place west of the Rockies. I was editing an anthology of California poetry—*Calafía*—from 1845 to the present and can only describe the range as astonishing. Nineteenth-century Latinos writing about trips to Chinatown; a black voodoo poet of the same period named Beulah Mae; a list of mine names as inventive as any poet's list.

After what seemed to me to be a disproportionately negative response to the remark made in the *Barb*, mostly said from humor and to stir up mischief, I began to think it might have some basis in fact. I felt like the cartoonist who'd issued an unflattering portrait of Rasputin and the Czarina and, as a consequence, was being hunted all over Moscow. I figured I'd do the hunting. I found out later that Bolinas was a mere watering hole for international artists, intellectuals, and people who grew up in households with five maids. Actually, there were some good writers there. It would be foolish to ignore the accomplishments of Di Prima, Kyger, MacAdams, Hawkins, and Rollins. There were much bigger fish around than Bolinas.

Some of the luminaries in this constellation were gay. Though I understand that there are some rather ardent, and extremely passionate, heterosexual relationships going on at Boulder, some of the people on the faculty are identified with Homosexual Studies. Bly's remarks about Burroughs representing the Death Principle. Bly, the exorciser, romping about the Greek Theatre with a Nixon mask on, muttering, "I am the soul of America," or something.

Anne Waldman was quoted in *Time* magazine, February 14, 1977, as saying that "Naropa was fast becoming the center of American poetics." I knew differently and so did Anne. What did they know that I didn't know? Was *Time* serious? Or was this merely a manifestation of the old, well-known Luce "Orientalism"? *Time* sounding like an underground newspaper circa 1967—ex-undergrounders were designing the editorial pages of the *New York Times*—said of Chogyam Trungpa, Rinpoche, that "when he appeared, according to legend, pails of water turned to milk and a rainbow spread across the sky."

When the 1960s East Village crowd returned from Millbrook where Timothy Leary was "guru," they'd talk about the children of famous people who were turning on. Had one of them grown up to influence *Time* magazine?

April 22, 1977

Twenty-two is a key number for me. It either sets me back or means a breakthrough. Today is a good 22 day. I arrive on the Boulder campus to hear Ron Sukenick *(98.6)* arguing with a spinster cartoon of the teacher, beak nose and everything. The argument is loud and can be heard through the halls. Ron comes back to us and tells me he's resigning from something. Appropriately, the students are celebrating the birthday of a Colorado cannibal.

After my reading, we have dinner at the Gold Hill Restaurant in the mountains above Boulder on a little strip that looks like Dog Patch. We share a table with a lady from *Time* magazine who's dressed in a frilled blouse and one of those coats Lord Byron used to wear. A man at the end of the table with Dali eyes is introduced to me as a photographer from *People*. The fiction reading I've given earlier at the University has excited my appetite and so I have a trout and some red wine. The restaurant was added to the bar, so the story goes, because the owner felt guilty about the people who drove off cliffs after drinking their liquor. We go to a party given me by two guys named Steve and David. The party jumps and some of the people from Naropa attend. I spend some time with a librarian who fills me in on some details about one of my heroes of antiquity, Julian the Apostate, who fought the good fight against official religion.

The next morning I've scheduled an interview with Dick Gallup and Michael Brownstein, Naropa teachers and poets, to take place at the Hotel Boulderado. At the party, I meet a Naropa dissident and invite him along. Turns out he's a reporter for *Soldier of Fortune* magazine and one of Idi Amin's employees.

The tape recorder is on the breakfast table. Not only will it pick up the voices of the speakers but the rock music in the background. Carol Berge described the rock singers as sounding like Pinocchio. Pinocchio supported by space-age electronics. A few months before, E. Power Biggs had died. The last holdout against the electric organ.

Brownstein tells me that Naropa grew out of a "high energy grab bag—everything arts festival held in the summer of 1974."

I remembered the 1960s love generation Be-Ins and Love-Ins which took place in Golden Gate and Tompkins Square Parks. This must have been something like those since it included the same personnel.

What is a clique? Brownstein argued convincingly that different "lineages" were represented at Naropa. Ginsberg was descended from the Beats while "Anne [Waldman] and me are more into a New York thing." I would hear more about New York in the hour-and-a-half interview than about Boulder.

When I asked Al Young, poet and novelist, whether he thought Boulder was "fast becoming the center of American poetics," he said, "None of those people are from Boulder, they're from the East." I found it curious that Colorado's cultural traditions weren't mentioned during the interview. Colorado is the Spanish for "red" but not once did I hear a reference to Hispanic poetry, though Hispanic poets were present in Boulder: Corky Gonzalez, Kris Guiterrez, Jesus Luna, and Arturo Rodriguez. Were the Naropa poets refugees from a dying planet unable to explore the New World? Sukenick said that the University at Boulder and Naropa were into a kind of cultural exchange: they shared teachers and poets. The relationship between Naropa and the University at Boulder didn't end there.

The Tibetan Buddhist Ceremony of the Vajra Crown was held on the University campus. Normally, according to the *Colorado Daily*, anybody raising revenue using the University must account for the money immediately and deposit it somewhere. The Buddhists claimed that, under Tibetan tradition, the money was "blessed," and if the money is put into an account and later withdrawn it loses its blessedness.

Brownstein, who sometimes looks like a guy who wore a prep school cap and shorts at one time, says he thought "the hottest scene in the country was taking place in Boulder," which he called an "energy center." Between sips of coffee, I sat there taking it all in while in the background that music, which always seems to include a loud drummer, pounded and crashed.

Gallup didn't say much. Silence is Buddhist, which right there prevents it from gaining any mass following in a rowdy country raised on noise. The land of the Hallelujah and the Yahoo. The country of Bang-a-Lang-a-Ding-Dong.

The publicity about Boulder was all wrong, said Brownstein, a poet from Tennessee. "We're not rich, the classroom equipment is inadequate and we're not paid very well. There's not enough for the programs." A teacher in the Poetics program receives $200 per week, I was told.

That information didn't square with what the All-Colorado Hamadryas News Agency was feeding me and what I was hearing from other sources. The suite Rinpoche rented in Chicago during an appearance. The real estate holdings.

Judith Hurley, a former disciple, complained in the *Colorado Daily* about the Boulder Buddhists' opulent living. In a piece called "Buddhism Schmoodism" she described what happened during the Gyalwa Karmapa's recent visit: "His Holiness," it seems, lived it up! She reported there were walls covered with satin, and sewn cushions, table cloths in satin and brocade; tickets to a Vajra Crown Ceremony went for $8; in the ballroom hung "floor to ceiling satin"; present to protect Rinpoche were the Vajra Guards, a para-military organization said by some to be a bully squad. "He's very charismatic," explained Buddhist Michael Brownstein.

Of the Crown Ceremony's audience, Hamadryas have said, "The men were dressed in starched white suits and formal neckties, and women in their Sunday best." Like a Kiwanis convention.

Hurley concluded her article, "So let me remind you that Tibet, where these people come from, was a theocracy. You know what that means? That means they're used to being treated like kings." Kings? That rings a bell. Camelot! The overwhelming image in the "liberal arts" books white boys are required to read. Toadying up to the court isn't anything new for the artist, the world over. Early art is sometimes described as "court art." They had some in Europe, in China, and in Africa. The musician had to write a concerto for his patron. Benin sculpture emerges from this tradition.

The descendants of Holy Roman Empire monarchies became feeble-minded in the twentieth century, and after World War I had been done in by the democracies; some were kept on to entertain the tourists, like the one they have in England. A lot of this "Lost Generation" whining is merely western writers mooning over the fact that they didn't have some Earl or somebody to pick up the bills. They viewed their taste as superior to that of the bourgeoisie.

They complained, and still do, about the stupidity of the bourgeoisie because to them the bourgeoisie doesn't have any smarts and won't bow down to their "genius." It was inevitable that they'd find a substitute, and so they adopted Shangri-la.

Brownstein disassociated himself from Rinpoche and the Boulder Buddhists and their "blessed" bank accounts and real estate holdings; Brownstein said that Rinpoche wasn't his guru but "Allen's." Brownstein and Anne had an Indian guru.

Although they file taxes together, and Rinpoche dominates the catalog, Brownstein insisted that the Poetics program was separate from the Buddhists and that the Poetics faculty had "carte blanche" to do what they wanted to do. What was going on here?

Would the Buddhists unite behind a presidential candidate and extend Naropa to the White House? Would the Vajra Squad become that candidate's Palace Guard? Would people get beat up for not attending the Inaugural party? Somebody at the party said, "Be careful of the Vajra Squad," when they heard I was writing an article. I told them that I wasn't a guest in this country. I had read about the silent deportation of the Moonies. When the upper-middle-class parents who run the nation find out what some of these kids are into, don't you think they're going to put pressure on the government to do something about Naropa? After they deport the Boulder Buddhists and the man *Time* called "The Precious Master of the Mountains," then, just as they have a white King of Swing, a white King of Rock (secret niggers say Jagger sold his soul to the devil for that spot and Altamont was the payoff), a white King of Rock and Roll, there will emerge a white "Precious Master of the Mountains."

Dillon and Brownstein got into a big quarrel about whether Buddhism was a religion. Brownstein claimed that Buddhism didn't have any gods, though the art associated with Buddhism, shown in Tibetan monasteries, depicts gods and goddesses, some of them of Indian origin, and some black. "It's all in here," Brownstein said, pointing inward. "Sort of like a psychological diagram," Dillon added. "What about a situation in which people are treated as gods?" Dillon said, obviously referring to Rinpoche, whose name, according to a text called *A Cultural History of Tibet,* by David Snellgrove and Hugh Richardson, was the one given "the most sacred of Tibetan images," the "Jopbo Rinpoche," "the Precious Lord," brought to Tibet by the Chinese wife of Srong-brtsan-sgam-po, the first of the great Buddhist kings, who died in A.D. 650. Unlike Boulder's Rinpoche, Srong-brtsan-sgam-po valued words and fixed a new script for the Tibetan language.

I had been an admirer of William Burroughs. As a joke I used to read his "Astronaut's Return" to largely black audiences and then ask them to identify the author. They'd usually say Elijah Muhammad or Malcolm X. Here was a white intellectual who was aware of the horrors visited upon the world by technology. Some of his ideas of history were quite consistent with those of pioneer, and outlaw, black historians like Hansbery, Rogers, and Van Sertima.

Where did Burroughs stand on Naropa? James Grauerholz, who signed a letter to me "Assistant to William Burroughs," wrote on August 21 that he had heard that I planned to discuss Boulder Buddhism in an article entitled "The Poetry Business." He wanted to be sure that Burroughs's viewpoint was accurately presented.

In the article "Obeying Chogyam Trungpa," Burroughs and Rinpoche disagree on some matters, the most important of which appears to be related to psychic phenomena, Burroughs feeling that astral projection and telepathy exist, while Rinpoche dismisses them as distractions. Much "evidence" would support Burroughs. Their essential disagreement can be summed up in what Burroughs wrote: he said that Rinpoche didn't give the matter of words as much importance as he did. Claiming that when Huxley got Buddhism, he stopped writing novels and wrote Buddhist tracts, Burroughs challenged, "Show me a good Buddhist novelist."

More and more investigation is being given to the matter of coincidence. Koestler argued in his *The Roots of Coincidence* that coincidence was not such a mysterious thing after all but something which happens in everyday life to such an extent that it can be measured.

Most people don't have the patience to concentrate on something which occurs every million times. I was beginning to believe this and had begun to record coincidences and found that they happened frequently. Victor Cruz *(Tropicalization)* didn't know that I was writing an article and called up on September 18 to tell me about a book called *The Job* written by William Burroughs. His criticisms sounded like those of Robert Bly. I turned on the tape recorder next to the phone.

In *The Job*, according to Cruz, Burroughs argued that there were cells inside a man's body which could produce a fetus. Vic thought that to be cold-blooded and accused Burroughs of advocating the elimination of women. It sounded cold-blooded to me, too. I finally understood why Mrs. Frankenstein cried her entire honeymoon night. "He's produced by heterosexuals and so his stance is contradictory," Cruz said. He felt that it was also anti-"Third World," a term both of us were uncomfortable with; it was created by politicians who hate culture and so permit words to become their traps. Our taxes support the American government and not the Third World Southern Hemisphere. We produced a multicultural magazine called *Y'Bird*. The literary wholesalers, those publications which forecast magazines and tell the booksellers what to buy, continually referred to the magazine as Third World, and black, when in the last issue we included twenty-six white contributors. We publish more "whites" than they do "Third Worlders." Who's ethnic? The white *Nation Magazine, The New York Colonial Review of Books* or us?

Cruz accused homosexuals of desiring to become women without paying the price. Without suffering labor pains, which I'm glad I don't have to suffer. "They just want the theatrics, and the gestures." He compared this attitude with that of disco music where you can learn a latin dance for $25 and an afternoon of your time. "Some of those dances, which originated in Africa, involve an hour's exercise of toe movement."

"Intricate lip-motions and eye-movement go with the Salsa, but you don't see these disco dancers doing it. It's the difference between the Tower of Power and Tito Puente," Cruz said. Cruz has written songs for Ray Barretto.

Boulder was where they wrote disco poetry, Cruz said. It's like the design art he associated with Andy Warhol in which one relies upon plastic formulas. "How can it be the center of American poetry when American poetry is more than one language." The new multicultural writing contained images, symbols, diction, and the textures of different traditions.

Anglo cultural moonies still contend that American art does not exist when there are literary, dance and art forms in the United States which have no European antecedent. The intellectuals of mass magazines couldn't respond to George Steiner's ignorant remark that America is the custodian of European art, with no art of its own because they agreed with him. The Beats and Black Mountain operate from basically a European tradition. Pick up the standard "American anthology" and you'll find included works from people who share similar values. The writers I interviewed at Boulder, Naropa critics and defenders, like French poetry and what happened among white exiles of the 1920s. Nonwhite poets knew that and more. If you were a victim of American superrace "education" you couldn't miss Shakespeare & Co. The nonwhite poets also seemed to be influenced by more than writing. Houston poet Lorenzo Thomas, who said some good things about Boulder, but didn't think it was the center, named among his influences "living down South in the country." New York, the traditional center of Afro-American writing, was not that any longer. A revolt had occurred in the early '70s which had sent Afro-American poetry into the West and the South. The first issue of *Callaloo*, a New Orleans magazine edited by former Umbra poet Tom Dent, Charles Rowell, and Jerry Ward, carried Dent's editorial which read:

So many of our friends are tired and disgusted with the New
York scene. . . . So one of the things we are about is redressing
the balance between the so-called advanced progressive N.Y.
& the backwards countrified South.

Cyn Zarco, a Filipino American, one of four poets included in
the internationally acclaimed anthology *Jambalaya,* said she
could sympathize with the 1920s expatriate movement, being an
expatriate herself, "but I'm not fascinated by it," she said.

I said in the same *Berkeley Barb* interview that the '70s would
bring about a multicultural poetry and that both the 1960s Black
Aesthetic and that of the counterculture were racist and limited.
When LeRoi Jones, the literary Black Power guru, became Amiri
Baraka, the Communist revolutionary, after a bold public recon-
sideration of his views, he left his groupies in intellectual dis-
array. Addison Gayle, Jr., the chief Black Aesthetic proponent,
sneaked away from his position via hardcover in a book where
he admits that he quoted Keats when faced with a crisis. So
much for the Black Aesthetic, which critic Larry Neal characterized as the spiritual sister of the Black Power movement in an
important anthology, *Black Fire,* he co-edited with Baraka.

Now, for the first time, a truly national poetry, made up of the
many writing cultures, was on the scene. It cut across gender,
race, and region. Music, painting, and dance had already been
there for about fifty years. A Japanese-American student said
that what he enjoyed most about dancer Twyla Tharp's "Dance
in America" show was the footage of black dancer Bill Robinson.
Tharp, in that sense, was a multicultural artist and synchronizer,
sometimes using the work of Fats Waller. Choreographer Carla
Blank had scored a number called "Eccentric Chorus Line," accompanied by Scott Joplin's music and performed in Tokyo,
long before the Joplin craze.

Besides knowing about "Modern Literature," the multicultural poets I interviewed mentioned dance, music, and other influences on their work.

They were influenced by Salsa, Be-bop, the Japanese avant-garde, the poetry of Latin America, Africa, and of the Harlem Renaissance, a movement probably more important than the 1920s expatriate one in terms of international influence.

On September 3, 1977, I invited Simon Ortiz *(Going for the Rain)*, David Meltzer *(The Two-Way Mirror)*, and Bob Callahan, publisher of Turtle Island Press and editor of the *New World Journal*, whose latest book is *Winter Poles*, to come to my home and discuss *Time* magazine's contention that Naropa was at the center of American poetry. Shawn Wong, head of the Combined Asian Resources Project, flew down from Seattle, Washington. He is the author of a novel and the editor of *Yardbird Reader*, Volume 3, which, according to Shawn, was the first publication to recognize an Asian American tradition which wasn't limited to exotica or mimicry.

Callahan didn't feel that Boulder had enough variety to be the center of American poetics. He said that it was merely the Saint Mark's project gone west. The Saint Mark's Church-in-the-Bowery on the Lower East Side in the middle 60s. The first reading happened because William Burroughs was persuaded to read there instead of at the Metro Cafe where a racist incident had occurred. Joel Oppenheimer was the first head of the poetry program; I headed the fiction program. Anne Waldman came on later and edited a magazine from there called *World* and St. Mark's, through her energies and talent, became famous. Recently, it was the scene of a reading including Allen Ginsberg and the late Robert Lowell, which, for literary politics, was equivalent to Begin sitting down for lunch with Arafat and reminiscing about mutual relatives. Robert Lowell, to some, represented the Academy the Beats sought to overthrow. He said that he and Ginsberg merely came from opposite ends of William Carlos Williams. At about the same time, the *New York Times Book Review*, in a daily review, divided the American poetry world between the Beats and the Academy. Women, "Third World," etc., according to the *Times* article, were on the outs. An article about a White House reception for poets, held by Rosalyn Carter, appeared in the neoconservative *New York Times* magazine section. In the article, the author, James Atlas, named the white poets who attended. The others were referred to as Japanese, Native American and black. Among the Japanese, Native American and black poets of Mr. Atlas's article were Rudy Anaya, Simon Ortiz, Lucille Clifton, and Lawson Inada, American poets with international reputations but barely known among the American-European readers because critics like Mr. Atlas can only see white.

David Meltzer said that the idea of Naropa being the center of American poetry sounded to him like someone's overblown enthusiasm. Kind of like baseball scorecards—baseball being a cult subject for the literary avant-garde—as in the expression "My team can beat your team."

Naropa, to Callahan, was part of a 200-year-old American tradition, "the dude ranch." Rinpoche's Dude Ranch!

Meltzer and Callahan were poets who worked in factories when they were fifteen. They don't look like young foolish money, to me. Meltzer is a Cabala scholar, and Callahan is Irish American. Both Meltzer and Callahan knew the riches of their backgrounds. So did the rest of those who met that day, at my house. We knew our heritages, and weren't having identity problems. We communicated because we were Americans, which meant that we knew about comic books, movies, World War II, Milton Berle, Redd Foxx, Yiddish theater, John F. Kennedy, Muhammad Ali, Toscanini, John Coltrane, Black Power, KKK, ice cream, Mickey Mouse, etc. We were also bookish and our reading didn't stop when we were "educated." Meltzer and Callahan were rare white poets who knew the works of other cultures. They didn't sneer at American culture as it was fashionable to do back East. After Jerzy Kosinski, the New York Intellectual's token dissident, made an ignorant tirade against American culture before a delighted French audience, I got up and asked him, as a truck driver would ask him,

"If you don't like the United States then why don't you go back to Poland and take Polanski with you." Muriel Rukeyser, that grand lady, criticized a letter I wrote saying that I couldn't relate to PEN, the writer's organization, because it was headed by Kosinski who couldn't possibly know the problems of an American writer. Now I feel justified in having written that letter kind Muriel called "lousy."*

Meltzer charged Naropa with adopting the slick merchandizing techniques of the modern corporation. Bob Callahan said that he had once asked Rinpoche why he was charging $50 for tickets, and Rinpoche told him that they had to operate Buddhism like an American business. Callahan, once Rinpoche's San Francisco host, found this enough reason to disassociate himself from Rinpoche, though he respects him and believes that he's good at TM. But charging $50 a ticket was foreign to Callahan's "communalistic principles."

When Robert Creeley was invited to a Rinpoche lecture, according to Richard Dillon, he refused; John Ashbery begged out claiming that "I'm Episcopalian." Why were Jewish intellectuals associated with Naropa? "Because they don't find enough reinforcement in their own backgrounds," Meltzer said.

"Literature belongs to the people," claimed Simon Ortiz, who often includes Acoma chants in his readings. "I would guide any Native American away from the idea that one place is the center of American poetry today." Ortiz wondered whether the CIA had anything to do with Naropa. Carl Bernstein had written in *Rolling Stone* that Luce's publications had something to do with the CIA. It was *Time* in which the "Precious King" article appeared.

---

*After reading Kosinski's novel, *Pinball,* I take it all back. In this novel, Mr. Kosinski seems to be aware of the major influence of Afro-American culture upon the American popular arts; for a white man to admit this is heresy. This is why *Pinball* received bad reviews from the Anglo establishment.

"There's always some story about a wealthy European going to Tibet only to return and start Nazism or something," Meltzer said.

What worried Shawn Wong about Naropa was its "official language."

Meltzer thought it ironic that those who had waged "holy war" against a former establishment, dedicated to white notions of literature, had themselves become victims of their own revolution and were in danger of being overthrown. "Maybe they're calling themselves the center because they're a hole in the clouds," Meltzer said.

The last publicized center of American writing was Manhattan. Its writers became known as the New York Intellectuals. With important connections to publishing, and universities, with access to the major book reviews, they were able to pose as the vanguard of American culture when they were so obsessed with the two Joes—McCarthy and Stalin—that they were to produce only two artists, Saul Bellow and Philip Roth, who left town. That's why everybody in the Berkeley theater laughed at the "Dysentery" joke in the Woody Allen movie *Annie Hall.* There was that sad issue of the *Partisan Review* (44, No. 2; 1977) called "New York and National Culture: An Exchange," in which a panel of New York Intellectuals claimed to represent National Culture when in reality they sounded like village people whispering about haunted houses. Forms they claimed to have invented were classical ingredients of American art, but they wouldn't know that because they hate "liberal Democracy" and popular cultures, and are still reading those books in the rusty trunks brought over from Europe. To them an intellectual is someone who uses big words, lives in the suburbs, and has read *Crime and Punishment* 88 times. Egoists that they are, to them the rest of us are stupid, and "simple-minded." California, to those culturally medieval mapmakers, is a place where "gurus" live.

When Charles Pruett asked from the audience why no blacks,

257

women, or Puerto Ricans were on the panel claiming to represent National Culture, he was wisecracked down by a demagogic Irving Howe, using a tactic the New Left he abused so much made famous.

Just as the Boulder minds are still in New York, the NYI mind was in France, or Russia, anywhere but in this—to them—disgusting place. Putting on airs, and claiming the rest of the country was "envious" of them. Another thing the panel agreed on. The New York Intellectual was dead.

Defying the NYI machine they embarrassed, the Beats originated in the Be-bop subculture, perhaps the most important modern "artistic" movement. Native Americans were doing "Abstract Expressionism" for thousands of years, even before somebody invented a critical term for it. "I don't know what they mean by Cubism," Picasso said. "My art is African art."

The Beats adopted the values of Be-boppers—the language as well as the interest in "Eastern Religion." Long ago, Lynn Hope, a Newark saxophonist, had quit the country for Egypt. Pre–Be-bopper Cab Calloway was singing "psychedelic" songs in the '20s. Bob Kaufman, the most admired Beat poet among the young multicultural poets, provided the bridge between the Beats and Be-bop. Armed with my tape recorder I ran into Kaufman on Broadway in San Francisco and asked him for an interview; he refused. He is still the enigma of the Beat movement and future multicultural critics will probably consider him the most important poet of the movement. For now, local criticism was in the hands of the Beat critical bureaucracy. They were white males. One had written up the KPFA reading as if the nonwhite poets hadn't even appeared.

Though he didn't originate it, Amiri Baraka, due to his strong publicity connections with Beats, and also because of the notoriety of his play *Dutchman*, was made the founder of the New Black Poetry. He was the first to admit, in the defunct *Diplomat* magazine, "there were others before me," but Richard Ellmann didn't read that and so, since Baraka had been influenced by

Olson and Williams, wrote, in *The Norton Anthology*, how the New Black Poetry was dependent upon white forebears, thus recalling the quaint racist American notion that heathens lack imagination.

Baraka's abstract Zen words were replaced by the abstract works of Kawaida, only to be succeeded by the abstract words of Marxist-Leninism. Everything other than the jargon showed brilliant, tight, original, witty, corruscating, even humorous work, which excelled as Be-bop did and, like African art, not on the basis of facts, but on the resemblances to facts. Somebody called it elliptical; Baraka was Miles Davis.

While Ginsberg took guruism into the counterculture, Baraka, who once described himself as Sammy Davis, Jr., to Ginsberg's Frank Sinatra, introduced it into "Black Arts." He built a cult around his personality. His public denial of the white Beats proved an effective strategy; for about eight years counterculture people kept asking me when Baraka was going to talk to them.

Now, he was back home on the front page of the *Village Voice*, renouncing his racist period. Ginsberg and Baraka, both from Newark, shared influences, and, shortly after *Dutchman* was produced, Baraka said on New Jersey television that he had read Pound before Marx.

Perhaps Pound led both Baraka and Ginsberg to the East. In David Meltzer's *The San Francisco Poets*, Kenneth Rexroth mentions the upside-down ideograms in Pound's *Cantos*. He told the publisher of New Directions about it who in turn passed it on to T.S. Eliot who, amused, said, "But, you know, no one pays any attention at all to that stuff. You know, that Chinese thing. Nobody reads Chinese anyway." Baraka was so good at the self-deprecating interior monologue that it was no surprise that he'd abandon guruism for "the people." He was just too much the New Yorker to take himself that seriously. His father was probably a Democrat like mine.

As for Ginsberg, he said of Rinpoche in the June issue of the short-lived *National Screw* magazine, that "he [Rinpoche] seems to have carried forward a practical, visible, programmatic practice of egolessness, and provided a path for other people to walk on." While Brownstein strove to separate the Poetics program from the Buddhist program, Ginsberg described the Kerouac School of Disembodied Poetics as "a branch" of Naropa. To the outside, all of this was confusing.

October 4, 1977,
Whittmore House, Washington University, St. Louis

Howard Nemerov buys me lunch. I have a Crab Louis. They say that Nemerov doesn't talk much, but I spring an interview on him anyway. He turns out to be one of the wittiest people I've talked to. He says that he was too involved in his own work to give much thought to a center of American poetry. Anne Waldman was his student at Bennington, but "She showed no signs of doing what she's doing now."

"Anne's ambitious," Nemerov says. "I think she wanted to be an actress." I thought of the Rita-Hayworth-circa-1940s poster that went up for her reading of "Fast Speaking Woman."

What were his opinions of contemporary American poetry? "I was a judge in last year's National Book Awards, and after reading one hundred books I doubted not only my judgment but my sanity." He characterizes much of today's poetry as "Kleenex poetry. You look at it and throw it away."

"Young people like to think of themselves as poets. If there are two million poets today, I'm partly responsible," Nemerov says. "I taught them and then they went out and taught others. Like a chain letter."

He says that Allen Tate had once told him that you had to be homosexual to get over in the poetry world. Fifteen years later you had to be asylum material. And by the 1970s you had to be dead, preferably by your own hand.

He says that literary Chinoiserie dates back to at least Pope's time in the eighteenth century and that he had studied Buddhism at Harvard long before it became fashionable.

"For someone who has survived five poetry movements and two wars, the idea of a Disembodied School of Poetics strikes me as funny."

His picture is in this week's *New York Times Book Review* in connection with the publication of *The Collected Poems of Howard Nemerov*.

The interview is over. They have a picture of Vincent Price in this faculty club. I've been told that the Price home is on this very street.

Later, Charles Wartts, Jr., wants to show me a short story and so we adjourn to Washington U's Rathskeller, which is celebrating its anniversary. There's a guy dressed up as an animal running around giving people free beer. In another room students are watching soap operas on the biggest TV screen I've ever seen.

Wartts says that he was in Boulder in the early '70s, when the Buddhists were sending a red van around to recruit people in pizza parlors and beer halls. He says that a sweet-looking blonde took him to a meeting where people were told that if they chanted long enough they'd get what they desired. The people started testifying like in the Baptist Church about what Buddhism had done for them. At the meeting, people talked about giving up all of their material possessions. The little blonde said that she was starving and that after she chanted somebody brought her a big pizza. Then they wanted to go to Denver to recruit people, he says, but he left.

When I tell Wartts, a director of Journalism at Webster College, about the lavish display accompanying the Vajra Crown Ceremony, he can't believe that this was the same ragged band of holy rollers he'd met in the early '70s.

When I returned to California, I called American Book Award winner Quincy Troupe, co-editor of the multicultural anthology *Giant Talk*, published by Random House, said that the guruism of Baraka and Ginsberg could be attributed to their "huge egos."

The New Black Poetry, Troupe claimed, had come a long way from the "burn down America" poems of the 1960s. He saw black poets returning to jazz, blues, folklore, and liberating themselves from "weighty diction."

"Poets fall into a guru complex," Troupe said, because their traditional role in some cultures has been that of "mediator between heaven and earth."

He did not see Boulder as the center; he found the poetry of blacks, Latinos, and some Asians to be much more interesting. Lorenzo Thomas and Troupe were both members of the New Black Poetry, which, like the Beats, broke away from the Academy. With the exception of Langston Hughes, Sterling Brown, and a few others, much of the poetry by blacks before that was indistinguishable from that found in an old *Oxford Book of Verse.*

Other American groups had found their "national voices" and the revolt begun by the Beats and picked up by the blacks was spreading. P. R. Felipe Luciano referred to black poets born between 1928 and 1938 as "Older Brothers."

The Beats influenced us. I read *On the Road* in my late teens and shortly afterwards took off for San Francisco. I thought that North Beach was where you went swimming. We discussed "Howl" in poetry classes at the University of Buffalo. I must have read Don Allen's *The New American Poetry* so many times that when I arrived in New York at twenty-two my copy was falling apart; my favorite was Helen Adam. The first apartment I lived in, on Spring Street, in 1962, had been abandoned a month before by Jack Kerouac, who told the other roommates that he was going to Las Vegas to get drunk.

During the meeting at my house Shawn Wong had said that in 1971 Asian American kids couldn't name a single Asian American writer and now some of them were writers themselves. "Asian American art isn't about business," Shawn said. "It's about educating artists."

Since Buddhism came out of Asia I was interested in what

some of the Asian Americans thought about American Buddhism.

Shawn said that Asian American writers were more interested in the Cantonese folk gods, the Chinese loas which had been suppressed by Christian missionaries. Kwan Kung was one. This folk god had become the loa of Asian American artists in San Francisco. He was the symbol of plunder, revenge, drama, and literature. Playwright Frank Chin invited me to purchase a statue of the fierce-looking god on display in a New York Chinatown shop window. It would have cost me $300. Chin, the leading spirit behind the Asian American Renaissance taking place in Seattle, San Francisco, Los Angeles, and New York, regarded the Buddhists as just another Christian sect.

Filipino American poet Cyn Zarco said that she was into a revolutionary Buddhism, which was gaining popularity among the Asian American avant-garde in San Francisco. It was called Nichiren Shoshu, and involved chanting twice a day. It was a religion in which one fulfilled one's goals and desires in the real world. She said that the idea of Boulder being the center of American poetics was "Bull!"

Some of the same crowd who were after Buddhahood were also into "shamanism," formerly an area for anthropologists and tourist poets; the Native Americans were now claiming their traditions for themselves.

Cherokee American writer Gerald Hobson, in his "The Rise of the White Shaman as a New Version of Cultural Imperialism," wrote: "knowledge of Indian cultures has, unfortunately, been formed too often by the romantic (and now the neoromantic) writers/artists/ethnologists who have avidly and imperiously staked out their claims as unequivocal experts on our Indian cultures."

The Hispanic American poets have been coming on so strong that soon Spanish will be a required language for those citizens living west of the Rockies. Their magazines are named *Tin Tan, Maize, Tejidos, Puerto Del Sol,* and *De Colores.*

I asked Ron Sukenick why someone at the Paris conference—
where Kosinski dropped his load on American culture—said
that Americans had no tradition when the Native Americans
were writing out of traditions which extended back 30,000 years.
Sukenick said that there was a tendency in America to ignore
traditions which weren't derived from Europe.

They've made me and Ron into bureaucrats and businessmen
because it's better that we have an influence on getting authors
published and magazines started than some people I know. His
remark that Naropa was the last stand of an important movement stuck with me. There's no center of American poetry. People in centers see themselves as the center because they can't see
the whole scene with an eye for detail. If the poetry scene were
the landscape at night and you were looking down at it, you'd
see flickering patches of light distributed over a great distance.
Knowing Anne, she was probably misquoted. Some of the
women out here asked, "Why did you publish that bitch?"
when I had "Fast Speaking Woman" in an anthology called
Yardbird Reader I used to edit. She's an important part of a significant culture. She's open-minded to show an interest in a variety
of cultures and art forms, as displayed in "Fast Speaking
Woman." I once wrote her a letter warning her, in green ink, not
to be Guinevere in somebody's Fairy Kingdom.

I'm convinced that Gallup and Brownstein are earnest, and
based upon the works I've read I believe Boulder to be an important center. Sympathetic critics ask them only to examine their
relationship to an official religion with its Abbots and its Hierarchy. Bob Callahan talked about how the old Druids handled the
situation: "whenever the Monkish drift ran too closely towards
one Godism and one Kingism—historically the two run hand-in-
hand—some old Druid would appear magically and cast an
oath or give a charm, and the Monks would all scatter back inside their castles again." A lot of American poets can't sit in one
position that long because they're itching from spirits and can't
keep still. Demons pour out of their mouths and issue from their

fingertips. Others may have their Fourth Estate but poets have their Estate of the Second Sight Seers.

In that 1972 book, Bhikku questioned whether Tibetan Buddhism could exist outside of Tibet. There was that famous encounter when Rinpoche and an old Zen Master who died the following year met on Page Street. They talked about the shape an American Buddhism would take. They opened a mental hospital in upstate New York. Millions of Americans are "depressed," that unmysterious word they created to describe what the old folks used to describe as a "haunt ridin' you" or "death on your back" or "bad loas in your head." TM may be one way of dealing with the increasing madness occurring in highly technological societies. It was almost as if the devil had become immune to the dominant psychiatric techniques of the last century. Buddhism, Voodoo, and other religions might provide some answers.

I understand that Rinpoche wants to get rid of the beards and long hair so that he might recruit some of the power elite: generals, industrialists, and politicians.

His abandoning them might be the best thing to happen to the Boulder poets, whom the publicity called the "center of American poetics."

When I asked Okinawan American poet Geraldine Kudaka, who reads with a band called Mugicha, featuring a musician named Snakepit Eddy, where she felt the center of American poetry was, she replied, "In every poet's heart."

1978

Distant Cousins

I *am* a native of the South, and it was not until last April that I began to understand how native I am. It's quite possible that I am a twenty-plus generation southerner.

Among my ancestors are those who roamed the mountains of Tennessee for thousands of years, Irish people who left the Irish frontier in the late 1700s, and at least one Danish woman from Stonewall, Tennessee, who for now remains a mystery. (When I discovered that, I began to realize why I had such an affinity for Kierkegaard in my late teenage years.) And that's what searching for the details of one's background is similar to: a whodunit. But every time I've found a new fact, a new lead, I've discovered that my fiction has been ahead of me.

The made-up moments in my creative work arising from another murky part of consciousness seem to have had a better take on my origin than I. For example, in the early 1970s I read of a state called Franklin that was almost admitted to the Union. All I knew about it was that its population was black, Indian, and white and that it was led by an idealistic governor named Sevier. I wrote a poem called "The Lost State of Franklin." This work was the basis for a performance created by Carla Blank and her Japanese collaborator, Susuhi Hanayagi.

When I visited my father's sisters and brother for the first

266

time, last year, I discovered that their homestead was located not too far from the site of Governor Sevier's home and that the street before the one they lived on was named Franklin.

I found that others knew details about me that were lost to me. Native Americans in the Southwest, Pacific Northwest, and Alaska knew about my ancestry before I was able to locate it. Leslie Silko, after hearing me read from my work, told me that I was an Indian. A group of Native Americans with whom we were joshing around in Ellensburg, Washington, removed a headdress from a white man who claims Native American ancestry and placed it on my head. That's more like it, they said.

After learning of my Cherokee great-grandmother, I phoned my friend Andy Hope and asked, in jest, why, given the fact that I had a Native American heritage, I wasn't invited to the Returning-of-the-Gift Festival held in Oklahoma City. Andy said he hoped I wouldn't be bitten by a mosquito so that my Native American blood would be drained. Some of the comments of these Indian writers came back to me in April as, en route to Alcoa from Knoxville, we passed through a section of land called the Old Cherokee Trail, and while discussing my ancestry, the lost part, with aunts I'd never seen, I was told that my grandfather's mother was a Cherokee who was spared the trip west, the Trail of Tears, during which thousands of Cherokee Indians were uprooted from their traditional homelands in Tennessee. I was informed that my grandfather attended Cherokee school.

The Afrocentric exploration of the black past only scratches the surface. A full examination of the ancestry of those who are referred to in the newspapers as blacks and African Americans must include Europe and Native America. The pursuit of this journey requires the sort of intellectual courage that's missing in contemporary, politically correct America, where certain words cannot be spoken and certain secrets cannot be unearthed and certain investigations are frowned upon.

Black Americans who desire to uncover their past face problems. They must encounter not only the intellectual timidity of some black Americans, but red racism (Native American novelist and critic Gerald Vizenor surprised me with his comments about the racist views some Native Americans hold toward blacks). Yet probably the thorniest impediment to the discovery of the black past is southern denial. The inability of some southerners, not only laymen but academicians, to face the fact of miscegenation is such an explosive issue that this word, which simply means "mix," has taken on a sinister meaning. The denial that generations of southern white men have lived in polygamous arrangements is a hypocrisy that exists to this day. As someone whose fiction plays with the hypocrisy, I was delighted to point out in my latest novel, *Japanese by Spring*, that among the recent candidates for president who were running or about to run on the "immorality in the inner city" ticket, two were fathers of out-of-wedlock children, two were accused by a blond lobbyist of having engaged in assignations with her, and one was accused by a beauty queen of receiving more than a massage from her when he visited her in a New York hotel. In fact, a Civil War writer named Martha Higgens wrote that plantation owners still thought of themselves as good husbands and fathers. Maybe this is why an exploration of the African American past can become so dangerous: an exploration that would reduce the newspaper, bureaucrat, and think-tank idea of a Black America, a place inhabited with people of an uninterrupted African genealogy, to speciousness.

Black people growing up in the 1940s and 1950s were told by their education that if they behaved like Anglos and assumed an Anglo identity, opportunities would appear. In order to become this other identity, one had to reject one's past. I think this is why there appears, frequently, a scene in the novel of assimilation, by those not only of black but of white ethnic background, in which the narrator invites college friends home and is ashamed of his or her parents speaking English with a German, Italian, Irish, or Yoruba syntax. Our parents were viewed by our education as dumb and backward, and the sooner we abandoned their attitudes and style, it was proposed, the better our chances for success. It took me many years to understand that my parents' style was in some ways hipper and more sophisticated than mine. In the 1950s, they were listening to the blues, Charles Brown, and others, while I was listening to West Coast jazz.

An exploration of those ancestors who lay behind their generation was considered unthinkable. You'd find yourself in some cotton field, and if you went back further than that, you might find yourself in a jungle surrounded by these teeth-gnashing natives. My education told me that I was an uncivilized infidel and that I could be redeemed only by cutting all ties to my background.

Travel, world events, and my contact with black intellectuals would change my outlook. At the age of fifteen, I traveled to Paris as part of a YMCA delegation and, while there, met with Africans for whom my education had not prepared me: students who were studying at the Sorbonne, articulate and intellectual.

The type of colonialism that today's students could only imagine began to fade in the 1960s. New and dynamic leaders arose in Africa—Patrice Lumumba and Kwame Nkrumah. I remember watching a shaken Adlai Stevenson being interrupted by black demonstrators as he sought to defend some backward American African policy. I excitedly turned to my mother and shouted at her that some black people were interrupting Stevenson's speech. Adlai Stevenson had been my hero.

In high school, when the teacher asked students to select countries to represent during United Nations Day assembly, we black students were too embarrassed to choose Africa. We preferred to represent someplace like Norway.

At the beginning of the 1960s, African Americans were claiming Africa. I met Malcolm X, who put it plain. In what was to be the beginning of a number of exchanges I had with him in both Buffalo and New York City, he said that black history was cotton-patch history as it was being taught. He was right. In the textbooks we read, the blacks seemed to be having a great time. Real party animals. So what was the fuss? We hadn't read W. E. B. Du Bois's *Black Reconstruction,* and so the Reconstruction period became another source of embarrassment, since our view of the Reconstruction period was framed by D. W. Griffith.

During the early 1960s, African Americans changed their style. Many stopped straightening their hair in favor of an Afro fashion. I went to New York and joined a black writers' workshop called Umbra, and we wrote poetry about the greatness of African civilization. I began to name my style after that of nonacademic folklore based upon the secret allusions to the Hoodoo culture I'd heard the old black people whisper about. If folklore was a despised culture, then I would embrace it. I would base my literary style upon a culture that embarrassed middle-class blacks and of which the white literary culture knew little, at least the northern white literary culture. I would wave this lost aesthetic in their faces. My use of what I called Neo-Hoodooism was an act of literary defiance. Little did I know that I was embarking on an aesthetic journey that would ultimately take me to the Yoruba people of West Africa.

Black Pride did wonders for the emotions. It was a great intellectual high. It made you feel good. It's significant, I think, that after the collapse of the Black Power movement, some of its leaders turned to physical drugs. But however exhilarating Black Power was, it could not put out of one's mind those rumors: family stories of ancestors who "could have been white," or who were white.

I was in my late thirties when one day, sitting at a table with my eighty-year-old grandmother, I asked her the identity of her father. (To this day, I wonder why it took me so long.)

She said he was an Irishman who had to leave Chattanooga for his role in organizing the pipe workers. It all came back to me—the early years, 1940, 1942, when I lived with my grandmother's brother on 1019 Elm Street in Chattanooga, before my mother returned to take me to Buffalo, New York. There was a pipe manufacturing plant located at the bottom of a hill from the house. Across the street from my uncle's house sat a huge mansion that dominated the neighborhood. It must have been about twenty acres. Built in the Spanish hacienda style, it was owned by the eccentric owner of the pipeworks. His name was pronounced Montegue, and my grandmother's brother remembered him as a man who, despite his wealth, walked down the hill toward his factory wearing overalls and a dirty rag around his neck. I remember staring for hours at the mansion, wondering what lay behind those walls. There were rumors that the mansion was haunted, but not, I was beginning to discover, as haunted as my genealogy. Nobody had ever told me that there was a connection between this man and an ancestor of mine.

When I hired a professional genealogist to trace my ancestry on my mother's side, I discovered that the name of the man whom my grandmother identified as an Irishman was Marion Shaw Coleman, who was born in December of 1869 in either Alabama or Georgia. The surprises wouldn't end with this discovery of an Irish American on my grandmother's side. In an interview I conducted with my mother and her cousin, I uncovered another ancestor of Irish American background, on my grandfather's side. My mother's cousin, whom we call "Sister," said that her grandfather, my mother's father's father, was a mean Irishman. My genealogical chart identified this man as Ezekiel Hopson or Hopkins, born in Alabama between 1854 and 1859. His father, Pleasant Hopson, was born in about 1830.

These European ghosts in the African American past have been shoveled under by the passionate claims made by the "pure race" theorists, black and white, who hold so much sway over our political and cultural life. These relatives would prove that racial supremacy is, as you say down here in Little Rock, a dog that won't hunt.

The late humanitarian John Maher introduced me at a meeting of the Celtic Foundation as an Irish American poet. His reasoning was that if a drop of black blood made me black, why didn't a drop of Irish blood make me Irish? The people at my table—Irish American celebrities—seemed stunned. Pete Hamill, however, shook my hand. Feminist Dierdre English stunned both me and the audience by announcing that I was an Irish American, all right, because I was a "liar and a thief." I then understood why her last name was English. Ms. English is ignorant of the fact that blacks and whites have been sneaking back and forth across the racial fences since they came in contact with each other in the early seventeenth century. Later I wasn't surprised to read her comments—printed in the *New York Times*—about the African slave trade, comments that must be the most ignorant on record.

I asked the late Sarah Fabio, a poet who was called the mother of black studies and whose features betrayed a European heritage, how one would reconcile the obvious European strain in the blood of an African American with the African American's identification with Africa, and she said that she was black because it was the black people who nurtured her. She had a point. Marion Shaw Coleman left his African American wife, whose maiden name was Mary E. Hardy, with a number of children whom she had to support by operating a restaurant in Chattanooga for more than twenty years. White American males may be the original runaway fathers of the African American experience.

In the census report of about 1870, Ezekiel Hopson's/Hopkins's children's names are listed. Under "Racial Classification," some children are listed "Black." Other children are listed "White." On the document, *White* has been crossed out and the letter *M* for *mulatto* is substituted. According to family oral history, the children who looked white or near white were beneficiaries of the family's assets and eventually abandoned their darker relatives. Don't look for a story in the *Atlantic Monthly,* *Harper's,* or the *New York Times Magazine* about how darker relatives were cheated out of millions of dollars in assets by white and near-white relatives. There are millions missing from the

American black family. These millions have long since passed over into whiteness.

In 1983, I came in contact with family members whom I'd never seen. Children of a father I'd never met. And this is how I found that there were Europeans and Native Americans on this side of the family tree.

The complex racial background of those who are referred to as black Americans has seldom been submitted to serious scrutiny. One could understand why the Identity Crisis nonfiction is a popular genre among assimilated intellectuals, but the fact that I could obtain as much information as I did for only $100 indicates that Identity Crisis intellectuals aren't seriously interested in discovering their roots, or are afraid of what they might find. Besides, millions of dollars are involved in continuing the black-white polarization. Think of all of the journalists and op-ed writers, along with a profit-feeding media, that would be out of business were there a fresh and revised look at race in America. If one allows the Native American ancestry of blacks, then W. E. B. Du Bois's theory of double consciousness, which has thrilled black intellectuals for decades, would fold.

I still haven't pieced together all the strains of my identity, but I'm much closer than I was before that day when I decided to ask my grandmother about her father, and his father. I know now why it took me so long to ask her the question. I also know that there's no such thing as Black America or White America, two nations, with two separate bloodlines. America is a land of distant cousins.

Index

A

ABC news, 29, 30, 31, 61, 63, 67
Abe, Frank, 51
abolitionists, 40, 58, 121–126, 168
Adams, Terry K., 14
Adler, Margot, xv, 61, 62, 64
Affirmative Action, 3, 27, 52, 100, 236
Africa, John, 144–145
African Americans, xviii, 28, 33–36, 40–42, 44, 47–48, 50, 51, 62, 77, 101, 109, 121, 131, 160, 174, 217, 220, 223, 229, 230, 231, 260, 267–268, 271. *See also* black
African Methodist Episcopal Church, 121
Afrocentrism, xviii, 36, 38, 39, 87, 267
Against Our Will, 56
AIDS, 42, 47, 62, 64, 138
alcoholism, xi, xii, 5–6, 7, 17, 22, 51, 64, 106, 163. *See also* drugs
Algren, Nelson, 105
Ali, Muhammad, 68, 73, 106, 176–205

All God's Chillun Got Pride, 153
All the Rest Have Died, 112
Allen, Don, 262
Almanac of the Dead, The, 10
Aluetta, Ken, 19
Ambrose Bierce, 127
American Poetry Review, 244
Amolaran, Adebesi, 166
Annie Hall, 257
anti-Semitism, 33–34, 37–42, 60, 61, 78, 133, 136. *See also* Jewish Americans
Aquarius Book Store, 50
Armstrong, Louis, 107, 114, 202
Asian Americans, xii–xv, 7, 9, 15–17, 30, 31, 44–45, 48, 50, 51, 60, 69, 81, 100, 125, 133, 218, 221, 254, 262–263
Atlantic Monthly, xii, 18
Atwater, Lee, 101
Auchincloss, Louis, 144
Auld, Hugh and Sophia, 120, 123

Auw, Ivan von, 136
Axelrod, Beverly, 97

B

Babbitt, Tom, 220
Baker-Fletcher, Karen, 73
Baldwin, James, 10, 48, 52, 69, 73, 99, 100, 119, 137, 149, 154, 162, 167
Bambara, Toni Cade, 147, 165–171
Banks, Russell, 50
Baraka, Amiri, 48, 99, 104, 115, 116, 149, 250, 253, 258, 259, 262
Barnes, Albert C., 185
Barry, Marion, 63, 93, 141, 142, 230
BCCI scandal, 4, 63, 99
Before Columbus Review, 11
Bellow, Saul, 41, 257
Bennett, William, 4
Berkeley Barb, 244, 253
Berkeley in the Sixties, 103
Berlet, Chip, 34
Berman, Paul, 230
Bernal, Martin, 50
Bernstein, Carl, 256
Bernstein, Leonard, 97–98

Bhikku, Kina Murti, 242, 265

Bierce, Ambrose, 126–132

Big Aiiieeeee, 9

Big Book of the American Irish, The, 22

Birth Dearths, 37

black
  Aesthetic, 253
  bashing, xii–xv, 3–11
  behavior, 3–4
  feminists, 58–59, 150
  Irishman, 240–243
  mayors, 143–144
  men, xii–xv, 3–7, 12, 13, 26, 29–30, 37, 41, 43, 56, 59, 64, 72, 95, 118, 123, 150, 152–153, 168, 180, 233
  nationalism, xvii, 121, 142, 152, 218
  newspapers, 123
  Pride, 243
  self-esteem, 151, 233

black. *See also* African Americans

Black Fire, 253

Black Panthers, 88–93, 97–98, 100, 102, 187

Black Picture Show, 112–114

Black Reconstruction, 270

Blank, Carla, 65, 79, 210, 211, 214, 253, 266

Bly, Robert, 243, 245, 251

Bond, Julian, 93, 230

Bontemps, Arna, 138

Borderline, 109

Boston Review, 149

Brashford, Walter, 106

Brinkley, David, 46, 62, 71

Brock, David, 54

Brokaw, Tom, 151, 240

"Bronzewille Woman in a Red Hat," 105

Brooks, Gwendolyn, 104–106, 209

Brown, Cecil, 53, 115

Brown, Clifford, 221

Brown, Drew Bundini, 179, 186

Brown, Elaine, 13, 87–94

Brown, Gov. Jerry, 73

Brown, Rap, 49, 201

Brown, Sterling, 262

Brown, William Wells, 14

Browne, Don, 30

Browne, Nick, 193, 194

Brownmiller, Susan, 56, 57, 70

Brownstein, Michael, 246–249, 260, 264

Buchanan, Patrick, 34, 37–39, 61

Buckley, William F., Jr., 21, 22–23, 37

Bullins, Ed, 48, 69, 93

Burnett, Charles, 48, 93

Burroughs, William, 243, 245, 250, 251, 254

Byrne, David, 146

C

Calafía, 244

Callahan, Bob, 22, 50, 240, 254, 255, 258

Callaloo, 252

Cannery Row, 157

Carter, Jimmy, 170, 171, 202

CBS news, 28, 31, 61, 191

Celestine, Jerry, 177

Chamberlin, Wilt, 70

Chameleon Street, 98

Chan, Jeffery Paul, 9

Children of the Night, 158

Chin, Frank, 8–9, 51, 263

Chin, Vincent, 16

Chinatown, A Portrait of a Closed Society, 8

Chinese Americans, 8–9, 16, 17, 40, 72, 77, 82. *See also* Asian Americans

Chissell, Dr. John T., 31, 233

Chistie, Alix, 29

civil rights, 240–243

Cleaver, Eldridge, 10, 91, 95–103

Cleaver, Kathleen, 101

Clinton, Bill, 35

Clinton, George, 144

CNN news, 7, 15, 18, 27, 29, 34, 46, 49, 59, 70, 72, 133, 161

Co-Evolution Quarterly, 243

Cohen, Jack, 33

Coleman, Marion Shaw, 271, 272

Color Purple, The, xiv, xv, 57, 113, 114

Colorado Daily, 247, 248

Columbus, Christopher, 224–228

"Columbus Controversy, The," 226

Communist Party, 88–89, 108, 111, 257

Complete Short Stories of Ambrose Bierce, 127

Conrad, Harold, 188, 189

Coogan, Tim Pat, 239, 240

corporations, 4, 32, 47

Cotton Club, 21

Couric, Katie, 54

Creed, Apollo, 68

Creely, Robert, 256

crime, 7, 8, 10, 15–18, 20–22, 30, 32, 49, 60–63, 87, 99, 108, 133, 138, 140. *See also* drugs

Crisis of Possession in VooDoo, The, 148

Crisis of the Negro Intellectual, The, 88

Croly, David Goodman, 37

Crossings, 93

Crumb, Robert, 97

Cruse, Harold, 88

Cruz, Victor, 243, 251–252

Cullen, Countee, 138, 148, 149

D
Dameron, Tadd, 221
Davis, Arthur, 98
Davis, George, 46
Davis, Miles, 101, 139, 144, 220, 222, 259
Davis, Ossie, 95
Davis, Sammy, Jr., 218
Davis, Thulani, 69
Dechter, Midge, 3
Demby, William, 69
Dent, Tom, 252
DePasse, Suzanne, 93
Depestre, Rene, 148
Devlin, Bernadette, 239
Dillon, Richard, 243, 249–250, 256
Dimarsky, Sherry Berliner, 19
Dinkins, David, 23, 61, 141–142
Donahue, Phil, 79
Donaldson, Sam, 25, 172
Doolittle, Hilda, 109
Douglass, Frederick, 94, 120–125
Driving Miss Daisy, 114
drugs, xii–xiii, 4, 5, 8, 15, 30, 45, 50, 51, 61, 106, 133, 151, 159, 226
  among Asian Americans, xiii, 49
  among blacks, xii, 5, 21, 91, 133
  among gays/lesbians, 64
  among whites, 5–6, 13, 46, 162–163
  cocaine (crack), xiii, 5, 13–14, 27, 29, 30, 64, 92, 141, 209, 213, 231
  heroin, 138
  legalization for, 165
  in prison, 91
  psychedelic, 159
Drum, 176

Drummond, Bill, 29
Du Bois, W.E.B., 270, 273
Duberman, Martin, 107
Dudley, James, 196, 201
Duke, Bill, 152
Duke, David, 37, 38, 47, 72, 171, 172, 174, 226
Dundee, Angelo, 184, 187, 194
Dutchman, 258, 259

E
Early, Gerald, xv
Ehrenreich, Barbara, xvi
Eisenberg, Lee, 19, 21
Eisenhower, Dwight, 107, 130
Ellington, Duke, 139
Elliot, Delbert, 59
Ellis, Jimmy, 184
Ellison, Ralph, 88
Ellmann, Richard, 258
Ellwood, David, 12
Emperor Jones, 109
English, Deidre, 272
English, T.J., 22–23
Esquire, xi, 20, 174, 230
Evans, Mari, 105
Everybody Knows What Time It Is, 167

F
Fabio, Sarah, 272
"Fallen Champ, The," 73
families, black, 12–15, 19, 27, 44, 45, 51, 79, 159–160, 177, 270–271, 273
"Fanfare for an Avenging Angel," 96
Fanning, Charles, 154
Farrakhan, Louis, 91
Farrell, James T., 49, 105
"Fast Speaking Woman," 260, 264
FBI, 17, 40, 70, 89, 93–94, 108, 142. *See also* Hoover, J. Edgar
Federman, Ray, 172

Feinstein, Dianne, 57
feminism, xiv–xv, xvii, 4, 13, 41–42, 54–57, 61, 64, 69–73, 83, 89–91, 97, 103, 121, 137, 148, 150, 155, 167, 174, 180, 210, 235, 272. *See also* individual feminists
Fight Doctor, 203
Fight, The, 189
Fire Next Time, The, 99
Fishbein, Dr., 37, 38
Fitzwater, Marlin, 44, 46
Flaherty, Joe, 186
Foley, Jack, 50, 159
Foote, Shelby, 124
Forbidden City, The, 112
Foreman, George, 198, 200
Forest, Gen. Nathan Bedford, 38, 124
Fort Pillow, 37, 124
Fox, Bob, 50
Frank, Barney, 59, 60, 61, 63, 64
Frazier, Joe, 180, 194–195, 202
Freedom Road, 201
Freeman, Morgan, 114
Fried, Albert, 21
Friedman, Sonya, 34
Frost, Robert, 224
Fuentes, José, 191
Fujii, Milton, 16
Fuller, Hoyt, 105
Furstenberg, Frank, 11

G
Gallup, Dick, 246, 247, 264
gangs
  Asian American, xii, xiii, 10
  black, xv
  Chinese American, 8
  corporate, 32
  Irish American, 22–23
  Latino, 10
  organized, 20

gangs *(cont'd)*
  The Little Rascals, 161
  The Westies, 22–23, 49
  white, 22
Ganja and Hess, 112, 114, 115, 116
Gant, Johnny, 196
Garnett, Henry, 122
Garrison, Greg, 17, 69, 70
Garrison, William Lloyd, 121
Garvey, Marcus, 121, 142, 241
Gates, Daryl, 46
Gates, Henry Louis, Jr., 13, 33–35, 37, 162
Gaye, Marvin, 229
Gayle, Addison, Jr., 253
gays, 28, 63, 64, 101, 137, 244–245, 251, 260
Gender Monthly, 13
Giachetti, Richie, 189
Giddens, Gary, 107
Gilks, Dr. Charles, 62
Gillespie, Dizzy, 222
Ginsberg, Allen, xviii, 50, 243, 245, 246, 254, 259, 260, 262
Glazer, Nathan, 23, 230
Goggins, Pat, 238
Golden Age of the Moors, The, 227
Golden, Stephanie, 175
Goldman, Emma, 111
Goldwater, Barry, 102
Golindez, Victor, 193
Gonzalez, Corky, 247
Goode, Eslanda Cardozo, 108
Goode, W. Wilson, 141, 142
Goodman, Ellen, 37
Goodman, Walter, xiv, 14, 28, 32
Gordone, Charles, 114
Gore, Mrs. Al, 232–234
Granz, Norman, 221
Grauerholz, James, 250
Greenberg, Stan, 35

Greenfield, Jeff, 61, 62
Gregory, Dick, 177, 182, 198, 199
Gremander, M.E., 126
Griffin, Noah W., 124
Gross, Terry, xv, xvi, 66
Guare, John, 93
Guiterrez, Kris, 247
Gullen, Nicholas, 230
Gumbo Ya Ya, 230
Gunn, Bill, 69, 112–119
Gurr, Ted Robert, 21

H
Hacker, Andrew, 8–9, 100
Halperin, Charles J., xvi, 227, 229
Hamill, Pete, xi, xii, 17, 20–23, 174, 272
Hampton, Fred, 89
Hanayagi, Susuhi, 266
Hanrahan, Kip, 146
Hansen, William W., 230
Harder They Come, The, 189
Hardy, Mary E., 272
Harley, Judith, 248
Harper's, 3, 18
Harrington, Walt, 93
Harris, Barbara, 19
Harris, Elihu, 80, 214
Harris, Kathleen Mullan, 11
Harris, Wendell, 98
Hattori, Yoshihiro, 16
Haworth, Steve, 29
Hayden, Tom, 93, 101, 230
Headwaiter, 154
Henderson, David, 77, 243
Hentoff, Nat, 35, 40–41
Hernton, Calvin, 154
Hewlett, Sylvia Ann, 100
Higgens, Martha, 268
Hill, Anita, xvi, 19, 53–55, 57, 58, 71, 174, 210, 214
Hillard, David, 91

Himes, Chester, 48, 135, 137, 149, 152–156, 163, 165
Hinckle, Warren, 240
Hing, Bill Ong, 8
Hispanic Americans, xvii–xviii, 7, 10–11, 25, 26, 27, 30, 43, 45, 47, 63, 69, 73, 79, 125, 174, 218, 221, 244, 247, 263
  history, 87, 226–229, 252, 270–72
Hitchens, Christopher, 175
Hobson, Gerald, 263
Hockenberry, John, 34
Holmes, Larry, 188, 189, 194, 199, 201, 205
homelessness, xiii, 6, 161, 177
Hong, Peter, 80
Hongisto, Richard, 45
hooks, bell, 55
Hoover, J. Edgar, 94, 108, 137. *See also* FBI
Hope, Andy, 267
Hope, Lynn, 258
Hopson, Ezekiel, 271, 272
Horne, Lena, 136
Horton, Willie, 35, 37, 61, 63, 68, 101
Howe, Irving, 258
Hubbard, Don, 181, 187, 188, 202, 203, 204
Huggins, Erica, 91
Hughes, Langston, 106, 138–141, 149, 230, 262
Hughes, Robert, xvii
Hurston, Zora Neale, 88, 109, 137, 138, 146–151
Huston, Angelica, 49

I
Ice T, 232
If Beale Street Could Talk, 100, 167
Inada, Lawson Fusao, 9, 255

Inniss, Carlton, 91
intellectuals
 Asian American, 8
 black, xvi, 39, 40, 41, 62, 82–83, 95, 96, 108, 124, 135, 138, 142, 152, 217, 239, 273
 Jewish, 256
 multicultural, 51, 53, 87
 New York, 255, 257, 258
 white, xvii, xviii, 6, 47, 50, 98, 186, 217, 224, 226, 238, 244, 252, 257
 women, 56
Invisible Man, 88
Ireland, 240–243
Irish Americans, xi, xii, 20–24, 36–40, 49, 61, 77, 238–241, 255, 266, 270–272. *See also* Scottish Americans
Irish Cultural Center, 77, 238, 240
"Irish Voice in America, The," 156
Islands in the Street, 22, 161
Italian Americans, 12, 19, 20, 48, 182

J
Jackson, George, 90
Jackson, Jesse, 34, 35, 38, 124, 171, 218
Jackson, Milt, 220
Jahn, Janheinz, 230
Jankowski, Martin Sanchez, 22, 161
Japan Times Weekly, 48
Japanese Americans, 8, 16–17, 41, 73, 79, 253, 255. *See also* Asian Americans
Japanese by Spring, 268
Jefferies, Leonard, 37
Jefferson, Thomas, 14, 97

Jewish Americans, 19, 20, 23, 35, 36, 40–42, 48, 61, 71, 78
Job, The, 253
Johannas, 112
Johnson, Jack, 68, 73, 181, 184, 197–198, 200, 205
Johnson, James Weldon, 148
Johnson, Lyndon, 102
Johnson, Robert, 48
Jones, Leroi, 253
Jordan, Frank, 45
Jordan, Winthrop D., 50–51

K
Kakutani, Michiko, xvi–xvii, 41
Kane, Big Daddy, 232
Kanelos, Nicolas, 11
Karenga, Maulana, 88, 89
Katzman, Allan, 242
Kaufman, Bob, 104, 258
Kaus, Michael, 18, 62
Kennedy, Jay, 88
Kennedy, William, 21
Kenyatta, Jomo, 109
Kerouac, Jack, 186, 260, 262
KGO-TV, 30
Killens, John O., 69, 106, 119
Kim, Elaine, 79
King, Dennis, 34
King, Don, 71, 73, 184, 185
King, Larry, xvi, 71, 72
King, Martin Luther, Jr., 40, 95, 116
King, Rodney, 3, 16, 43, 45, 47, 49, 50, 52, 67, 82, 90, 238
Kinkead, Gwen, 8
Klan, The, 37
Klein, Joe, xiii, 17, 36, 61, 62
Kohn, Jakkov, 242
Konch, 9

Kopage, Eric, xi, xiii, xix
Koppel, Ted, 19, 45, 60, 79
Korean Americans, xiii–xiv, 44, 51, 77–83. *See also* Asian Americans
Kosetile, Willie, 106
Kosinski, Jerry, 255, 256, 264
KPFA, 213, 245, 258
Krim, Seymour, 99
Kristol, William, 35–36
Ku Klux Klan, xiv, 37, 40, 64, 70, 73, 160, 161, 243
Kudaka, Geraldine, 265
Kwong, Peter, 8

L
Lafferty, Charles, 239
Lampham, Lewis H., xii
LaRouche, Lyndon, 34
Lee, Bob, 10
Lee, Shirley J., 58
Lee, Spike, 61
Legge, Wade, 222
Lehmann-Haupt, Christopher, 41
Lenoir, Dr. Michael, 46, 212
Lenz, Gunther, 10
Letter to a Black Friend, xi, 23
Levin, Tamar, 14
Lewis, Butch, 188, 205, 206
Lewis, Emma, 241
Lewis, John, 230
Lewis, Reginald, 134
Life, xvii, 5
Life of Langston Hughes, The, 138
Lipsyte, Robert, 69
literature, 10, 88, 217, 257. *See also* poetry
 African, 230
 Asian American, 9–10, 11

literature *(cont'd)*
  black, xvi, 5, 10, 48, 88,
    139, 144, 151
  Hispanic, 10–11,
    174–177, 256
  Native American, 10
  satirical, 156
  slave, 168
Locke, Alan, 88
Los Angeles riots,
  xiii–xiv, 3, 16, 37, 43,
  46, 50, 51, 79–81
"Lost State of Franklin,
  The," 266
Louis, Joe, 69, 182,
  197–198, 200
Love, Eula, 50
Lowell, Robert, 254
Luciano, P.R. Felipe, 262
Lumumba, Patrice, 269
Luna, Jesus, 247

M
MacAdams, Lewis, 50,
  243, 244
McDaniel, Hattie, 115
MacDonald, Andrew, 40
McFeely, William, 120,
  123
McKay, Claude, 88, 89,
  138
MacKinnon, Catherine,
  71
McLaughlin Report, 18
"MacNeil/Lehrer News
  Hour," 26, 27, 61
McPherson, Aimee
  Semple, 136
McPherson, James Allen,
  xii
McQueen, Michel, 60
Madhubuti, Haki, 105,
  106, 209
Maher, John, 77, 271
Mailer, Norman, 96, 100,
  178, 185, 186
Malcolm X, 93, 95, 101,
  161, 171, 181, 201, 218,
  250, 269

Mandingo, 176
Marcus in the High Grass,
  112
Mars, Dr. Louis, 148
Martin, Dr. Reginald,
  165–171
Marvin, Jay, 29
Matthews, Anne, 7
*Meanest Cop in the World,
  The*, 153
media, xii, xvi–xvii, 3–11,
  15–16, 18, 25–27, 34, 43,
  50–53, 55, 60, 69, 71, 73,
  114, 133, 138, 161, 170,
  192, 212, 214, 233, 236,
  273
  television news
    boycott, 26–32
media myths, xii–xiv, 9,
  92, 174
Meltzer, David, 50, 254,
  255, 256
men. *See* black, men;
  white(s)
Metzger, Tom, 175
Micheaux, Oscar, 109
Milken, Michael, 72
Miller, Jerome, 60
Minelli, Liza, 196
minorities, 4, 8–10, 30,
  38, 100. *See also* specific
  minority
misogyny, xiv, xv, 5, 13,
  19, 23, 38, 41, 54, 56, 89,
  133
*Money and Class in
  America*, xii
money laundering, 4–5,
  63, 99
Monk, Thelonious, 220,
  221
Moore, Archie, 184, 195,
  224
Morgan, Joan, 69
Morganthau, Robert, 4
Morial, Ernest N., 179
Morley, Jeff, xvi, 71
Moses, Bob, 230
Moses, Gilbert, 93

MOVE, 140–145
Mowry, Jess, 157–164
Moynihan, Daniel, 21,
  22, 28, 45
Ms., xiv–xv, 56, 64, 70
Muhammad, Elijah, 142,
  250
Mulligan, Gerry, 49
multiculturalism, xvii,
  xviii, 11, 53, 87–88, 101,
  253, 255
Murray, Charles, 22, 46

N
NAACP, 110
Nakasjima, David, xiii
Naropa Institute,
  xviii–xix, 243, 245–247,
  254, 256–259, 266
Nation, 14, 251
National Review, 8, 94
National Rural
  Development Institute,
  13–14
Native Americans, xvi,
  10, 47, 160, 220,
  226–230, 257, 258, 260,
  263, 264, 267
Naziism, 23, 34, 35, 38,
  39, 40, 47, 64, 70, 72, 88,
  99, 165, 170, 177, 182,
  224–227, 239, 255, 257
NBC news, 16, 27, 28, 30,
  31–32, 59, 63, 71, 110,
  133, 134, 151
Negritude movement,
  137
Nemerov, Howard,
  260–261
Neo-African Literature,
  230
neoconservatives, xii, 3,
  14–16, 30, 45, 48, 50, 61,
  100, 121, 138, 140, 226,
  238, 255
*New American Poetry
  Review, The*, 262
New Chinatown, The, 8
New Negro, The, 185

New Republic, The, 8, 10, 18, 23, 100, 134, 175, 230
New World Journal, 254
New York Magazine, 18, 41, 204
New York Post, 23
New York Review of Books, 23, 94, 100, 237, 251
New York Times, xi, xiv–xvi, 3, 5–6, 11, 13–16, 27–28, 33–35, 41, 45, 51, 59, 60–61, 63, 69, 71, 73, 89, 93, 97, 101, 134, 162, 175, 183, 230, 245, 254–255, 261, 272
New York World, 36
New Yorker, 99, 241
Newsday, 31, 70, 72
Newsweek, xiii, 61, 71, 105, 203, 204
Newton, Huey, 90–93, 102
Nicosia, Gregory, 26
Nixon, Richard, 38, 62
Nkrumah, Kwazi, 44, 269
Norton, Ken, 176, 189
NPR, xv, xvi, 4, 25, 29, 34, 45, 55, 61–63, 66, 71, 89

O

Oakland, 67, 75–83, 88–93, 102, 126, 142, 159, 161–163, 165, 187, 209–215
Oakland Tribune, 29
Oh, Angela, xiv, 79–83
O'Hara, Frank, 49
Olivella, Manuel Zapata, 173–175
On the Blanket, 239
On the Road, 262
One Hundred Amazing Facts about the Negro, 217
O'Neill, Eugene, 110
op-ed articles, xii, xv, xviii, 4, 6, 12, 13, 26, 30, 38, 41, 45, 62, 63, 73, 134, 273. *See also* media
Oppenheimer, Joel, 254
Order, the, 40
Ortiz, Simon, 243, 253, 255, 256
Otalda, Claire, 26
Our Time, 242

P

Pacifica Radio, 44, 56
Park, Ann, 78, 80
Parker, Charlie, 137, 221, 230
Partisan Review, 257
pathology
 Asian American, 10
 black, xi, 18, 24, 61, 63, 133, 138, 140, 163, 174, 230
 social, xi–xii, xv, xix, 7, 18, 20–22, 27, 28, 30, 42
 white, 7, 11, 22
Paul Robeson, 107
PBS news, xiii, 3, 9, 22, 71, 128
PEN West, 26–27, 78, 159, 256
People (magazine), 69, 70, 245
Peretz, Martin, 10, 11, 100
Perot, Ross, 52, 171
Perry, Bruce, 101
Personal Problems, 112, 115, 116–118
Phelan, Anna Hamilton, 101
Phelps, Timothy, 70
Philadelphia Fire, 140–145
Podhoretz, Norman, 19
poetry, 104–106, 139, 184, 242–265. *See also* literature
 American, 244–267
 black, 115, 137, 257, 262
 Hispanic, 247
 Native American, 257, 260, 265–267

New Black, 260–261, 263–264
police brutality, 43, 49, 50, 57, 61, 65–67, 89–91, 102, 140, 235, 237, 241
Polish Americans, 23–24
poverty, xii, 6, 10–15, 17, 20, 23, 24, 45, 141
Pratt, Geronimo, 102
Pruett, Charles, 257
"Pulse of the Morning," xv

Q

Quinn, Sally, 61

R

"Race and Reason," 63
Racial Matters, 89
racism, 9, 15, 18, 21, 23–25, 28, 29, 32, 36–38, 47–48, 49–52, 57–63, 67, 69, 70–71, 79–80, 89, 92, 95–96, 107, 109, 114–115, 135, 138, 142, 151, 155, 170, 177, 189, 202, 216–219, 233, 244, 253, 259
 against black writers, 114, 138, 151, 157
 as psychiatric problem, 122
 red, 268
Rage in Harlem, A, 152
Rahman, Aishah, 48
Rampersad, Arnold, 138–139
rap music, 144, 164, 221, 232–234
rape, 13, 17, 54, 56, 64, 70, 71, 73, 81, 96, 131, 157, 212, 232
Rare Bird Indeed, A, 189
Rats on the Roof, 158, 159
Ravitch, Diane, 173
Reagan, Ronald, 35, 38, 141, 144, 150, 170, 224, 236, 240

Real Anita Hill: The Untold Story, The, 54
Reckless Eyeballing, 41
Redmond, Eugene, 28
religion
  African, xviii, 38, 109, 146–151, 153, 169, 171, 174, 221
  Buddhism, 242–243
  Chinese, 265
  Christianity, xviii, 38, 42, 94, 98, 120, 121, 123, 136, 148, 151, 265
  Islam, 178–179, 192, 201, 224
  Native American, 221, 265
  Santaria, 201
  Voodoo, 146–151, 246
Rexroth, Kenneth, 259
Rhinestone, 112, 113
Rhinestone Sharecropping, 112, 113, 114, 115
Rice, Ann, 230
Rich, Frank, 47
Rise and Fall of the Jewish Gangster in America, The, 21
Rivera, Geraldo, 40
Rizzo, Frank, 140–141
Roach, Max, 137, 222
Roberts, Cokie, 62, 63
Roberts, Sam, 7, 28
Robertson, Pat, 52, 64, 171
Robeson, Paul, 106, 107–111
Robinson, Bill, 253
Robinson, Dolores, 93
Rodriguez, Arturo, 247
Rogers, A.J., 217
Rolling Stone, 101, 229, 230, 256
Roots of Coincidence, The, 250–251
Rose, Axil, 101
Rosenblatt, Roger, 19, 26
Roth, Philip, xv, 43, 257

Rowan, Carl, 6, 73, 237
Rowell, Charles, 252
Rudd, Hughes, 191
Rukeyser, Muriel, 256
Russia and the Golden Hordes, 227, 229

S
Saint is Born in Chima, A, 174
Salas, Floyd, 26, 159
Salt Eaters, The, 147, 167, 168
San Francisco Chronicle, 8, 15, 78
San Francisco Examiner, 15, 124, 126
Sanchez, Sonia, 104
Sanders of the River, 109
Sands, Bobby, 240
Sansome, Mary, 19
Saroyan, William, 157
Sarvich, Vincent, 102
Satchmo, 107
Sawyer, Diane, 62
"Scapegoating the Black Family," 14
Schott, Marge, 62
Schulberg, Bud, 178
Science, 12
Scottish Americans, 36, 38, 39, 40. *See also* Irish Americans
SDS, 94, 100
Seale, Bobby, 89, 91, 92
Seaver, Lynda, 31
segregation, 41, 74, 107, 237
  in media, 35, 52, 74
  at NPR, xv, 55, 64
Senghor, Leopold Sedar, 137
Senno, Jane, 191
Serra, Luis, 198
Sevier, Gov., 266, 267
Shange, Ntozake, 104
Shee Atika Lodge, 77
Shorenstein, Walter, 55
Showboat, 109

Sidney Poet Heroical, The, 114
Silko, Leslie, 10, 267
Silver, Joel, 93
Simon, Scott, 63
Sims, Patsy, 37
Sister Souljah, 35
Skinner, Sam, 189
slavery, 39, 120–121, 125, 147, 166, 176, 183, 226, 274
  among Asian Americans, xiii
  sexual, 5
Sleeper, Jim, 7–9, 18, 61, 62
Smith, Barbara, xiv
Smith, William Kennedy, 56, 71
Snipes, Wesley, 93
Soldofsky, Alan, 243–244
Sollars, Werner, 50, 230
Soul on Fire, 98
Soul on Ice, 96, 97, 98, 99, 100, 101, 103
Soviet Union, 111, 138
Soyinka, Wole, 230
Spady, James, 90
Specter, Arlen, xv, 57
Spence, Gerry, 32
Spinks, Leonard, 179–207
Spitzer, Julie, 1, 19
Sports Illustrated, 69, 72, 203
Spousal Abuse in Rabbinic and Contemporary Judaism, 19
Spy (magazine), 71
Stallings, Rev. George A., Jr., 147
Stallone, Sylvester, 194
Staples, Brent, 10
Stark, Evan, 59
Steel, Ronald, 45–46
Steele, Shelby, 3, 62
Steffens, Lincoln, 6
Steinbeck, John, 157
Steinem, Gloria, xv, 56
Stephens, Bill, 114

Stevenson, Adlai, 269
Strangers From a Different Shore, 8
Streep, Meryl, 93
"Street Scene," 138
suicide, xii, 10, 106
 among men, 17
 among whites, xvii
Sukenick, Ron, 245, 264
Sullivan, Louis, 12, 161
Sunday Examiner & Chronicle, 15–16
Swados, Harvey, 97
Sweeny, Tim, 243
Sze, Hoyt, 8

T
Taboo, 109
Tailhook convention, 54
Takaki, Ronald, 8, 51
Tales of Manhattan, 109
Taste of Power, A, 89, 91
Tate, Allen, 260
Tatoo the Wicked Cross, 159
Tatum, Wilbert A., 23
Taub, Sam, 183–184
Taylor, Susan, 209
technicals, 89–90
television news boycott, 26–32
Tell My Horse, 146–151
Tharp, Twyla, 255
Their Eyes Were Watching God, 150
Thernstrom, Stephen, 227
Third Generation, The, 152
"This Week with David Brinkley," 46, 62
Thomas, Clarence, xv–xvi, 50, 53–56, 57, 64, 70, 71, 210
Thomas, Lorenzo, 252, 262
Thompson, Hunter, 183
Thompson, Robert, 146
Thompson, Robert Ferris, 50

thought-control, 3, 4
Tikkun (magazine), 8, 18, 77
Time, 59, 240, 245, 249, 254, 256
Tolson, Melvin, 137
Torres, José, 15, 184–185
Totenberg, Nina, 55
Toure, Askia Muhammed, 96
Transition Center, 19
Tropicalization, 251
Troupe, Quincy, 261–262
Truman, Harry, 110, 235–236
Trungpa, Chogyam Rinpoche, 243–266
Turner, Nat, 123
Turner, Ted, 29
"20/20," 62
Tyson, Mike, xiv, 50, 54, 56, 57, 69–74

U
Ueberroth, Peter, 83
underclass, xi–xii, 19, 20, 25, 34, 39, 66, 107, 115, 142, 174. *See also* minorities
 Asian American, xii–xiii
 black, xii, 14, 17, 19, 20–21
 Irish, 22–23
 Jewish American, 23
 white, xii, 11, 20
U.S. News & World Report, 53
urban society, 14–18, 76–77, 238
USA Today, 15, 162
Utne Reader, 64, 175

V
Vanity Fair, 55
Varney, Stuart, 48
Vechten, Carl Van, 138
Ventura, Michael, 146
Vidal, Gore, 39

Vietnamese Americans, xii–xiii, 8. *See also* Asian Americans
Village Voice, xi, 17, 19, 35, 69, 70, 259
violence, 6–7, 16, 49, 162
 to Asian Americans, 17
 drug related, 77, 163
 in family, 15, 17
 Jewish American, 19
 professional, 20
 rural, 164
 in schools, 16
 white perpetrated, 15–18, 44, 141
Vizenor, Gerald, 160, 268

W
Waldman, Anne, xviii, 245, 246, 251, 254, 260, 264
Walker, Alice, 13, 56, 90
Wall Street Journal, 17, 53, 60, 79, 134
Wallace, George, 171
Walters, Barbara, 54, 70
Ward, Jerry, 252
Wartts, Charles, Jr., 261
Washington, Desiree, 54, 56–57, 69–72, 73
Washington Post, xvi, 71
Washton, Dr. Arnold, 13
Wattenberg, Ben, 19, 23, 37, 38
Way Past Cool, 158, 159, 160, 161
welfare, 6, 11, 12, 14, 24, 36, 44, 45, 47, 60, 62, 116, 175, 236
West, Cornel, 13, 38
Westies, The, 22–23, 49
What Lisa Steinberg Knew, xv
White Negro, The, 96
White over Blacks, 50
white(s), 7–8, 28
 campus crime involvement, 7
 child abuse, 13

white(s) *(cont'd)*
  cocaine pregnancies, 5
  control of drugs, 60, 92
  control of media, 4
  crime, 15–16
  drug addiction, 5–6,
    13, 164
  ethnics, 144
  family problems, 5–6,
    12
  gunshot death, 17, 18
  in justice system, 61
  in L.A. riots, xiii,
    45–46, 80
  males, xiii, xvii, 14–15,
    54
  poverty, 11, 12, 14, 15, 20
  rapists, 17
  suicide rates, xvii
  underclass, xii
  violence, 15, 16, 17, 44,
    133, 141, 164
  welfare, 47, 63, 175
Wiborg, Mary Hoyt, 109
Wideman, John Edgar,
  140–145

Will, George, 25, 46, 71
Willis, Ellen, 69
Wilson, Lionel, 92
With Justice for None;
  Destroying an American
  Myth, 32
Wolfe, Tom, 93, 97, 172
Wolfson, Mark, 220
women, 23, 97, 101, 253
  black, xiii, 44, 151
  on welfare, 44, 177
  in poverty, 12
  unwed mothers, 14–15
  violence to, 5, 12–13,
    16, 17, 19, 56
  violent, 13
Wong, Shawn, 9, 254,
  257, 262–263
Wong, William, 8, 51
Woods, Larry, 30
Wright, Richard, 10, 48,
  104–105, 116, 149, 160,
  167
writers, 9, 10, 162, 172.
  See also literature;
  poetry; specific writers

African, 165
  black, 48, 88, 137–138,
    149, 154–158,
    159–171
  black female, 151–152,
    164
WTKN Radio, 29

Y
Yabusaki, Ken and Ann,
  79
Yardbird Reader, 254,
  264
Y'Bird, 251
Yeakel, Lynn, 57
Year of the Dragon, The,
  9
Yoruba, 166, 169, 172,
  173, 226, 270, 272
Young, Al, 159, 246
Young, Coleman, 142
Young, Martha, 221

Z
Zarco, Cyn, 253, 263
Zwerdling, Daniel, 25

Grand Canyon
Living Single
Fresh Prince
Sports story online?

Continued from front flap

network news ("electronic junk food"), the editorial page of *The New York Times* ("a black bashing hangout"), or National Public Radio ("about as integrated as a Georgia Country Club"), whether profiling Bill Gunn ("a prince among philistines"), Jess Mowry ("the Homer of inner city youth"), or Gwendolyn Brooks ("the Gods will bless her"), Ishmael Reed's incisive intellect, his vigorous repartee, and his often hopeful and generous spirit is always present.

In a style that encompasses both Coltrane and Rap, Reed's criticism, his profiles of African Americans as diverse as Elaine Brown and Reginald Lewis, his meditations on being a Black Irishman, the Be-Bop revival, and the Oakland fires all combine in *Airing Dirty Laundry* to reveal one of America's most provocative and irrepressible minds at work.

Ishmael Reed grew up in working-class neighborhoods in Buffalo, New York, attended Buffalo public schools and the University of Buffalo. He has taught at Harvard, Yale, and Dartmouth, and for twenty years now has been on the faculty at the University of California at Berkeley. He is a Harvard Signet Fellow, and a Yale Calhoun Fellow. He is the author of more than twenty books —his most recent being *Japanese By Spring*—including novels, essays, plays, and poetry. He has been a finalist for the Pulitzer Prize and was twice nominated for the National Book Award. Reed is the founder of the Before Columbus Foundation and is also one of two Americans to receive the 1993 Suzukinu Hanayagi Award from the Osaka Community Foundation. He lives in Oakland with his wife Carla and their daughter Tennessee.

Bantam Books by David Reuben, M.D.

EVERYTHING YOU ALWAYS WANTED
   TO KNOW ABOUT SEX
ANY WOMAN CAN